THE INDIAN FRONTIER OF THE AMERICAN WEST
1846–1890

The Indian Frontier
of the American West 1846 - 1890

Robert M. Utley

Histories of the American Frontier

Ray Allen Billington, General Editor
Howard R. Lamar, Coeditor
Martin Ridge, Coeditor
David J. Weber, Coeditor

University of New Mexico Press / *Albuquerque*

Library of Congress Cataloging in Publication Data

Utley, Robert Marshall, 1929-
    The Indian frontier of the American West, 1846-1890.

    (Histories of the American frontier)
    Bibliography: p.
    Includes index.
    1. Indians of North America—Wars. 2. Indians of
North America—Government relations. 3. West (U.S.)—
History—1848-1950. I. Title. II. Series.
E81.U747   1983   978'.02   83-12516
ISBN 0-8263-0715-9
ISBN 0-8263-0716-7 (pbk.)

Library of Congress Catalog Card Number 83-12516.
International Standard Book Number:
    0-8263-0715-9 (cloth)
    0-8263-0716-7 (paper)
Eighth Printing, 1993

To Bob Garvey

Contents

Illustrations

Maps

Foreword

In the past quarter century, no figure associated with the American frontier has attracted more attention from scholars and laymen alike than the American Indian. Before this century a sympathetic understanding of their own history and culture was limited to a relatively few scholars, many of them anthropologists, and some sensitive and enthusiastic amateur admirers. Yet the name of Massasoit is linked to that of the Pilgrims, that of King Philip to a tragic colonial war of extermination, and those of Powhatan and Pocahontas to the fortunes of the first Virginia settlers. Similarly the chronicle of British and Revolutionary America would not be complete without reference to such Iroquois figures as Joseph Brant and Red Jacket, Pontiac's Rebellion in 1763, and the revitalization movement led by Handsome Lake, the Seneca religious leader, at the beginning of the national period. These impressive northern leaders had their southern counterparts in the brilliant Alexander McGillivray of the Creek Nation, and Osceola, Seminole chief. The careers of early nineteenth century American heroes and public officials have also been intimately associated with Indian leaders and events: Daniel Boone with the battle for Kentucky between 1775 and 1778, William Henry Harrison with the Shawnee brothers, Tenskwatawa and Tecumseh, Andrew Jackson with the Battle of Horseshoe Bend and the policy of removal, and Sam Houston with the exiled Cherokees, with whom he lived for a time.

But no span of years in the nation's past has produced as many famous figures and as many historic encounters between Indians and whites as the period from 1846 to 1890. In this brief time, the names of John Ross of the Cherokee Nation; Sitting Bull and Red Cloud, spokesmen respectively for the Hunkpapa and Oglala Sioux; Mangas Coloradas, Cochise, and Geronimo, Apache leaders; and Chief Joseph of the Nez Perce, became household words. Each has been the subject of so many sensational accounts as well as scholarly studies that they have become legends. The conflicts and battles with whites in which one or more of these were engaged are even better known. Any American who could read a newspaper knew about Colonel Chivington's massacre of the Cheyennes at Sand Creek in 1864, or later of the Battle of the Little Bighorn in which George Armstrong Custer and his command were wiped out. In 1877 the nation followed for weeks on end the heroic retreat of the battered and starving Nez Perces across the Pacific Northwest. Reporters and journalists were on the scene when the last battle between the Sioux and the Americans took place at Wounded Knee in 1890.

Curiously at the same time that these violent encounters were taking place, American government officials and religious reformers were engaged in intense efforts to solve the so-called Indian problem peaceably. Thus we also associate this period with the Quaker Peace Policy, the rise of the reservation and annuity system, the granting of lands in severalty to Indians, and the Americanization of Indian youths either on the reservation at day and boarding schools, or at off-reservation institutions such as the Carlisle Indian School in Pennsylvania.

It is the story of this dramatic, wide-ranging, multifaceted interaction between the 360,000 Indians west of the Mississippi River and American Soldiers, government bureaucrats, religious reformers, and an overwhelming number of white settlers between 1846 and 1890, that the distinguished student of Indian history, Robert M. Utley, has made the focus of this newest volume in the Histories of the American Frontier Series.

When Ray Allen Billington began his search for the most appropriate scholar to write the volume on the last Indian-white frontier, he did not have to look far. In 1963 Robert Utley, a graduate of the University of Indiana—where he had worked with Oscar O. Winther—produced a seminal book entitled *The Last Days of the Sioux Nation,* which depicted with rare sensitivity and moving eloquence the years leading to the tragic confrontation at Wounded Knee.

That work alone would have qualified Utley for the task of writing a general scholarly and exceptionally readable history of Native Americans in the nineteenth century. But since then Utley, who became Chief Historian of the National Park Service in 1964, has written or edited many more volumes that deal with Indian history. His edition of General Richard H. Pratt's memoirs, *Battlefield and Classroom: Four Decades with the American*

Indian (1964), was followed by his magisterial *Frontiersmen in Blue: The United States Army and the Indian, 1848–1865* (1967) and *Frontier Regulars: The United States and the Indian, 1866–1891* (1973). Having already written about Custer in an earlier volume, *Custer and the Great Controversy* (1962), he then produced *Life in Custer's Cavalry* (1977), a splendid edition of the diaries and letters of Captain Albert Barnitz (who served with Custer at the Battle of the Washita) and his wife Jennie.

When Ray Billington and Robert Utley initiated discussions about the form and purpose of *The Indian Frontier of the American West, 1846–1890,* they agreed that it should combine Utley's own research of some twenty years with the findings of the hundreds of older scholars and the detailed monographic studies of contemporary scholars. As will be evident from the extensive bibliography in this volume, Utley has not only succeeded at this daunting task, he has also managed to describe in a remarkably efficient way the dozens of distinctive Indian cultures that thrived in the nineteenth-century West. Further, he has contrasted these actual cultures with the ideas and perceptions Americans had about western Indians before moving on to a discussion of the policies practiced by the American government, the Army, and the reformers in dealing with these truly distinctive Indian communities. Out of this approach comes one of the most arresting themes in this fine study; namely that two thought worlds existed neither of which ever understood the other. The consequence was that whether federal policies were based on military action or a peace policy, they were destined to end in failure. This is, then, a perceptive book about the mind-sets of the red and white participants as well as about their actions on the battlefield, on the reservation, or in joint councils.

In Utley's treatment, much that seems so familiar takes on new meaning. His dispassionate approach moves quickly beyond the level of praise or blame to a more complex and humane analysis of personalities and groups. And by his full coverage of the histories of all the major western tribes, he is able to demonstrate that both a popular and a scholarly preoccupation with Great Plains Indians has dominated earlier narratives to the exclusion of the story of the Five Civilized Tribes during the Civil War; in later years that same preoccupation with the defeat and near demise of the Plains Indians in 1890 obscured the fact that the Creeks and Cherokees had returned to stability and even prosperity in Indian Territory.

Perhaps the most arresting theme in *The Indian Frontier of The American*

West, however, is one that gives unity to the often disjointed and sensation-ridden chronicle of Indian-white relations. In a brilliant treatment of the paradoxical effects of the peace policy and the resulting reservation system, Utley argues that the Indian Wars, whether with the Modoc and the Nez Perce in the Pacific Northwest, or with the Sioux and Cheyenne in the Dakotas and Montana, or with the Apache in Arizona, were not directed so much against the whites as against reservation life. Whether it was in the form of military resistance or cultural resistance—as demonstrated by the Sioux response to the Ghost Dance religion—both were violent rejections of the reservation system. In so doing Utley not only provides a coherent explanation for the nineteenth-century Indian response, he gives us a disturbing insight into the debilitating resignation and despair that characterized Indian reservation life in the first three decades of the twentieth century.

Utley is equally superb in his penetrating analysis of the well-intentioned reformers who had such a powerful impact on Indian policy. In his final chapter he notes that they, like Frederick Jackson Turner in his famous essay on the "Significance of the Frontier in American History," were also simply expressing their own cultural values when they set out to save the Indian by substituting their culture for his.

Because it is both an engrossing, splendidly told narrative and a major new interpretation of the last Indian-American frontier, it is with particular pride and pleasure that the editors of the Histories of the Frontier Series present this volume to the public. Like other books in the Series it tells a complete story, but it is also intended to be read as a part of the broader history of western expansion told in connected form in these volumes. Each book has been written by a leading authority who brings to his task an intimate knowledge of the period that he covers and a demonstrated skill in narration and interpretation. Each is designed to provide the general reader with a sound but readable account of one phase of the nation's frontier past and the specialized student with a documented narrative that is integrated into the general story of the nation's growth.

The Series, originally conceived of as a multivolume narrative history of the American frontier in eighteen volumes, has been expanded to include comparative volumes such as Alastair Hennessy's *The Frontier in Latin American History* (1978), and thematic studies, such as Sandra L. Myres's *Westering Women and the Frontier Experience, 1800–1915* (1982). Whether the approach is narrative, comparative, or thematic, the hope of the authors and the editors remains the same as that expressed by Ray Allen Billington, founder of the Series, "that the full history of the most American phase of the country's past will help its people to understand themselves and thus be better equipped to face the global problems of the twentieth century world."

Howard R. Lamar
  Yale University
Martin Ridge
  The Huntington Library
David J. Weber
  Southern Methodist University

Spring 1983

Preface

In the spiritual life of the Pueblo Indians of the Southwest, the *kachina* plays a significant role. Whites would call the kachina a "doll," but this is only the tangible representation of a spiritual being or "god" that objectifies particular truths or dynamics of life. The Zuñis of western New Mexico have a kachina heavy with meaning for understanding the history of the Indian frontier. This kachina came out of the underworld fastened back to back with a person from an alien world. The deformity condemned the two to an eternity of physical union in which neither could ever see or understand the other.[1]

No more graphic emblem can be found to objectify the history of white-Indian contact in the American West. The frontier condemned the two to physical union, while a great cultural chasm condemned them never really to see or understand each other. As a thoughtful student has recently written, "Indian-White history is the process of two thoughtworlds that at the time were more often than not mutually unintelligible. Surely this is the most poignant message of Indian-White relations: 500 years of talking past each other, of mutual incomprehension."[2] A dominant theme of this book, then, is that the truths captured by this Zuñi kachina spawned forces that gave direction to the history of the Indian frontier of the American West.

Another theme is that this history involved two peoples—not just westward-moving whites for whom Indians were mere impersonal foils, like other fixtures of the wilderness. If the concept of frontier is to have validity, it has to be treated as a considerably more complicated phenomenon than first described by Frederick Jackson Turner. He saw a single Anglo-Saxon frontier advancing westward, taming a wilderness that happened to include Indians as well as wild beasts, and in the process shaping the distinctive character that set Americans apart from other peoples.

A more realistic construction is in terms not of a single frontier line, white on one side and lacking any discernible color at all on the other, but of groupings of frontier zones in which white and red met and mingled . They saw themselves as distinct peoples and usually on opposing sides in conflicts. These conflicts were sometimes violent and sometimes simply political, economic, and cultural competition. More often than generally appreciated, the contact was even friendly, or at least peaceful. The interaction almost always produced acculturation—changes in values, attitudes, institutions, and material culture. And, of vital import, acculturation was not confined to one side. Both peoples changed, often radically and in ways never really perceived as attributable to the other.

Students of this process differ on when to consider the frontier period closed. Some have pointed out that acculturation continues indefinitely, that political, social, economic, and cultural interaction and change do not end so long as distinct peoples are in contact. If the frontier concept is to have utility, however, there needs to be a generally recognized point at which to consider the frontier closed. The most useful interpretation, and the one adopted here, is to view the frontier period at an end when one side clearly established political domination over the other. For most (though not all) Indian groups, this point, as suggested in chapter 9, was reached in roughly 1890.[3]

This book is written less for specialists in the various fields of study from which it draws than for a readership of beginning students and interested lay people seeking an introduction to and overview of Indian-white relations in the Trans-Mississippi West during the final half-century of the frontier period, roughly 1846 to 1890. In this spirit I have designed the footnotes as a guide to pertinent monographic literature as much as to particular sources relied upon. I should point out, though, that the contents reflect more than twenty years of research and study for previous books in sources that I have not always felt called upon to cite here in the footnotes.

Of the many people who helped in one way or another, I want to give special recognition to the Reverend Francis Paul Prucha, S.J., of Marquette University. Anyone who deals with Indian-white relations in the nineteenth century must acknowledge a heavy debt to Prucha's writings on many facets of the subject. I have drawn deeply on virtually all his books and articles, which I admire greatly both in factual and interpretive content. In addition, I have profited immensely from his generous consent to review and criticize the entire manuscript in draft, although, of course, he cannot be held responsible for any of the final contents.

Others deserve my heartfelt thanks. In particular, Professor Wilbur Jacobs of the University of California at Santa Barbara made comments on early drafts of chapters 1 and 2 that led to extensive revisions. John C. Ewers of the Smithsonian Institution also importantly influenced these two chapters. And these and certain later chapters have profited from review by Professor Richard N. Ellis of the University of New Mexico, Harry Kelsey and Donald Chaput of the Los Angeles County Museum, and Professor Robert A. Trennert of Arizona State University.

Another special acknowledgment must go to Ray Allen Billington. He asked me to take on this project—appropriately, beneath a canopy of towering redwoods during a historical group tour of Muir Woods in June 1977. Together with Martin Ridge, Ray arranged a six-week visit to the Huntington Library for me in the spring of 1981, and scarcely two days before his lamented death he completed a critical review of the first three chapters. Both at the Huntington and as an editor of the Histories of the American Frontier series Martin Ridge merits thanks, as do the other two editors, Professors Howard Lamar of Yale University and David Weber of Southern Methodist University. Finally, gratitude is due Virginia J. Renner and her efficient staff at the Huntington for making my stay there so pleasant and rewarding.

Through professional publications chief Mark Carroll, the National Park Service made available most of the maps that appear in this volume. Drawn by Harry Scott for the Park Service publication *Soldier and Brave: Historic Places Associated with Indian Affairs and the Indian Wars in the Trans-Mississippi West* (and based on drafts I myself prepared many years ago), they seemed a good illustration for most of the matters dealt with in my book.

And I would be remiss indeed if I did not express the most sincere appreciation to my wife, Melody Webb, Regional Historian of the National Park Service's Southwest Region, both for professional criticism and for personal support and encouragement.

Santa Fe, New Mexico
September 1982

1

The Indian West at Midcentury

On August 29, 1846, a party of Cheyenne Indians pitched their conical skin tipis on the north bank of the Arkansas River near the bastioned adobe castle where the Bent brothers had traded since 1833. Among the party was Yellow Wolf. A hardened, wiry little man in his middle sixties, Yellow Wolf enjoyed an enviable record as a leader in warfare with the Kiowas, Comanches, Utes, and Pawnees, and as a chief of the prestigious Dog Soldier band he exerted great influence among his tribesmen. Few Cheyennes possessed his wisdom or intellect. It was Yellow Wolf who had persuaded "Little White Man" William Bent and his brothers not to locate their trading post farther up the river, beyond the buffalo range. Ever since, Yellow Wolf and his people had been the Bents' staunchest supporters among the southern Plains tribes, an affinity cemented when William Bent took a Cheyenne wife, Owl Woman.

Yellow Wolf reached Bent's Fort in time to witness the closing scenes of a momentous summer. Beginning in late July, the valley around the fort had begun to fill with white men. The tents of seventeen hundred soldiers sprouted for miles along the river. Rank upon rank of white-topped wagons drew up nearby. Twenty thousand horses, mules, and oxen covered the sandy plain. The soldiers were marching to fight the Mexicans, they told the Indians gathered at the fort to trade. In wonder, the tribesmen declared over and over that they had never supposed there were so many white people.

Most of the army had moved on by the time Yellow Wolf arrived, but the spectacle of its passage may well have crystallized his thinking. He had noted year after year the growing presence of white men in the Indian country. Each year more wagons made their way across the plains with goods for trade with the Mexicans in Santa Fe. The signs were

1

Yellow Wolf. This prescient Cheyenne chief shared his fears for the future of his people with Lt. J. J. Abert at Bent's Fort in 1846, and Abert, impressed with the Indian's character and intellect, prepared this sketch for later inclusion in his official report. Puzzlingly, although already in his sixties, Abert gave him a decidedly youthful aspect. Without success, Yellow Wolf tried to persuade his people that their only hope of survival lay in adopting the ways of the white people. Whites repaid him with a bullet at Sand Creek in 1864.

ominous, and they pointed to a conclusion no other Cheyenne leader was to acknowledge for years. He shared his thoughts with an army officer recuperating from an illness at Bent's Fort. Yellow Wolf, the officer wrote in his journal,

> is a man of considerable influence, of enlarged views, and gifted with more foresight than any other man in his tribe. He frequently talks of the diminishing numbers of his people, and the decrease of the once abundant buffalo. He says that in a few years they will become extinct; and unless the Indians wish to pass away also, they will have to adopt the habits of the white people, using such measures to produce subsistence as will render them independent of the precarious reliance afforded by the game.[1]

Yellow Wolf had good reason for apprehension. The march of these soldiers held great portent for the Cheyennes. This year of 1846 was one of profound significance, a year of decision. The army the Indians watched marching on the Santa Fe Trail—General Stephen Watts Kearny's Army of the West—was an instrument of decision. In the Mexican War of 1846–48 the United States seized the Southwest and California. Already, in 1845, Texas had been annexed; and on the eve of the war the resolution of the Oregon boundary dispute with Great Britain added the Pacific Northwest. With breathtaking suddenness, the United States flung its western boundary to the Pacific and transformed itself into a continental nation. Then, as if to light a powder train laid down by these events, on January 24, 1848, only ten days before diplomats at Guadalupe Hidalgo signed the treaty that ended the Mexican War, James Marshall spotted a golden glint in the millrace of a sawmill he was building on California's American River. Territorial expansion combined with the discovery of gold to place the Indian word of the Trans-Mississippi West on the threshold of enormous change.

For Yellow Wolf and his people, the march of Kearny's army marked the end of one era and the beginning of another. In his remaining eighteen years the old chief saw his fears realized. He continued to believe that the only hope for his people lay in learning the ways of the white man. In the frigid dawn of November 29, 1864, the crash of carbine fire awakened him. With others of Black Kettle's village, he sprang from his tipi to confront the charging soldiers. And there on Sand Creek, not far from the melting mud ruins of William Bent's long-abandoned trading post, Yellow Wolf died, cut down in his eighty-fifth year by a bullet fired by a white man.

The sudden leap of the nation's boundaries to the Pacific set off a process of confrontation and conflict between whites and the Indians of the Trans-Mississippi West. It was a process even then ending in catastrophe for the tribes of the eastern woodlands. Having destroyed one "Indian barrier," an aggressively westering America now faced another. In less than half a century this barrier too would be destroyed, and white civilization would reign unchallenged over the plains, mountains, and deserts of the Trans-Mississippi West.

At midcentury the prospective victims numbered about 360,000.[2] Seventy-five thousand ranged the Great Plains from Texas to the British possessions in buffalo-hunting peoples that have produced today's befeathered stereotype of the American Indian: Blackfoot, Assiniboine, Sioux, Cheyenne, Arapaho, Crow, Shoshoni, Pawnee, Kiowa, and Comanche, to name the most powerful. The nomads of the southern Plains shared their domain uneasily with some 84,000 Indians uprooted from their eastern homes by the U.S. government and swept westward to new lands beyond the ninety-fifth meridian. Most gave allegiance to what the whites, with unconscious patronization, labeled the Five Civilized Tribes: Cherokee, Choctaw, Chickasaw, Creek, and Seminole. Of the 200,000 Indians in the new U.S. territories, Texas claimed 25,000, most prominently Lipan, Apache, and Comanche. The Mexican Cession (California and New Mexico) contained 150,000, among them Ute, Pueblo, Navajo, Apache, Yavapai, Paiute, Yuma, Mojave, Modoc, and a host of tiny coastal groups that, whether or not wholly missionized, came to be known collectively as "Mission Indians." The Oregon Country (later to give birth to the states of Oregon, Washington, and Idaho) was home to 25,000 Indians, including Nez Perce, Flathead, Coeur d'Alene, Spokane, Pend d'Oreille, Yakima, Walla Walla, Cayuse, Umatilla, Palouse, Chinook, Squaxon, Nisqually, and Puyallup.

Opposed to these Indians, the United States at midcentury boasted a population of more than 20 million, a counting utterly beyond the comprehension of the western natives. By 1860, 1.4 million would live in the West; by 1890, 8.5 million.

Although a so-called Indian barrier influenced the speed and direction of the white people's westward movement, it was scarcely a monolithic barrier. For four and a half centuries Europeans had applied the label "Indian" to the indigenous peoples of the Western Hemisphere, but this

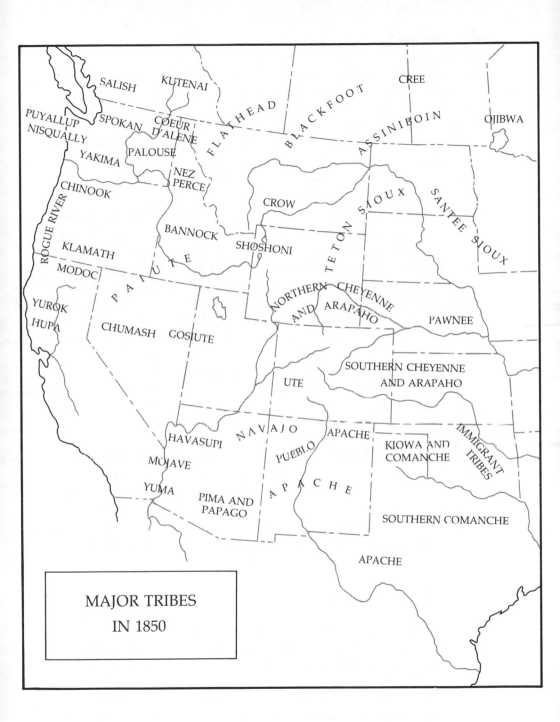

SALISH KUTENAI CREE

PUYALLUP SPOKAN CŒUR BLACKFOOT ASSINIBOIN OJIBWA
NISQUALLY D'ALENE FLATHEAD
YAKIMA PALOUSE
NEZ
CHINOOK PERCE CROW
TETON SIOUX SANTEE SIOUX
BANNOCK
KLAMATH SHOSHONI
MODOC PAIUTE
NORTHERN CHEYENNE
YUROK AND ARAPAHO PAWNEE
HUPA CHUMASH GOSIUTE
SOUTHERN CHEYENNE
AND ARAPAHO
UTE
NAVAJO IMMIGRANT
HAVASUPI APACHE TRIBES
MOJAVE PUEBLO KIOWA AND
COMANCHE
YUMA APACHE
PIMA AND
PAPAGO SOUTHERN COMANCHE

APACHE

MAJOR TRIBES
IN 1850

arbitrary collectivization obscured a profound cultural diversity. Despite cultural similarities, the native Americans were in fact many different peoples. Thus no group typifies the western Indians. The Nez Perce affords as useful a group as any for suggesting who these people were that unknowingly, or with the vague forebodings of a Yellow Wolf, stood on the threshold of catastrophe.[3]

The Nez Perces were a handsome people of three thousand or less in 1850. They occupied the eastern reaches of the recently disputed Oregon Country—from the rugged, forested mountains drained by the Clearwater and Salmon rivers to the high, open plateaus gashed by the Snake and Grande Ronde rivers and bounded on the west by the Great Bend of the Columbia. They formed a bridge between the powerful buffalo-hunting plainsmen to the east and the small, loosely organized fishing groups to the west, and not surprisingly, their culture partook of both. They lived in skin or brush lodges and dressed in finely tailored skin garments decorated with shells, elk teeth, beads, and other ornaments. "Lofty eligantly formed active and durable" horses, in Meriwether Lewis's words, furnished transportation and the origins of the distinctive Appaloosa breed.

A ceaseless quest for food ordered the life of the Nez Perces. They planted no crops but moved about to where food could be had. In early summer, *hillal*, "the time of the first run of the salmon," the people appeared on the banks of the rivers to spear or net salmon from the hordes fighting their way upstream to spawn. They gorged on fresh fish while drying and smoking supplies for leaner times. Then, as summer warmed the meadows and prairies, the bands came together at favorite camas grounds for festival-like gatherings in which fun and visiting alternated with digging the onionlike camas root, a staple food of the tribe. Spring was also a time of harvest, when other roots and wild plants ripened. Throughout the year hunting engaged the men, as with powerful bow fashioned of mountain sheep horn they stalked elk, deer, mountain sheep, and bear, and with snare or net they captured rabbits and grouse. Each autumn some bands on the east trekked across the great rampart of the Bitterroot Mountains to chase buffalo on the plains of Montana.[4]

In addition to hunting and gathering, trade was an important element of the Nez Perce economy. They traded constantly with neighbors and periodically gathered at popular centers to meet more distant people. An annual truce in the warfare between the Nez Perces and their southern neighbors, Shoshonis and Paiutes, permitted a short period of trade. The Nez Perces' most important trade, however, occurred at the fixed fishing villages of the Wishram, Wasco, and Wyampam Indians at The Dalles of the Columbia. Here Nez Perces met with Chinookan-speaking coastal peoples to exchange dried meat, furs, hides, roots, bear claws, and elk teeth for dried clams, fish oil, baskets, carved wooden implements, and dentalium shells. Equally significant, the barterers exchanged techniques, skills, and methods as well as legends, traditions, and lore that subtly but strongly reshaped intangible aspects of their cultures.

Living in intimate and precarious equilibrium with the environment, the Nez Perces pursued a spiritual life given form by nature and the individual's relations with nature. The land, especially their homeland, compelled a worshipful, mystical veneration. "The earth is part of my body," declared old Toohoolhoolzote. "I belong to the land out of which I came. The earth is my mother."[5] Every feature of it, animate and inanimate, contained unseen spirits that formed a brotherhood of which the Nez Perce was part and to which he looked for that ingredient most essential to progress through life—power. Almost every man and woman had a *Wyakin*—an eagle, a rock, thunder, a cloud—with which an intimate, personal, spiritual relationship was established and from which assistance and protection—power—could be drawn. "It is this way," Many Wounds explained to a white student. "You have faith, and ask maybe some saint to help with something where you are probably stalled. It is the same way climbing a mountain. You ask *Wyakin* to help you."[6] An elaborate body of belief and practice, undergirded by a rich mythology, governed war and the hunt and political, social, and family relationships. Holy men worked miracles, aided healing, and advised in spiritual matters, but religion was still, for the individual, an intensely personal matter, between him, his *Wyakin*, and all the phenomena of nature.

The Nez Perce accorded his loyalty and allegiance first to his family, then to his band, and finally to his tribe, but rarely beyond. These institutions provided the framework for the political system. It was a policy- and decision-making mechanism for which the word *government* calls forth misleading connotations, for leaders did not "govern" in the sense that inheritors of the European tradition understand. Social and spiritual sanctions and the persuasion and example of leaders constrained and guided individual behavior. The autonomous bands looked to chiefs and headmen who counseled but did not command, and who spoke for their followers only as their followers consented. When bands came together, tribal councils made decisions and determined policy. Exalting the individual, rejecting authoritarianism, often fostering factionalism in both tribe and band, the political system made decisive or unified action difficult, especially in times of danger or crisis.

Though less combative than some other natives, the Nez Perces none-theless knew how to make war. With lance, bow and arrow, warclub, and shield, they fought fiercely with their enemies on the south and sparred with the Plains groups to the east. Their weapons, techniques, and goals resembled those of the Plains Indians, from whom they had been largely borrowed. As with food gathering, religion, and the politi-cal system, warfare accentuated the individual. Leadership depended on personal influence rather than command, warriors obeyed or disobeyed as personal inclination dictated, and combat usually took the form of an explosion of personal encounters rather than a collision of organized units. With the Blackfeet, Crows, Sioux, and Assiniboines east of the Rocky Mountains, the Nez Perces, often in alliance with the Flatheads, conducted the sporadic raid and counterraid characteristic of the Plains war complex, in which the principal aims were wealth in horses and other plunder and the war honors on which one's rise to prominence so greatly depended. Against Shoshonis, Paiutes, and Bannocks to the south the hostility was chronic and deadly. The same aims prevailed, but fortified by genuine historic animosities rooted in overlapping hunting grounds. In these wars, which were both offensive and defensive, the Nez Perces also joined with their friendly neighbors on the west, Umatillas, Walla Wallas, and Cayuses.

The Nez Perces differed in many ways from Apache, Navajo, Pueblo, Cheyenne, and Mandan, as likewise these people differed from one another. In language, dress, shelter, food, means of transportation, spiri-tual beliefs, political and social organization, and other cultural traits, the groups displayed variations rooted in environmental and historical in-fluences. Navajos lived in log-and-sod hogans and herded sheep. Apaches preferred to travel on foot. Pueblos lived in communal apartments of adobe and planted corn and beans.

Yet for all the differences there were significant similarities. Most groups, for example, even the agricultural Pueblos and Caddos, practiced a pre-carious subsistence economy and depended on a simple technology. Most worshipped deities residing in nature and strove for a life in balance with the natural world. Most exalted war and fought in ways that exalted the individual warrior. Most placed a premium on individual freedom and government by persuasion and consensus and withheld from their chiefs the power to command or enforce. All the natives, like the Nez Perces, venerated their homeland and looked upon it with a keen sense of possession. It was a group posession, however, recognizing the right of

Sun Dance. This ceremony lay at the core of the Plains Indian's spiritual life. To the whites, its most spectacular feature was self-torture. Warriors suspended themselves from a pole by strips of rawhide inserted beneath the chest or back muscles. The weight of their bodies at length tore them loose. Frederic Remington here depicts the ritual among the Sioux. *Courtesy Harold McCracken.*

all to partake of its bounty. No individual could "own" any part of it to the exclusion of others. Use privileges might be granted or sold, but sale of the land itself was a concept foreign to the Indian mind. The earth, Chief Joseph told treaty commissioners, was "too sacred to be valued by or sold for silver and gold."[7]

Perhaps the most critical similarity in the struggle with the white people was a strong sense of group identity. Indians saw themselves as many different peoples rather than as a single Indian people with common interests and, especially to the point, a common danger from the whites. Indeed, a group's name for itself frequently meant *"the* people," and its word for a neighboring group as often translated into "enemy." A Flathead or Lipan looked upon himself above all as Flathead or Lipan, and only dimly if at all as Indian. In his mind the differences that set him

Buffalo. Not only did the huge herds provide a mobile commissary for the Plains Indians, they furnished almost every other material want and gave shape to other cultural institutions as well. In the 1870s, white hide-hunters cut down the buffalo by the millions, and by the early 1880s only a few hundred survived. *Painting by W. J. Hays, Library of Congress.*

apart from other natives, though often as much form as substance, over-shadowed the similarities.

The feeling of unity and identity implicit in the grouping of bands in a tribe is evident in the armed conflicts that pitted native people against native people. Alone or in alliance with neighbors, they contended for honors, plunder, captives, and above all hunting grounds. Chronic fighting occurred where areas of occupation met or overlapped. Revenge for injuries inflicted by enemies also furnished an important motivation—indeed, a culturally prescribed obligation, although this word implies a mindless savagery foreign to the underlying rationale.[8] At times such warfare brought about major shifts in a regional balance of power and the traditional ranges of groups. The westward surge of the Sioux in the early nineteenth century is a classic example: driven from Minnesota by Chippewas, they seized territory from Iowa, Ponca, Pawnee, Arikara, Mandan, Hidatsa, Assiniboine, and Crow and emerged the monarchs of the northern Plains. Thus the wave of white migration did not wash against a wall of Indian opposition but rather broke over a congeries of scattered groups that had been fighting one another for generations and would continue to fight one another to the day of their final conquest by the whites.[9]

In all their diversity, then, these were the people whose lives were about to be transformed by the final westward leap of the American frontier. None of them, however, not even those who had never laid eyes on a white man, was a pristine aboriginal group, untouched by white influence. On the contrary, for nearly four centuries the European presence in North America had been beaming forces of change either directly or indirectly into the cultures of the Trans-Mississippi peoples. None, however remote, remained immune.

Indians on the southern and western rims of the West, the "Spanish Borderlands," had contended with Spaniards ever since the day in 1540 when Coronado's conquistadors clashed with the warriors of Hawikuh. Those most directly affected were the Pueblos of the Rio Grande and the scattering of small coastal groups that came to be called "Mission Indians." Despite intensive missionary effort and military and political domination, the Pueblos nourished their ancient institutions and traditions through a process anthropologists have called "compartmentalization." With the proscribed customs and beliefs they simply went underground while externally adopting the forms imposed by the Spanish. In time these new forms took on their own cultural meaning, but without serious damage to the old. The result was a compartmentalized culture, or a "dual tradition."[10]

In California, by contrast, Indians unlucky enough to live where Spaniards colonized were corralled at the missions rather than the missions introduced into existing native villages. Put to forced labor, weakened by radical dietary changes, ravaged by diseases, subjected to cruel punishments and even death for infractions of the many rules, the Indians found mission life scarcely the "beneficent servitude" of conventional historical interpretation. Half a century of such devastation left them unable to cope with whites and other Indians following secularization of the missions in 1834, and they all but vanished as recognizable groups.[11]

Because they were nomadic, most natives of the Trans-Mississippi West escaped the direct and continuous impact of Spain endured by the sedentary Pueblos and the missionized Californians. Even they, however, had experienced many and profound changes because of Europeans, changes that anthropologists and ethnohistorians still have not entirely sorted out.

European diseases, for example, did not depend on direct contact yet had cataclysmic consequences for the population and thus also for culture. Indians had no immunity to these diseases, and epidemics of smallpox, cholera, plague, typhus, influenza, malaria, measles, and yellow fever swept away millions of people and destroyed entire groups. Recent scholarship suggests that nearly ten million natives inhabited North America in 1492. By the middle of the nineteenth century this population had dwindled by more than ninety percent, chiefly because of European diseases. A force so catastrophic, it has been contended, deserves to be viewed as a "disease frontier" that rolled across the continent in front of the other frontiers identified by Frederick Jackson Turner.[12] Just how this depopulation affected social, political, and economic institutions remains only suggestive.

The European impact also strengthened political institutions. Tribes and bands were probably much more loosely organized before the advent of Europeans. But as the newcomers advanced they demanded institutions reflective of their own with which to relate and through which to manipulate and ultimately dominate. Thus they gave stronger form to nascent institutions or called forth new institutions. Again, this process did not require direct contact with whites; it could be set off by the development of such forms in neighboring groups.[13] Even as late as the middle of the nineteenth century, the peoples called Nez Perce or Paiute or Apache associated only loosely in tribes. The tribe of our modern understanding took shape under the pressures of white societies just then beginning the period of serious encroachment.

Related to political organization are warfare and the institutions of war. Indian groups unquestionably fought bitterly with one another in prehistoric times, but the appearance of Europeans greatly intensified hostilities. First, their presence strengthened stratified political systems and thus the organization to make war. Second, they crowded groups into the traditional ranges of other groups. Third, they gave rise to territorial ambitions in groups hitherto content with their own areas of occupation, for now Indians killed game not only for their own needs but to pile up hides and furs for barter with the whites. The trade had another effect as well, in stimulating hostility between groups that enjoyed direct trade with the whites and those forced to deal through intermediaries. The one strove to preserve its advantage, the other to break the monopoly and establish its own direct relationship. All these influences had been at work since 1492, and they had undoubtedly produced momentous changes in all the Indians of North America.[14]

Two other European contributions were also of enormous consequence—the horse and the gun. The Spanish brought horses to the Rio Grande. Some escaped, and Indian raiders seized others. By the opening of the eighteenth century the grasslands of the Great Plains nourished multiplying herds of wild horses. Trade and raids hastened their spread north and east. By late in the century virtually all the Indians of the Trans-Mississippi West had horses. Replacing dogs as beasts of burden, horses gave their owners undreamed mobility and laid the foundation for the buffalo-hunting culture that overspread the Great Plains and even reached into the Rocky Mountains.

The horse wrought a revolutionary cultural transformation. It enabled peoples of varied geographical origin and great cultural and linguistic diversity to move on to the Great Plains as a place of residence rather than as a place of occasional resort. Within scarcely more than two generations, the horse and the buffalo worked an extraordinary homogenizing effect on these diverse peoples. By the middle of the nineteenth century, Algonkian Cheyennes, Siouan Dakotas, Caddoan Pawnees, and Uto-Aztecan Comanches shared fundamentally the same culture. It owed its very existence to the white man's horse, and in little more than a century it collapsed, the victim of the white man's slaughter of the buffalo.

Guns came from the east and north at the same time horses advanced from the opposite directions. Originating mainly with the French, guns spread from group to group by trade and war. Until the development of metallic cartridges they were not much used for hunting, but they af-

The horse gave the Indian mobility to match the buffalo's. Together, horse and buffalo gave rise to the culturally rich way of life of the Plains Indians. It flourished for little more than a century, then collapsed as suddenly as the herds were obliterated. Left, horse-mounted Blackfoot woman pulls travois with family and belongings. Right, in an 1873 drawing by F. O. C. Darley, hunters down buffalo. *Smithsonian Institution National Anthropological Archives* and *Library of Congress.*

forded a decisive weapon in warfare with enemies who were not yet equipped. Guns forged another bond of dependence, however, for powder, lead, and repairs could only be obtained from the white man.

For thousands of Indians who had yet to see their first white man, horse and gun brought revolutionary change to culture and balance of power. "The horse frontier rolled across the West from New Mexico far in advance of most white traders and sometimes as much as a century and a half in advance of tangible white frontiers," writes a modern scholar. "The gun frontier, moving from the east, reached the Great Plains at about the same time. The convulsions of these several Indian-versus-Indian frontiers sent reverberations rolling in all directions, changing in myriad ways

the Indian world and thus affecting in myriad ways the setting and course of American history."[15]

The first whites to appear in the Indian camp were usually traders or, more rarely, missionaries. Trade and traders injected a particularly volatile ingredient into relationships both within and among groups. All Indians had well-developed trading patterns and readily adapted them to white trading initiatives. French and English traders advanced from the east, while Spaniards traded in the Southwest and Englishmen and Russians on the Pacific Coast. Early in the nineteenth century, Americans began working their way up the Missouri River and westward to the Rocky Mountains, and they entered the coastal trade as well. The traders sought robes, skins, and above all furs—chiefly otter and seal on the coast and beaver inland. At shifting seasonal rendezvous, in the Indian camps themselves, and later at trading posts that sprouted in every corner of

Lawyer.
Hal-hal-tros tsot.
Head Chief of the Nez perce Tribe.

Lawyer. The advent of white people in the Indian world intensified and complicated the factionalism that had always divided the tribes. The Nez Perces were
especially affected because missionaries came among them early and labored long.
For a generation Lawyer headed the Christian or "progressive" faction that coop-
erated with the whites. Gustave Sohon sketched this likeness in 1855. *Washington
State Historical Society*.

the western wilderness, Indians made their first significant contact with white men.[16]

What the traders offered in exchange, directly or indirectly through intermediaries, was a wondrous range of manufactured goods—guns, metal knives and hatchets, iron cooking pots and other utensils, European fabrics, new foods such as sugar and coffee, and ornamental items such as dyes and beads. These innovations greatly altered the Indians' material culture but did not (except for horse and gun) seriously affect social, political, religious, economic, or military institutions. They simply substituted more efficient tools or created new tastes and wants. They made life easier, more varied, and more interesting without basically changing it. Of unrecognized portent, however, the skills that had produced the native versions of the items now obtained in trade fell into disuse and, untaught to later generations, began to die out. Bonds of dependency formed that fastened Indians firmly to whites.

The traders brought other innovations that had less happy results. Besides disease, liquor was the most disruptive. The literature of the fur trade from colonial times well into the nineteenth century documents in vivid and voluminous detail the dramatic susceptibility of the Indians to the attractions and effects of liquor. Scene after explicit scene portrays them resorting to almost any extremity to obtain it, drinking compulsively to get drunk, and when drunk giving vent to violence and self-abuse almost without limits. Liquor functioned more as a lubricant to the trading ritual than as a trade item in itself, but, especially in situations of intense competition between trading companies, it became one of the white man's most destructive gifts to the natives. As a recent authority has written, "In epidemic force it ravaged tribe after tribe until the drunken, reprobate Indian became a fixture of American folklore."[17]

The stereotype is simplistic. Frontier whites indulged in drunken debauchery and mayhem too. Indeed, Indians may have learned from them how to behave when drunk. Drunken behavior may take a variety of forms and may be as much a learned as a physiological response. The trappers' annual rendezvous, for example, featured an abundance of vivid role-models. In addition, Indians believed that liquor contained a hidden spirit or demon that took possession of the imbiber. The perpetrator of injury or even death inflicted while drunk could hardly be held responsible for actions caused by evil spirits. Within certain limits, therefore, drunkenness was "time out" from ordinary social constraints.[18]

Another gift of the traders was themselves. Through intermarriage, as one contemporary observer explained, traders "soon learn the Indian

Fort Union Trading Post. Significant contacts between Indians and whites occurred at fur trading posts such as Fort Union, the American Fur Company's
station at the confluence of the Missouri and Yellowstone rivers. This is an 1833
view by artist Carl Bodmer. *Montana Historical Society.*

tongue, keep a friendship with the savages, and besides have the satisfaction of a she-bedfellow."[19] In addition to forming a conduit for the exchange of cultural influences, intermarriage had two important results.
First, cementing political alliances in pursuit of commercial goals, it introduced external political factors into internal political relationships, inten-
sifying factionalism and helping to shape policy. Second, intermarriage
spawned a growing population of mixed-bloods who, with a foot in both
red and white worlds, wielded great influence, for good or bad, in native affairs.

In contrast to the traders, missionaries sought fundamental change in
the Indian way of life—conversion to Christianity and adoption of European civilization. Also in contrast to the traders, however, missionaries
had but lightly intruded on the Indian world. For the Pueblos and the
California coastal groups, Spanish friars had been a fact of life until Mexico secularized the missions in 1834. Among others, only those of the

Comanches. "Lords of the South Plains," the Comanches have been called. Frequently allied with the Kiowas, they ranged from the Arkansas River south into Texas. For almost a century they ravaged the Texas and northern Mexican frontier, finally succumbing in the Red River War of 1874–75. Of all the mounted nomads of the Plains, the Comanches were almost universally regarded as the finest horsemen. William S. Soule caught this family in front of their tipi sometime in the late sixties or early seventies. *Smithsonian Institution National Anthropological Archives.*

Pacific Northwest had important associations with missionaries. Here, beginning in the 1830s, Presbyterians and Methodists competed with Jesuit "Black Robes" for Indian allegiance. Some groups, notably the Nez Perce, had rewarded their labors with growing Christian or "progressive" factions that stood in opposition to the "pagan" or "nonprogressive" factions. Other western tribes had yet to be so afflicted, but ultimately this source of dissension would disrupt the unity of virtually all in their struggle to cope with the white threat.[20]

Traders and missionaries afforded the Indians their first close look at this strange and puzzling race that more and more affected their lives. Indian views of white people defy generalization because they differed

Apaches. These tough, wily people performed as well on foot as Comanches on horseback. In tribes such as Chiricahua, Mimbres, Mescalero, and Jicarilla, they ranged the southwestern deserts and mountains from western Texas to central Arizona and deep into Mexico as well. For white frontiersmen, no Indians proved as formidable foes as these tenacious people who excelled at exploiting the environment to their advantage and the enemy's disadvantage. Ben Wittick photographed this Mescalero warrior with his pistol and beltfull of rifle cartridges. *Museum of New Mexico*.

so vastly throughout the West. Generally they changed from positive to negative in proportion to increasing familiarity. At first contact, Indians stood in awe and admiration of the white man, often even attributing divinity to him. But "a little familiarity destroys this illusion," observed trader Pierre Antoine Tabeau, who went on to identify three stages in Indian-white relations: "the age of gold, that of first meeting; the age of iron, that of the beginning of their insight; and that of brass, when a very long intercourse has mitigated their ferocity and a little of our trade has become indispensable to them."[21]

In all three stages, however intense the enmity, Indians looked in wonder and envy on the white man's technology. Horses and guns were but the precursors of a splendid, endless, and often mysterious variety of goods, machines, and other possessions. Steamboats, "iron horses," "talking wires," artists' portraits, writing, compasses, clocks and watches, cannon, and "lucifer matches" were but a few of the marvels of the whites that amazed, amused, mystified, and sometimes frightened the Indians. Trader James Kipp in 1833 translated the Mandan word for white man, *wasschi*, as "he who has everything, or everything good."[22]

Not surprisingly in a people for whom all things animate and inanimate possessed some form of spiritual power, the white innovations, and even the whites themselves, were seen as endowed with supernatural qualities. Father Pierre Jean De Smet told of a Sioux chief whose most valued war medicine was a large color portrait of a Russian general who had fought in the Napoleonic Wars. Once acquired and put to daily use, most white manufactures lost their supernatural character, but some of the more inexplicable remained mysterious and sacred.

Much white behavior and many white beliefs defied the Indian's comprehension. "They laughed outright when we affirmed that the earth was round and revolved about the sun," wrote Prince Maximilian of upper Missouri natives in 1833.[23] Equally mystifying, though not so ridiculed, were white religious beliefs. Doctrinal differences especially prompted puzzlement. Artist Paul Kane recorded the bemusement of Cree Chief Broken Arm in 1848: "Mr. Rundell had told him what he preached was the only true road to heaven, and Mr. Hunter told him the same thing, and so did Mr. Thebo, and as all three had said the other two were wrong, and as he did not know which was right, he thought they ought to call a council among themselves, and then he would go with them all; but until they agreed he would wait."[24]

As the last half of the nineteenth century opened, all the Indians of the Trans-Mississippi West had experienced the white presence in vary-

Apaches lived in brush wickiups well adapted to their harsh desert homeland. Ben Wittick photographed this domestic scene at San Carlos Reservation about 1885. *Museum of New Mexico.*

Navajo. Navajos herded sheep and cultivated fruit orchards in the plateau country west of the Rio Grande. For two centuries they warred first with Spaniards,
then Mexicans, and finally Americans, as well as with Ute and Pueblo neighbors.
Kit Carson conquered them in 1864, but it was the four-year ordeal at Bosque
Redondo that ended Navajo wars forever. Back in their homeland, they achieved
fame as silversmiths and weavers. This man stands beside his rock-and-timber
"hogan." Ben Wittick photo, *School of American Research Collections, Museum of
New Mexico.*

ing degree. Some had but recently entered Tabeau's "age of gold," others had progressed to his "age of iron," and those most accessible to whites
were deep into the "age of brass." Whatever the age, the generalization
of a recent scholar seems applicable to all: "The Indian perceived and
alternately envied and feared the sophistication of the white man's religion,
customs, and technology, which seemed at times a threat and at times
the logical development of the principles of his own society and religion.
Each culture viewed the other with mixed feelings of attraction and
repulsion, sympathy and antipathy."[25]

The changes wrought in Indian life by white influences varied in kind
and magnitude from tribe to tribe. Paradoxically, many tribes that in
1850 boasted strong, viable institutions owed a heavy cultural debt to

the white man. The Blackfoot experience may serve to illustrate the *process* by which white influences helped guide the course of a people's history and culture.[26]

The Blackfoot divided into three tribes—Piegan, Blood, and Siksika (or Blackfoot proper). The vanguard of Algonkian-speaking peoples emerging from the woodlands to the grasslands, they came to rest early in the eighteenth century on the northern Great Plains at the eastern base of the Rocky Mountains, on both sides of the present international boundary. They hunted buffalo and other game on foot, with stone-tipped weapons, and they fought their enemies on the south and west—Shoshonis, Kutenais, and Flatheads—in the same way. Dogs provided transport, and all possessions had to be scaled proportionately. Even today, this period in Blackfoot history is remembered as "When we had only dogs for moving camp."

About 1730 a war party of Shoshonis stormed into a Piegan camp astride great galloping beasts and, smashing skulls with stone war clubs, put the hapless victims to rout. Terrified, the Piegans turned to their Assiniboine and Cree friends to the east. Warriors came to help launch a counterattack, and they brought with them a weapon even more wondrous than the Shoshonis' "Big Dog"—a metal tube that spurted flame and hurled a deadly little iron ball at the enemy. Thus fortified, the allied warriors confronted a Shoshoni force. Now the Shoshonis reacted in terror, as the blazing muskets felled fifty warriors and put the others to flight.

Within but few years the Blackfeet had acquired their own "Big Dogs" and firearms. Horses probably came in trade from tribes to the west. Guns came in trade from Assiniboines and Crees, who obtained them from French traders farther east. Other metal tools and utensils accompanied the guns. By midcentury the Blackfeet had become true horse-and-gun Indians, embarked on the rich life these innovations made possible.

By the 1780s the Blackfeet no longer had to rely on intermediaries for trade goods. The bearded white *Napikwans* (Old Man Persons) appeared in their country. On the North Saskatchewan River they built trading posts. Cutthroat competition flourished as the Hudson's Bay Company and the North West Company vied for the Blackfoot trade. At the posts the Indians obtained the coveted goods in direct trade with the white man. In exchange, since they did not trap beaver themselves, they offered buffalo meat and horses for the use of white hunters who worked out of the forts.

The trade also introduced the Blackfeet to "white man's water." They proved so susceptible to its effects that traders concocted a specially wa-

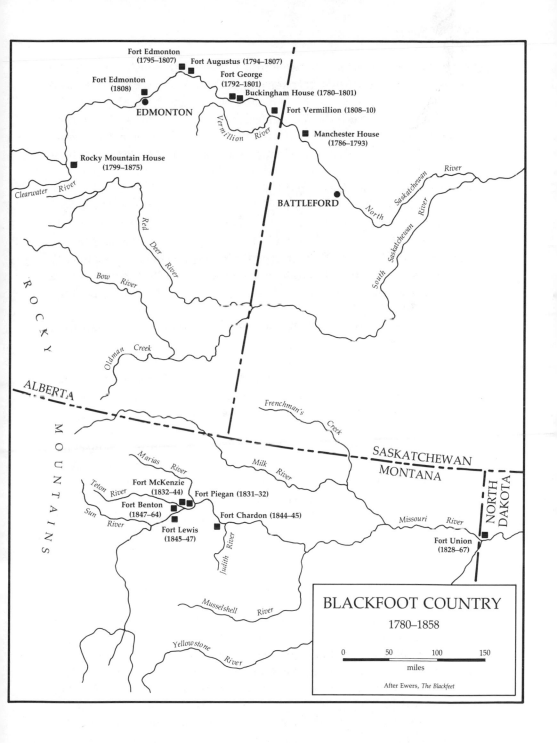

Fort Edmonton
(1795–1807)

Fort Augustus (1794–1807)

Fort Edmonton
(1808)

Fort George
(1792–1801)

Buckingham House (1780–1801)

Fort Vermillion (1808–10)

EDMONTON

Vermillion River

Manchester House
(1786–1793)

Rocky Mountain House
(1799–1875)

Clearwater River

North Saskatchewan River

River

BATTLEFORD

Red Deer River

Bow River

South Saskatchewan River

R
O
C
K
Y

Oldman Creek

ALBERTA

M
O
U
N
T
A
I
N
S

Frenchman's Creek

Marias River

Milk River

SASKATCHEWAN

Teton River

Fort McKenzie
(1832–44)

Fort Piegan (1831–32)

MONTANA

NORTH
DAKOTA

Fort Benton
(1847–64)

Fort Chardon (1844–45)

Sun River

Fort Lewis
(1845–47)

Missouri River

Judith River

Fort Union
(1828–67)

Musselshell River

Yellowstone River

BLACKFOOT COUNTRY

1780–1858

0   50   100   150

miles

After Ewers, *The Blackfeet*

tered mixture known as "Blackfoot Rum." Even that (consistent with the theory that Indians learned drunken comportment from whites) produced monumental drunks, invariably a feature of the trading ritual. As competition intensified, so did the use of Blackfoot Rum as a weapon of competition. By 1810 a trader observed of the Blackfeet: "That power for all evil, spiritous liquor, now seems to dominate them, and has taken such hold on them that they are no longer the quiet people they were."[27]

The Blackfeet also discovered the devastating effects of smallpox. In 1781 a Piegan war party chanced upon a seemingly abandoned Shoshoni village. Warily scouting it, they finally launched a dawn attack, only to find the tipis full of dead and dying Indians. Ascribing to supernatural causes the horrible sores that covered their foes' bodies, the Piegans collected their war trophies and rode home in triumph. Half the Piegan tribe paid for the victory with their lives as the scourge swept lethally through their camps.

After the epidemic the Blackfeet recovered more quickly than their neighbors. In the closing decade of the eighteenth century they turned on their enemies to the south and west. Lacking firearms, ravaged by smallpox, the Shoshonis gave way under the assault and withdrew far to the south, abandoning rich hunting grounds to the aggressors. Similarly, the Kutenais and Flatheads proved no match for the Blackfeet and, retreating west of the Rocky Mountains, yielded large areas. Confident and powerful, by the first decade of the nineteenth century the Blackfeet boasted a fully developed horse-mounted, buffalo-hunting culture. Alexander Henry called them "the most independent and happy people of all the tribes E. of the Rocky mountains. War, women, horses and buffalo are their delights, and all these they have at command."[28]

The Blackfeet needed all the power they could summon, for the pressures generated by the fur trade kept tribal ranges and relationships in constant flux. The Blackfeet entered the nineteenth century almost friendless and increasingly beset on all sides. The Crees and Assiniboines, once allies, began to encroach from the east as beaver and game gave out in their country, and bitter fighting erupted. To the south Shoshonis and Crows and to the west Kutenais and Flatheads obtained firearms and began to challenge their once-invincible foes.

The Blackfeet also took on the Americans advancing up the Missouri River in the early 1800s, seeking beaver. The Lewis and Clark expedition collided with Piegans in 1806 and killed one. Thereafter, for a quarter of a century, the Blackfeet effectually denied the rich beaver country of the upper Missouri to the "Big Knives," whose occasional forays into this

Pueblos. These people lived in adobe and stone villages, often picturesquely terraced, and cultivated corn and beans. They threw the Spaniards out of New Mexico in 1680 but after the reconquest accommodated with their neighbors. U.S. officials honored their Spanish land grants but thereby excluded them from U.S. Indian law. Not until the twentieth century was the injustice rectified and the land muddle untangled. These are dancers celebrating St. John's Day at Ácoma Pueblo in 1883. photographed by Ben Wittick. *School of American Research Collections, Museum of New Mexico.*

The advent of white traders intensified traditional animosities between tribes. Here, at the American Fur Company's Fort McKenzie, in the Blackfoot country of the upper Missouri, Assinniboines fell on Blackfeet in a bloody surprise attack, August 28, 1833. Carl Bodmer recorded the scene. *Montana Historical Society.*

region invariably ended in disaster. Blackfoot hostility persisted and intensified in this period because American traders supplied the guns and ammunition that enabled Shoshonis and others to contest Blackfoot pretensions.

Blackfoot opposition dissolved in the early 1830s. The peace maker was Kenneth McKenzie, who had charge of Fort Union, the American Fur Company's post at the confluence of the Missouri and Yellowstone rivers. McKenzie promised the Blackfeet to keep white trappers out of their country and offered them premium prices for buffalo robes. The "Northern White Men" had never been much interested in the heavy robes because they were difficult to transport, but the Americans could easily float them down the Missouri to St. Louis. Also holding forth surpassing quantities of "white man's water," the American Fur Company in the 1830s and

1840s almost entirely weaned the Blackfeet from the Hudson's Bay Company, in the process prompting a significant shift southward of the Blackfoot range. Most of the trade was conducted at Fort McKenzie, on the Missouri at the mouth of the Marias, but the Blackfeet journeyed even to Fort Union itself.

Significant in keeping Blackfoot allegiance were the alliances between traders and Indian women. The most influential was Alexander Culbertson's marriage to a woman from a prominent Blood family. Culbertson's presence at Fort McKenzie proved crucial in persuading the Blackfeet not to blame the whites for the terrible smallpox epidemic of 1837. Reaching the upper Missouri on a company cargo vessel, the infection spread virulently through all three Blackfoot tribes, carrying off two-thirds of the people, six thousand in number. Later, in 1846, after blunders of company officials at Fort Union had turned the Blackfeet hostile again, Culbertson was sent back to the upper Missouri and successfully restored peace and trade.

By the middle of the nineteenth century the Blackfeet had grown dependent on trade for a great variety of manufactured goods, both necessities and luxuries. In many less tangible ways, too, the Blackfeet of 1850 were products of a process set in motion by white people. The more wives a man had, for example, the more buffalo robes could be prepared for trade and the more wealth he could amass. In the 1820s he would have had three or four; in 1850 he might have had many more. Wives had to be paid for in horses, which spurred their accumulation in vast herds. The economic premium on horses in turn gave horse-stealing raids against other Indians a prominence in warfare absent in earlier times. Also, the horse and gun wrought basic changes in the techniques of warfare. Massed encounters on foot, involving heavy casualties, gave way to mounted hit-and-run forays by small parties. The war chief of old disappeared in favor of the temporary leader who organized his own war party. Political chiefs too were vulnerable to the trade. A monopoly firm strengthened the authority of a chief by dealing through him. Competition undermined a chief because competitors went "to the very tipi doors."

In these and countless other subtle ways Blackfoot institutions, customs, and beliefs had undergone change in response to forces loosed by trade and traders. The changes, however, mostly amounted to a strengthening or evolution of traditional ways rather than a fundamental transformation or substitution of new for old. Just as a metal arrow point was simply a better version of the stone point, the new emphasis on women and horses simply gave further development to institutions that had ex-

isted for nearly a century. Thus the Blackfeet of 1850, despite dependence on trade goods and despite a century of profound white influence,
remained a culturally and politically viable people: proud, self-confident,
firmly in control of their destinies.

So were many of the other natives of the Trans-Mississippi West. Like
the Blackfeet, they had changed in many similar ways and many different ways in response to the presence of white people in or near their
world. Until now the changes had been evolutionary and mostly within
the bounds of traditional culture. Henceforth they would be revolutionary and finally destructive of traditional culture.

With good reason did the prescient Yellow Wolf, pondering the meaning of the sudden passage of so many white soldiers through the Cheyenne hunting grounds in the summer of 1846, fear for the future of his
people.

2

Foundations of a New Indian Policy, 1846–1860

A sleepy village of low adobe buildings, Las Vegas nestled among piñon-dappled foothills of the Sangre de Cristo Mountains. It marked the northeastern frontier of New Mexico, the first Mexican settlement reached by Missouri traders after the long journey over the Santa Fe Trail from Independence. On August 15, 1846, Las Vegas played reluctant host to the Army of the West.

The morning sun shown brightly on the blue columns of horsemen, their banners unfurled for the first time since leaving the Missouri River. As they trooped through the dusty plaza under the apprehensive gaze of the assembled citizens, General Kearny and his staff confronted the alcalde and other town functionaries. Together they climbed to the top of a flat-roofed building on the north side of the plaza. The townspeople gathered below to hear the American general take possession of New Mexico in the name of the United States. No longer did they owe allegiance to Governor Manuel Armijo in Santa Fe, he told them. His troops would not take a pepper or an onion without pay. All would be free to follow their Catholic religion. And, a matter of almost daily concern to this pastoral people: "From the Mexican government, you have never received protection. The Apaches and the Navajos come down from the mountains and carry off your sheep, and even your women, whenever they please. My government will correct all this. It will keep off the Indians, protect you in your persons and property."[1]

The promise so unqualifiedly delivered in the Las Vegas plaza that sunny August morning was to be repeated as the army made its way westward. Indeed, the promise to eliminate the Indian menace to white settlement was implicit in the nation's westward expansion to the Pacific. If an experienced frontiersman like Stephen Watts Kearny could betray

31

On August 18, 1846, from a rooftop overlooking the plaza of Las Vegas, New Mexico, General Stephen Watts Kearny took possession of New Mexico for the United States. He also promised to protect the inhabitants from Indian raiders—a promise neither he nor his successors were to fulfill for four decades. From Twitchell, *Military Occupation of New Mexico.*

so little sense of the complexity of the obligation thus assumed, and of the tribesmen who for three centuries had scourged the New Mexican colonists, his countrymen could hardly be faulted for lacking the knowledge and understanding on which to base enlightened national policies toward the Indians.

However distorted, whites did possess distinct images of their Indian neighbors. For four centuries the two races had shared the North American continent. If the white presence had changed the Indians, so the Indian presence had powerfully affected the whites. In ways that few white Americans of Kearny's time would have recognized or understood, their conceptions of themselves and their destiny had been influenced by this experience. These conceptions shaped white images of the Indian, white attitudes toward the Indian, and, ultimately, white policies and institutions for dealing with the Indian.[2]

Central to white thinking was the idea of progress, which had been flowering through successive mutations since germinating in seventeenth-century Europe. Progress marked human history, the theory went, as peoples learned from their forebears and marched onward and upward to ever greater attainments. The scientific, intellectual, cultural, and even political achievements of the Renaissance and the Enlightenment seemed to confirm the idea, and by the end of the eighteenth century it had firmly embedded itself in European and American thought.

In purely American terms, progress demanded the conquest of the wilderness, an imperative fortified by God's command to "Be fruitful and multiply, and fill the earth and subdue it." It was not truly a wilderness, of course, for it supported thriving civilizations and networks of constantly traveled roads and trails, all markedly at variance with the meaning of "wilderness."[3] But Indians and their works did not qualify as human in the same sense as Spaniards or Englishmen, even though the latter secured a foothold in this wilderness only with the crucial aid, freely given or forcibly compelled, of its human inhabitants. Still, from the European perspective a wilderness such as God had in mind confronted and challenged them. A progressively westward struggle with this wilderness had in fact been a dominant theme of American history since the advent of Columbus.

The idea of progress focused on the Indian in two ways. First, he was a central feature of the wilderness, and, by definition, conquest of the wilderness entailed conquest of the Indian. Second, he was living confirmation of the very idea of progress itself. Progress came to be seen as rise from savagery to civilization. In the Indian whites saw the lower order from which they themselves had progressed, and thus in themselves they saw the higher order to which the Indian might one day progress. Of the American Indians a Scottish philosopher wrote in 1767: "It is in their present condition that we are to behold, as in a mirror, the features of our own progenitors."[4]

As whites saw the Indian as progenitor, they described him not in observably objective terms but in terms of what whites were not. They collectivized diverse groups of natives into a generic "Indian," labeled him "savage," and defined savagery as deficiencies, both cultural and moral, as measured against the standards and ideals of "civilization." By this term they meant their own civilization, for they recognized no other. Of this formulation, then, with its value-laden nomenclature, was born an image of the Indian as substandard, even subhuman, that was to endure in the American consciousness.

This so-called deficient Indian assumed two persistent, contradictory forms—the good Indian and the bad Indian, the Noble Savage and the Ignoble Savage. The bad Indian was barbarous, cruel, lecherous, deceitful, filthy, lazy, and superstitious. The good Indian, though still deficient, was wise, dignified, handsome, hospitable, courageous, eloquent, and tender. These opposing conceptions took form partly as devices in a larger debate over the validity of European values and institutions. Critics of the established order portrayed the Noble Savage as a simple child of nature dwelling idyllically in a forested paradise, a living reproach to the artificiality and decadence of industrial society. Defenders of the established order pointed to the bad Indian, the "red devil," the Ignoble Savage, as living testimony to the rightness of what they deemed to be civilization.

The Noble Savage-Ignoble Savage dichotomy was but one manifestation of ambivalent white attitudes toward the Indian and the wilderness. Another was the rise in American literature of the "Boone figure"—the white frontiersman who acquires the outdoor skills of the Indian, indeed becomes part Indian, as an essential weapon in the white conquest of the wilderness. Daniel Boone sired a large progeny, real and fictional, of mythical figures who combined Indian and white traits. "It is out of this tradition," observes a close student, "that America's greatest hero figures have come—the Indian guide, the scout, ranger, mountain man, plainsman, and, finally, the cowboy."[5] Like the Indian, however, the Boone figures aroused mixed feelings of admiration and revulsion in their countrymen, and in the end, having fulfilled their appointed task as civilization's cutting edge in the wilderness, civilization had a place for them only in its literature.

Both the Boone figure and the Noble Savage achieved their clearest definition and widest public acceptance in the first half of the nineteenth century. James Fenimore Cooper cast the first in classic form in the character known variously as Natty Bumppo, Deerslayer, Leatherstocking, and Hawkeye, and the second in Uncas, "The Last of the Mohicans." Significant also were the paintings of Charles Bird King, George Catlin, and Seth Eastman and the ethnological studies of Henry R. Schoolcraft. Henry Wadsworth Longfellow brought the strands together in Hiawatha, a figure another modern commentator sees as carrying to "its logical conclusion the paradoxical premises at the heart of the Boone myth: that the American hero is simultaneously hunter and farmer, wanderer and citizen, exploiter and cultivator . . . a mediating figure between mythological conceptions of the old and the new Americans—like Daniel Boone."[6]

Besides roaming deeply, darkly, and mirrorlike through the American psyche, the Indian also roamed through the American wilderness. He thus posed a practical problem that had to be dealt with. About his ultimate fate none disagreed: progress demanded his destruction along with the wilderness. About the means of destruction, however, there was disagreement. He could be either destroyed outright by killing or, consistent with the tenets of progress, elevated from savagery to civilization. In either event, since the generic Indian (like savagery and civilization) was a white conception, he ceased to exist.

From the birth of the American nation, public sentiment overwhelmingly favored destruction by civilization rather than by killing. Thomas Jefferson gave clear and persuasive expression to the idea and laid the foundations of governmental policy that he and his successors carried forward. Strangely, the Jeffersonian underpinnings of this policy, a product of Enlightenment thought, came to be replaced by the dogma of the evangelical Protestantism that swept America in the early decades of the nineteenth century; though very different rationales, both dictated the same policy.[7] Despite vocal agitation for extermination by a minority, usually those closest to the frontier, basic Jeffersonian aims never aroused serious challenge.

Other than a vague assumption that Christianity would lead to civilization, policy makers at the midpoint of the nineteenth century had not seriously confronted the problem of how to civilize the Indian. The rhetoric about incorporation into white society skirted the question of whether incorporation meant racial assimilation and, if so, whether white Americans were ready for interracial marriages on the necessary scale. Rather, so long as vast lands lay vacant beyond the frontier, the precise means of civilizing the Indian did not have to be worked out. As in colonial times, therefore, white concern in the formative years of the United States remained more with how to possess the Indian's land than with how to civilize him.

At the heart of the land issue lay starkly differing attitudes toward land. Indian attitudes sprang in large measure from religious concepts. Worshiping deities residing in nature, Indians in effect worshiped the natural world and strove for a life in balance with it. Whites, on the other hand, worshiped otherworldly abstractions. The Christian God in His heaven, the place of all goodness, ruled over a natural world below that was the source of all evil. Far from encouraging His children to seek harmony with the wilderness, He commanded them to subdue and destroy the wilderness and make it blossom with the fruits of their industry.[8]

Absolute individual ownership of the land ran deep in European tradition and formed the cornerstone of the white economic system. To minds steeped in concepts of private property, the Indians' communal use of large areas of land could scarcely be regarded as a basis for true ownership, especially when they used so little of it in the approved fashion. John Quincy Adams surely spoke for his countrymen when he asked in 1802: "What is the right of a huntsman to the forest of a thousand miles over which he has accidentally ranged in quest of prey? . . . Shall the field and vallies, which a beneficent God has formed to teem with the life of innumerable multitudes, be condemned to ever lasting barrenness?"[9]

The answer, of course, was no. But the land could not be simply seized without some rationalizing cloak of legality and humanity. The colonial powers and then the United States repeatedly acknowledged Indian "title" to the land. They recognized the tribes as possessing some, but not total, sovereignty—Chief Justice John Marshall aptly characterized them as "domestic dependent nations." With such "nations" the true sovereign might treat for transfer of title.

This very recognition, in turn, speeded the evolution of the tribe as the Indians' socio-political organization, and in its demand for governing authorities with whom to negotiate it had a twofold effect on the institution of chief: it truly strengthened the internal authority of the native leaders, but it also led white officialdom to assume for them a greater authority and representative character than they could possibly possess. Thus did seeds of endless misunderstanding and recrimination take root.

Treaties were the mechanism for describing and legitimizing the manipulation of Indian land title. "The purpose of the treaty-making process," notes a recent scholar, "was to benefit the national interest without staining the nation's honor."[10] More bluntly, a governor of Georgia explained it in terms many of his countrymen would have approved: "Treaties were expedients by which ignorant, intractable, and savage people were induced without bloodshed to yield up what civilized people had the right to possess by virtue of that command of the.Creator delivered to man upon his formation—be fruitful, multiply, and replenish the earth, and subdue it."[11]

But there was bloodshed. When government emissaries could not persuade, coax, or trick Indians into selling title, wars broke out. The killing so foreign to the Jeffersonian ideal occurred. Title then passed based on conquest rather than diplomacy; more accurately, both war and diplomacy usually led to transfer of title. War and diplomacy alternated throughout the colonial period and into the decades following American independence.

The Jeffersonian answer to the recurring bloodshed was removal: Remove the Indians of the East to the West, to lands not inhabited by whites or included within the boundaries of any state. Give them new lands in the unorganized territory beyond the ninety-fifth meridian. Protect them there from white encroachment either on their domain or their way of life. In this officially designated "Indian Country," separated from the rest of the nation by a "Permanent Indian Frontier," the Indians could dwell in free and happy isolation from their tormentors, absorbing civilization at their own pace or rejecting it altogether if they wished. Under Presidents James Monroe and Andrew Jackson, removal became the dominant feature of U.S. Indian policy. Throughout the 1830s and 1840s the eastern Indians were uprooted and moved westward. Some fifty thousand people made the trek, many at great cost in suffering, hardship, and impoverishment. They yielded 100 million acres of eastern home land in return for 32 million western acres and 68 million dollars in annuity pledges.[12]

History has spotlighted the ordeal of the so-called Five Civilized Tribes—Cherokee, Creek, Choctaw, Chickasaw, and Seminole—who lost land and property in Georgia, Mississippi, and other southern states and finally came to rest in what would soon become Indian Territory and later Oklahoma. But many other groups made the move, too, often concluding a westward odyssey that began on the East Coast and featured pauses enroute on lands first granted, then taken away as westering whites encroached.

A chain of military posts extending from Fort Snelling, Minnesota, to Fort Jesup, Louisiana, defined the so-called Permanent Indian Frontier. Otherwise, it existed mainly as a tantalizing abstraction, and even this crumbled under the tread of General Kearny's Army of the West and collapsed altogether under the wheels of wagons bearing goldseekers to the new U.S. possessions on the Pacific.

Throughout the decade of the 1850s a stream of travelers flowed westward. Few got rich, but gold and silver dramatized the new territories, invited immigration, and stimulated agriculture, commerce, transportation, and ultimately industry. By 1860 settlers beyond the ninety-fifth meridian had multiplied more than threefold, with Texas alone claiming 604,215 and California 379,994.[13] California and Oregon had joined Texas in statehood, and nearly all the rest of the land west of the Missouri River had been organized into the territories of New Mexico, Utah, Washington, Kansas, and Nebraska.

The migration sent whites coursing through the homeland of some tribes

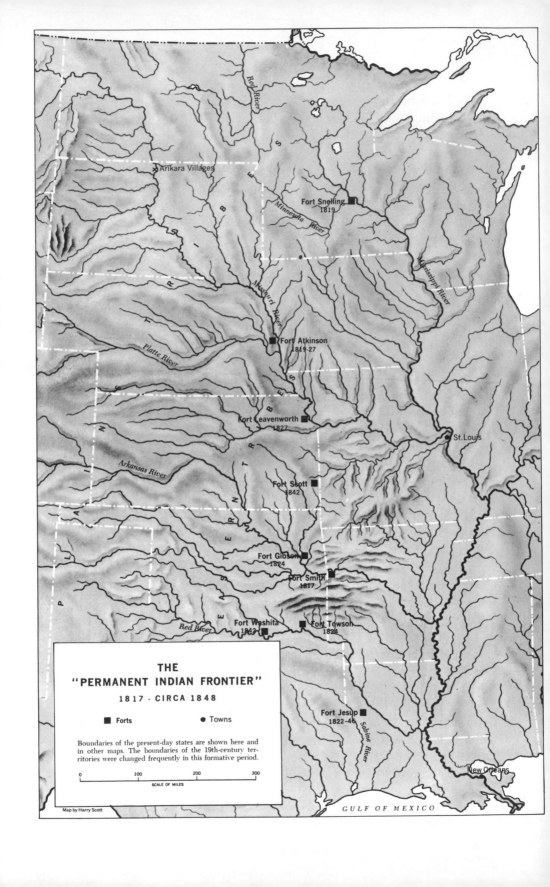

Arikara Villages

Fort Snelling
1819

Minnesota River

Missouri River

Fort Atkinson
1819-27

Platte River

Fort Leavenworth
1827

St. Louis

Arkansas River

Fort Scott
1842

Fort Gibson
1824

Fort Smith
1817

Fort Washita
1842

Fort Towson
1824

Red River

Red River

Mississippi River

THE
"PERMANENT INDIAN FRONTIER"
1817 · CIRCA 1848

■ Forts   ● Towns

Boundaries of the present-day states are shown here and
in other maps. The boundaries of the 19th-century territories were changed frequently in this formative period.

0   100   200   300
SCALE OF MILES

Map by Harry Scott

Fort Jesup
1822-46

Sabine River

New Orleans

GULF OF MEXICO

Army wagon trains transporting supplies for General Kearny's army over the Santa Fe Trail were the vanguard of a great westward migration of whites that doomed the Permanent Indian Frontier. *Utah Historical Society.*

and deposited them, as settlers, in the homeland of others. Once again, as in the advance of the frontier across the Appalachians and down to the Mississippi, Indians complicated the lives of enough American citizens to lay on their government the task of dealing with an "Indian problem." From earlier frontier experience, and the public attitudes and assumptions it shaped, emerged the governmental policies and institutions for dealing with the Indians of the Trans-Mississippi West.[14]

The Mexican War had scarcely opened in 1846 before government officials began to recognize its implications for Indian policy. Consideration of measures focused on three major objectives that acquisition of the new territories imposed on federal Indian policy. First, military protection had to be provided to citizens threatened by Indians. Second, Indian title to lands coveted, needed, or already possessed by whites had

"Washing for Gold." The California gold discovery, followed by strikes through-out the West, drew hordes of prospectors to the mountain homeland of many tribes and brought heavy use to transcontinental trails that sliced through the homeland of others. More than any other whites, miners disrupted the Indian world of the American West. From Samuel Bowles, *Our New West*.

to be formally "extinguished." Third, now that removal beyond a Permanent Indian Frontier was no longer possible, some other humane disposition of the Indians had to be worked out.

Frontier military needs had been partly addressed in 1846 when Congress authorized a string of guardian forts along the Oregon Trail and the creation of a special unit to garrison them. Thereafter, however, both Congress and the executive branch failed to appreciate the demands the new possessions placed on the army. President James K. Polk said in 1848, as the army shrank to its prewar dimensions, that "the present military establishment is sufficient for all exigencies." And though modest increases came in 1850 and 1855, never in the years before the Civil War did the little regular army succeed in fielding more than seven or eight thousand officers and enlisted men for duty in a frontier West of two million square miles.[15]

They were a tough, diverse lot, these regulars. Boredom, isolation, slow promotion, and wretched living conditions on the frontier thinned the officer corps of much of its talent and discouraged all but life's most unfortunate from enlisting in the ranks. But a hard core of able officers, future generals of blue and gray, combined with a leavening in the ranks of adventurous youths and steady old veterans to provide a redemption sufficient to make the army a significant presence in the frontier West.

As the army emerged from the woodlands, it confronted a new geography and a new enemy. Vast distances and climatic extremes combined with sparsity of natural foods, fuel, and water to make geography a more formidable foe than the Indian. Few navigable streams afforded access by steamboat, as in the East, and supplies had to be hauled hundreds of miles by wagon. The enemy, too, was different—mostly mounted, masters of guerrilla warfare, nomadic or seminomadic, and so perfectly attuned to their environment as to exploit its every feature to their advantage.

The regulars did not wrestle very imaginatively with the strategic implications of their new task. The basic approach was an ever spreading network of small frontier forts, most so weakly manned as to accomplish little except to show the flag, and most located as much in response to demands of settlers for markets and visible protection as to strategic considerations. From such forts the army mounted small-unit patrols, scouts, and escorts, and occasionally it concentrated enough force to field an offensive column. Some succeeded, but most failed, mainly because of a hostile land and climate and a foe that rarely fought according to the white soldiers' rules.

Few looked to the little forts for a long-term solution of the Indian problem. The agency entrusted with this mission was the Bureau of Indian Affairs, organized in 1824 as a component of the War Department and in 1849 given a clearly civilian complexion by incorporation into the newly created Department of the Interior. As the so-called Indian problem became less and less a military problem, the Indian Bureau gained in strength and influence. By the close of the frontier period in 1890, it was the most powerful force in the lives of the Indians.

Headed by the Commissioner of Indian Affairs and a cadre of clerks in Washington, the Indian Bureau functioned mainly through a field force of superintendents and agents. In the territories, the superintendency was often combined with the post of territorial governor. This had the appeal of economy, but it usually subjected Indian affairs to neglect at best and partisan political manipulation at worst. Moreover, the Indian

Above and right: Throughout the 1850s and 1860s the covered wagons of emi-
grants bound for the Pacific crawled up the Great Platte Road past Chimney Rock
and other landmarks and across the continental divide via the broad portal of
South Pass. Their passage depleted the timber, grass, and game of Pawnee,
Sioux, Cheyenne, Shoshoni, and other tribes. W. H. Jackson paintings, *Denver
Public Library Western Collection.*

Bureau suffered the worst evils of the spoils system. Appointments usually went to men with no other qualification than faithful party service.
As a former agent crisply explained his appointment, "I could sing a good
political song."[16] Aside from lack of qualifications and the certainty of
replacement when the next President took office, all too many brought
to their assignments gross incompetence, a deliberate intent to profit by
corruption, or both.

The Indian Bureau had two major purposes: to extinguish Indian land
titles and to grapple with the vexing problem of what to do with the people whose title had been extinguished. The title question intruded ur-
gently because in Oregon, California, and New Mexico whites were
settling in growing numbers on lands still owned by Indians. To get to
the new possessions, furthermore, the immigrants traveled trails across

Indian lands that, if not needed now, soon would be. As Senator Ste-phen Λ. Douglas pointed out in the angry debates over the Kansas-Nebraska Bill, the new Pacific Coast possessions could never truly be a part of the United States without settled, organized territory in between, nor could the Pacific Railroad that almost everyone championed ever be a success. Only in Texas was there no immediate question of title; upon entering the Union, the state had retained jurisdiction over all its vacant land and refused to concede that the Indians owned any of it.

The treaty remained the mechanism for extinguishing title and defin-ing all other relations between the United States and a tribe. The system contained major flaws. When vital interests were involved, neither Con-gress nor the executive branch felt the same scruples about violating Indian treaties as they did in honoring treaties with foreign nations,

To protect the emigrants and settlers who headed west after the Mexican War, the U.S. Army scattered thin lines of "war houses" through the Indian country. So small was the army and so vast the country, they could do little more than defend their own parade grounds. This is Fort Duncan, Texas, the upriver limit of settlement on the Rio Grande border with Mexico. *National Archives*.

especially when the Indians seemed equally adept at violations. And indeed they were, with good reason. Chiefs who signed treaties did not always understand what they had agreed to. "Boone came out and got them to sign a paper," recalled the Arapaho Little Raven, "but they did not know what it meant."[17] Often such misunderstanding had no more sinister explanation than simply a bad interpreter, but often, too, negotiators intentionally concealed or deceived. Furthermore, chiefs rarely represented their people as fully as white officials assumed, nor could they enforce compliance if the people did not want to comply. And chiefs and people alike sometimes failed to see compelling reason to keep promises when the other party to the agreement so often broke promises. All in all, the treaty system piled up mountainous troubles for both sides, but as long as Indians retained enough power to resist the government's

An enduring institution of Indian-white relations was the treaty council, in which government commissioners sought cessions of Indian lands and guarantees of peace. Gustavus Sohon here depicts Governor Isaac I. Stevens' council with Flathead Indians of Montana in 1855. *Smithsonian Institution National Anthropological Archives.*

dictates, there seemed no better way of coming to terms with each other's existence.

An insidious by-product of the treaty system was the annuity system—the practice of paying for land with cash dispensed in annual installments over a period of years. It was a system highly vulnerable to abuse by politically well-connected traders, who sat at disbursing tables each year to collect real or fictional debts run up during the year by the Indians. Aggravating the abuse was the custom of making lump-sum payments to chiefs for distribution to their people (another of those outside influences that strengthened the institution of chief), especially when a chief formed a corrupt alliance with unscrupulous whites. Finally, cash annuities lubricated the commerce in liquor, affording traders enhanced opportunity for fraudulently siphoning off the payments and exacerbating the curse of drunkenness. Despite the efforts of successive Commissioners of Indian Affairs backed by a succession of acts of Congress, the annuity system and its concomitant abuses persisted.[18]

What to do with dispossessed Indians now that a Permanent Indian Frontier no longer offered a solution posed a thorny problem. The answer evolved out of a proposal by Polk's Commissioner of Indian Affairs, William Medill, in his annual report for 1848. Medill's scheme for Indian "colonies," in which to gather Indians while the whites filled up the country around them, swiftly matured. Reservations of sorts existed east of the Mississippi River, but not until the 1850s did the idea flower into established policy. It gained the strong and consistent support of successive Commissioners of Indian Affairs, largely through the influence of the Indian Bureau's longtime chief clerk, Charles E. Mix, who energetically promoted the concept during a tenure that lasted from 1850 to 1869.

In broad outline, the reservation policy called for concentrating the Indians on small, well-defined tracts of land, protecting them from white contamination, teaching them to become self-sufficient farmers, and conferring on them the blessings of white Christian civilization. The policy met both practical and moral objectives: it would clear the Indians from the travel routes and settled areas while also advancing what one official called "the great work of regenerating the Indian race." Congress and the President and his Indian officials often disagreed on which lands to set aside and how much to pay for them, but the policy itself attracted broad and consistent support.[19]

Besides the army and the Indian Bureau, a third institution of government dominated Indian relations: the Congress. The legislation that guided and the appropriations that fueled all activities of the executive branch originated in the Congress, and in addition the Senate had to consent to presidential ratification of Indian treaties in the same manner as for treaties with foreign nations. Both House and Senate maintained Indian committees to give direction to their deliberations in these matters.

In still another way did the Congress exert powerful influence. Agents and other field employees of the Indian Bureau usually owed their appointments to a member of Congress. All too often this patronage spawned a three-way alliance that fed on the annuity system. Senators and representatives placed their protégés in official posts, and they in turn, in league with local traders, contractors, and other claimants, pursued schemes for harvesting the appropriations that their mentors in Washington assiduously cultivated. All three profited, often spectacularly. The Indian lost, often spectacularly.

From the brown ridges bordering the valleys and the green cottonwood groves along the rivers, the Plains Indians watched as whites flowed westward on the transcontinental trails. On horseback and foot they came, in white-topped prairie schooners, in lumbering freight wagons, and in swift stagecoaches.

Ambivalence marked the reaction of these observors. On the one hand, the splendid array of white-man goods, to be had in exchange for hides and furs at trading posts like Bent's Fort and Fort Laramie, furnished a powerful lure. Moreover, as treaties established annuity obligations for the government, official gift-giving extravaganzas took place yearly that greatly appealed to social and acquisitive instincts. And apart from tangible gain, the endlessly surprising and puzzling behavior of the queer white-skinned people proved irresistibly fascinating. On the other hand, although few of the travelers paused to make their homes on the Plains, they left a mark of their passage increasingly disturbing to the Indians. Their campfires consumed entire stands of timber at favored camping places. Their stock stripped bare the valley grasses and ate their way up the benches. Most threatening, their rifles felled buffalo, deer, and antelope by the thousands to supply meat for hungry travelers. "Since the white man has made a road across our land," complained the Shoshoni chief Washakie as early as 1855, "and has killed off our game, we are hungry, and there is nothing for us to eat. Our women and children cry for food and we have no food to give them."[20]

Much less ambivalence pulled at the Indians who lived at the end of the trails, for here the threat was immediate and direct. In California and Oregon, Texas and New Mexico, whites did not merely make a road across Indian lands; they settled in the midst of them. Yet even here natives could not entirely free themselves from white attractions.

The groups thus threatened by travelers and settlers reacted differently at different times and places. Some accommodated. Some retreated or scattered. Some fought back, in lightning raids or in open war, not solely in defense but for the opportunities in plunder, adventure, and honor that war afforded. Some combined all reactions at once. Some, notably in the gold-bearing regions of California's Sierra Nevada, simply vanished.

Whatever a group's experience, sooner or later it involved a treaty council. Government emissaries appeared, treaty in hand, and the bargaining began over the transfer of title to a large share of the group's traditional range and the definition of a smaller tract, increasingly called a reservation, within which the people were now to live. The details varied, but such councils had enough in common for one to suggest the nature of all.

Chief negotiators at the Laguna Negra council of 1855 were New Mexico Governor David Meriwether (1853–56) (above), who concluded treaties with all the New Mexico tribes only to have them rejected by the U.S. Senate, and Navajo Chief Manuelito, (right) just rising to the commanding leadership he exerted for a generation. At first an advocate of peace, Manuelito turned hostile under repeated provocations and during the war of 1863–64 was the principal war leader. He surrendered in 1866 and, after the Bosque Redondo experience, returned to the Navajo homeland to function as a revered elder statesman. This picture was taken by Charles Bell 1874. *Museum of New Mexico.*

The Laguna Negra Treaty of 1855 was the handiwork of David Meriwether, governor of the Territory of New Mexico and ex-officio Superintendent of Indian Affairs. A hearty, big-framed man with thick white hair, he had ranged the West for a decade as a youthful fur trapper and, following a successful career in Kentucky politics, returned at age fifty-three as territorial governor. Meriwether set forth in 1855 to negotiate treaties of cession with all the major New Mexico groups. One was the Navajo, a brawny nation of twelve thousand people who herded sheep on the red mesa-studded plateaus stretching westward from the Rio Grande toward the Grand Canyon. A weakly manned military post with the brave name

Fort Defiance watched tentatively over the eastern fringe of the Navajo domain. More influential in maintaining a precarious peace was an unusually able agent, Henry Dodge, who had repudiated the life of his father and brother, both U.S. senators, to take an Indian wife and devote himself to the welfare of the Navajos. Accompanied by a dragoon escort, Governor Meriwether and his party arrived at the Laguna Negra council grounds on July 13, 1855.[21]

The little band of whites pitched their tents beside a pretty lake nestled in grassy meadows and surrounded by timbered hills. Menace hung over them as between fifteen hundred and two thousand well-armed, well-mounted Navajos gathered. At one point, while the governor parleyed with the chiefs, a handful of studiedly insolent men took over his personal tent and, when the sergeant of the guard protested, ostentatiously fitted arrows to bows and intimidated him into silence. Also, a rumor ran through camp that the Indians planned a nighttime ambush and massacre. But the night passed without incident, and all such talk evaporated next day with the arrival of General John Garland and a battery of field artillery from Fort Defiance.

The deliberations took place on open ground near Meriwether's tent. About twenty chiefs represented the Indians. At first Zarcillos Largos (Long Earrings) spoke for them. A wise and respected leader of about sixty, consistently a proponent of peace, he had been looked upon by white officials as head chief of the tribe ever since the American conquest in 1846. As symbols of this distinction, he carried a cane given him by one of Meriwether's predecessors, and around his neck he wore a beribboned medal presented by Meriwether himself two years earlier. Midway in the proceedings, however, Zarcillos Largos abruptly sent his cane and medal to the governor's tent with the explanation that he had grown too old to lead his people and had asked the headmen to select another. Fortunately the choice fell on Manuelito, a vigorous giant of about thirty-seven years and also a champion of peace. Another difficulty arose, however, as described by Meriwether's private secretary: Manuelito "would not receive the staff the other chief had surrendered, nor allow the medal to be suspended from his neck by the same string, giving as a reason that his people had a superstition about such things, and that, if he should receive them, he would lose his influence over the tribe."[22] Meriwether deftly solved this problem by presenting Manuelito with his own cane and supplying the medal with a new cord.

The purpose of the conference, Meriwether explained through an interpreter, was to "agree on a country the Navajos and whites may each have, that they may not pasture their flocks on each other's lands. If we have a dividing line . . . , it will keep us at peace." From this seemingly sensible proposition, the meeting moved through two days of increasingly bewildering deliberations. The "dividing line," of course, marked off the lands to be ceded to the United States as well as those to be retained by the Indians. In return for the cession, the government would confirm the Navajos in the ownership of their new reservation—subject to such wagon roads, railways, and military posts as might be needed at any time—and promised annuity payments of $10,000 a year for two years, $6,000 a year for another two, and $4,000 a year for a final sixteen. In the discretion of the President, this money could be paid directly to the Navajos or "expended for such beneficial objects as in his judgment will be calculated to advance them in civilization."

Just how much of what transpired the Indians understood can only be surmised. Meriwether and Dodge used a map to explain the boundaries, a proceeding both puzzling and distressing to the chiefs. Manuelito made enough objections to the boundaries to show that he grasped at least some of the implications. But it is unlikely that he or any of the other chiefs fully perceived that about two-thirds of their traditional homeland, almost fifteen thousand square miles, was to be yielded and that they were all now to live within an area about half that size. In any case, the chiefs assented to the terms without serious debate, and on July 18 twenty-seven of them lined up to scratch their marks on the document while the army officers signed their names as witnesses.

Then came the eagerly awaited distribution of presents. Each headman received his share, and each then turned his followers loose on it. A wild, shouting melee followed. Bales flew apart, packages sailed through the air, dust roiled about pounding hooves, and bolts of cloth billowed behind galloping horses as the Laguna Negra council dissolved in pandemonium.

The Navajos made no attempt to live by the new treaty. None moved to the Indian side of the "dividing line." Few demonstrated any awareness of the other obligations they had taken on. This failure to honor the commitments of Laguna Negra furnished white officials in New Mexico with the pretext for subsequent aggressive measures. In this attitude there resided a large inconsistency, for the United States Senate, balking at the monetary cost, had refused to consent to ratification of any of the Meriwether treaties. Legally, the Treaty of Laguna Negra was binding on neither party.

More than any other influence, conditions in California crystallized official thinking about Commissioner Medill's incipient reservation policy. Assaulting the western foothills of the Sierra Nevada, goldseekers crashed with explosive effect into the fragile little worlds of loosely organized "tribelets" that pursued a quiet fishing and gathering economy among the gold-bearing streams. No considerations of humanity restrained the newcomers. "If the tale of the poor wretches . . . could be impartially related," wrote an army officer in his journal, "it would exhibit a picture of cruelty, injustice and horror scarcely to be surpassed by that of the Peruvians in the time of Pizarro."[23] In 1852 a citizen of San Francisco told the newly assigned military commander on the Pacific, as he recorded it in his diary, that "Providence designed the extermination of the Indians and that it would be a good thing to introduce the small-pox among them!" And that, he added, "is the opinion of most white people living in the interior of the country."[24] If the tribes were to be saved from swift obliteration, something had to be done at once, and reservations seemed the answer.

During 1851 three commissions concluded 18 treaties covering 139 little tribes and bands and setting aside almost 12,000 square miles in a network of reservations. On them the people were to gather and, over a five-year period, be taught how to farm. During this time they would be rationed by the government, for, as the commissioners observed, "It is, in the end, cheaper to feed the whole flock for a year than to fight them for a week."[25]

The fate of these treaties revealed some of the obstacles to inaugurating the reservation policy in places where whites were actually settling rather than merely passing through. Californians loudly protested giving Indians any lands that might hold agricultural or mineral potential. Aided by a widely held belief in legal circles that the Indians in the Mexican Cession possessed no valid title to land, California's senators in Washington easily scuttled the treaties when they came up for ratification debate in the summer of 1852.[26]

For the remainder of the decade a succession of federal officials labored to work out a reservation system that could overcome such opposition, at the same time amassing a record of fraud and corruption remarkable even for the Indian Bureau. By 1858 they had established eight reservations, embracing a total of scarcely more than two or three thousand acres of sterile soil and claiming scarcely more than that number of Indians. "As far as anyone can see," commented a disgusted army officer, "the whole system is turned into a speculation for the benefit of the Agents."[27] A measure of the failure of the reservation policy in California is revealed in an Indian population that, through disease, starvation, malnutrition, and simple homicide, plummeted from 150,000 in 1845 to 100,000 in 1850 to 50,000 in 1855, and to 35,000 in 1860.[28]

Similar obstacles blocked the reservation policy in Oregon, where whites settled in the fertile valley of the Willamette River and trickled northward toward Puget Sound. Settlers carried vivid memories of the massacre by Cayuse Indians in 1847 of Doctor Marcus Whitman and his followers at the Presbyterian mission on the Walla Walla River, east of the Cascade Mountains. The war that followed had left Oregonians with rankling bitterness and no more sympathy for the native fate than their California neighbors.

In 1851 officials set forth to negotiate treaties for the cession of all land west of the Cascade Mountains and the relocation of the natives to east of the mountains. They concluded a total of nineteen treaties that accomplished the first aim but not the second. The Indians refused to move to the sterile lands to the east, where other groups greeted the prospect belligerently. A search for reservations west of the Cascades ran afoul the Oregon Donation Land Law of 1850, in which Congress had sanctioned homesteading without regard to Indian title. A few parcels of land not yet encumbered by white claims were finally located, but in the end the Oregon treaties fell prey in the Senate to the same forces that killed the California treaties.[29]

Serious trouble occurred in the Rogue River country, a tangle of mountains beyond the head of the Willamette, near the California border. Here mineral strikes brought goldseekers to lands occupied by a group of bands known collectively as the Rogue River Indians. Treaties negotiated at the Table Rock council grounds in 1851 and 1853 sought to contain the conflict by setting aside reservations. The Table Rock Treaty of 1853 furnished the prototype for a series of treaties, and these, finally, gained Senate consent. The Table Rock Treaty, however, failed in its principal aim, for friction worsened between Indians and settlers. In 1855 full-scale war erupted.

For the army, the Rogue River War became entangled with another, to the north, that found its origins in still another treaty-making enterprise. Authored by Isaac I. Stevens, brash and energetic young governor of the newly created Washington Territory, it aimed at clearing his domain of all Indian land titles, concentrating the natives on reservations, and teaching them how to farm. In 1854 and 1855 Stevens staged one treaty council after another, all the way from Puget Sound to the headwaters of the Missouri River. His methods featured fast talk, bluster, and intimidation, and when he finished he had stampeded virtually all the groups of the territory into signing treaties. Not for four years did the Stevens treaties win Senate approval, but even before the governor had concluded his negotiations a gold strike on the upper Columbia River brought whites swarming across the Cascade Mountains. The Yakimas rose in violent protest.

The Rogue River and Yakima hostilities confronted the army with a two-front war in the Pacific Northwest. Sharp-tongued, combative little John E. Wool, the general who commanded the Pacific Division, regarded both as unjustly thrust on the Indians, particularly by the governors of Washington and Oregon, and with them he conducted a battle of words whose echoes reverberated all the way to the national capital. In the Rogue River country, by 1856 Oregon volunteers and U.S. regulars had deci-

Kamayakhen
head-chief of the Yakimas

Kamiakin. This Yakima chieftain, sketched here by Gustavus Sohon, headed the opposition in his and allied tribes to the treaties of Washington Territory Governor Isaac Stevens, then led his people in the war of 1855. *Washington State Historical Society*.

sively ended the war and exiled the Indians to new reservations in the Coast Range. Amid the verbal pyrotechnics of General Wool and Governor Stevens, the Yakima War petered out inconclusively in September 1856.

A year and a half later the legacy of the Yakima War and the still-unratified Stevens treaties festered into another war. With the conspicuous exception of the Nez Perce, infiltrated for two decades by Jesuit and Presbyterian missionaries, most of the tribes of the Columbia Basin united to contest the continuing invasion of their homeland. At the Battles of Four Lakes and Spokane Plains in September 1858, however, Colonel George Wright's howitzers and new long-range rifles put the foe to flight. Wright then marched grimly through their country, peremptorily hanging chiefs and others deemed guilty of fomenting war.[30]

Isaac I. Stevens. Brash, mercurial, opinionated, young for his post, the governor of Washington Territory stampeded most of the Indians of the Northwest into signing treaties of cession, only to have them fight for their lands when white settlers tried to enter them. Stevens and General John E. Wool engaged in a celebrated war of words over the resulting Indian hostilities. A Union general, Stevens was killed in an early battle of the Civil War. *Library of Congress.*

Wright's victories and his ruthless follow-up marked the end of Indian warfare in the Pacific Northwest. By the close of the 1850s all the Oregon and Washington treaties had been ratified, eight reservations established, and the noble experiment of converting Indians into Christian farmers begun.

No such success attended the efforts of federal authorities to introduce the reservation system in Texas. Since Spanish times Kiowas, Comanches, and Apaches had ravaged Texan settlements, and few citizens harbored generous sentiments toward them. Joining the Union in 1845, the state retained control of all its vacant lands and acknowledged no Indian ownership. Although federal agents began negotiating treaties as early as 1846, none could have much effect because the state would not relinquish any land for reservations. A Texan version of the Permanent Indian Frontier proved short-lived: the weakly manned chain of military forts defining it could not keep Indian raiders on their side of the line or discourage settlers from pushing beyond it into the Indian country. In fact, most Texans favored the removal of all Indians from the state.[31]

In 1854, after six years of prodding, the Texas Legislature relented and authorized federal officials to survey 53,136 acres of unclaimed state land for Indian reservations. The task fell to Robert S. Neighbors, a veteran Indian agent of uncommon ability and probity. High on the Brazos River, Neighbors marked out a reservation for the Southern Comanches and another for the Anadarkos, Caddos, Tawakonis, Wacos, and Tonkawas.

From the first, pressures built against the reservations as more and more settlers took up residence nearby and as raiders continued to stab at frontier settlements from Red River to the Rio Grande. Citizens refused to believe that the culprits came from north of Red River and not, in part at least, from the reservations. At last, self-styled "rangers" mobilized to take matters into their own hands. Although federal troops interposed, an embittered Neighbors had to concede the failure of his reservations and face the likelihood that none could ever succeed in Texas.

For the Indians of these reservations, the government leased land north of Red River, in Indian Territory, from the Choctaws and Chickasaws. Sadly, Neighbors shepherded his charges northward to their new homes. "I have this day crossed all the Indians out of the heathen land of Texas," he wrote his wife on August 8, 1859, "and am now out of the land of the Philistines." Returning home, Neighbors paused in the village of Fort Belknap, where an Indian-hating townsman stepped from behind a building and fired a shotgun into his back. Thus ended the reservation experiment in Texas. Henceforth the government would have to look elsewhere for places to settle the Texas Indians.[32]

In New Mexico David Meriwether was the third territorial governor to seek treaty solutions to the Indian problem. Like Meriwether, James S. Calhoun and William Carr Lane failed, in part because they could not make good their promises, and in part because the Indians were not ready to make good theirs.[33] Meriwether mounted the most determined and comprehensive effort of the decade to introduce reservations in New Mexico. He concentrated on the nomadic people that for three centuries had waged sporadic war on Spanish, Mexican, and now American colonists—Utes, Apaches, and Navajos. The treaty he negotiated with the Navajos at Laguna Negra was but one of six concluded during 1855. Similar accords with two tribes of Utes and three of Apaches pledged reservations, rations, and other presents in exchange for land titles. Rejection

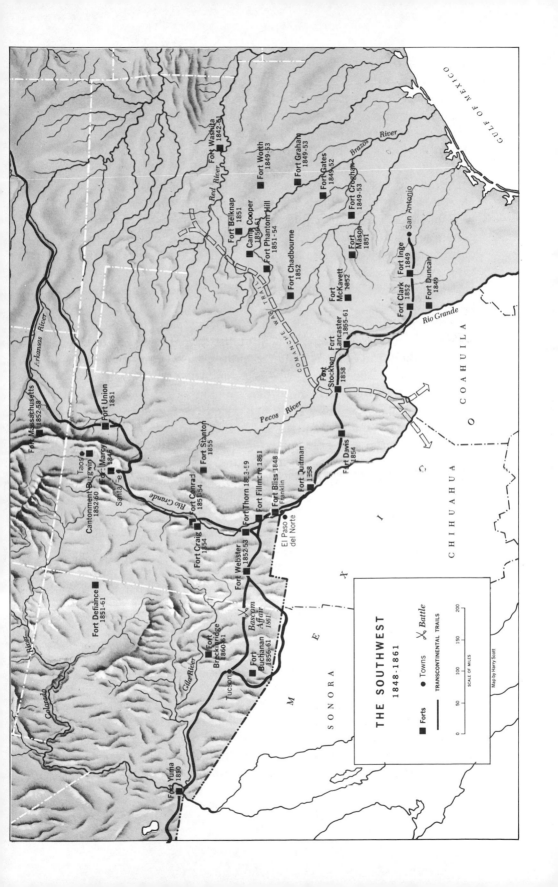

THE SOUTHWEST
1848-1861

Forts ■
Towns ●
TRANSCONTINENTAL TRAILS

Battle ✕

SCALE OF MILES
0   50   100   150   200

Map by Harry Scott

GULF OF MEXICO

Fort Washita 1842-61
Red River
Fort Worth 1849-53
Fort Graham 1849-53
Brazos River
Fort Gates 1849-52
Fort Croghan 1849-53
San Antonio
Fort Belknap 1851
Camp Cooper 1856-61
Fort Phantom Hill 1851-54
Fort Mason 1851
Fort Inge 1849
Fort Chadbourne 1852
Fort McKavett 1852
Fort Clark 1852
Fort Duncan 1849
COMANCHE WAR TRAIL
Fort Lancaster 1855-61
Rio Grande
Fort Massachusetts 1852-58
Fort Union 1851
Pecos River
Fort Stockton 1858
COAHUILA
Taos
Cantonment Burgwin 1852-60
Fort Marcy 1846
Santa Fe
Fort Stanton 1855
Fort Conrad 1851-54
Fort Thorn 1853-59
Fort Fillmore 1851
Fort Bliss 1848
Fort Quitman 1858
Fort Davis 1854
Rio Grande
Fort Defiance 1851-61
Fort Craig 1854
Fort Webster 1852-53
El Paso del Norte
Franklin
CHIHUAHUA
Arkansas River
Fort Breckinridge 1860-61
Bascom Affair 1861
Fort Buchanan 1856-61
SONORA
Gila River
Colorado River
Tucson
Fort Yuma 1850

of the Meriwether treaties by the Senate in 1856 discouraged his successors from pursuing a systematic reservation program. Reservations came
and went almost at the whim of agents and as enough food and other
presents could be scraped together to lure groups into abandoning their
roving ways and settling, however temporarily, near an agency.

Despite ripples of apparent progress, the history of Indian relations in
New Mexico during the 1850s is largely a military history. Even consistent,
well-financed civil policies could not have overcome the patterns in which
generations of hostility had locked both Indians and colonists—patterns
of raid and counterraid, of plunder and pillage, and of enslavement of
captives by both sides. From the little forts strung down the Rio Grande
and flung east and west into Indian country, the troops campaigned
against the elusive foe.

Official preoccupation with Navajos, Apaches, and Utes penalized the
peaceable Pueblos, sedentary agriculturalists since prehistoric times. For
some ten thousand Pueblos scattered among twenty mud villages down
the Rio Grande Valley from Taos to Isleta and westward to Ácoma, Zuñi,
and the Hopi towns perched on their three mesas, this was the beginning of several generations of official neglect. The Pueblos suffered from
the incursions of the nomadic tribes as much as the Hispanics and An-
glos and for thirty years sided with them in the wars with other Indians.
Such cooperation did gain U.S. recognition of their land "grants" from
the king of Spain. But legal title did not discourage illegal encroachment
on their irrigated farm lands. The Pueblos quickly discovered that the
Americans could not protect them from Apache, Navajo, and Ute raiders and would not protect them from Hispanic and Anglo squatters. As
a Zuñi elder later remarked resignedly, perhaps if the Pueblos stole like
the Navajos they might get something from the Americans.[34]

By 1861 New Mexicans and Pueblos alike might have recalled General
Kearny with a touch of irony. In the fifteen years since his bright promise to keep off the Indians, the toll of lives exacted by Indians ran between two and three hundred, and property loss, principally in sheep,
cattle, mules, and horses, approached a million dollars. Three thousand
soldiers and five Indian agents worked hard to make the promise come
true, but the end was nowhere in sight and the toll continued to mount.

In New Mexico as in Texas and on the Pacific Coast, the drive for a
reservation system attained momentum because white settlers contested
Indian occupancy. The same was true along the western borders of Iowa
and Missouri. Here a collection of small groups, native as well as trans-
planted easterner, found themselves caught between the advancing agri-

cultural frontier of the whites on the east and the powerful Plains groups on the west. The plight of these people, in fact, seems to have been a major inspiration of Commissioner Medill's Indian colony proposal of 1848. Occupying lands white farmers wanted, the border tribes were obvious targets for the reservation program. In a series of treaties in 1853–54, they gave up thirteen million acres of land in exchange for annuities and tiny reservations scattered through eastern Kansas and Indian Territory.[35] But even here they were not to be left in peace. The deadly combination of settlers, townsite boomers, and above all fiercely competing railroad corporations proved irresistible, especially when leagued with puppet "government chiefs." Treaty after treaty ate away at the Kansas reservations, beginning a process that by 1870 would shunt most of their ten thousand Indian residents southward into Indian Territory.[36]

In Indian Territory, by the 1850s the Five Civilized Tribes were beginning to flourish. For the Cherokees, Creeks, Choctaws, Chickasaws, and Seminoles, these years before the Civil War were not a time of serious friction with whites, although white whiskey runners, horse thieves, and other kinds of desperadoes took their toll. Rather, it was a time of making homes in the new country, evolving social, political, and economic institutions, and above all quieting internal factionalism. In the 1830s and 1840s all five tribes had fractured badly amid the trauma of removal from their eastern homelands. Those who had opposed the removal treaties and those who had favored them now had to compose differences made all but irreconcilable by violence, bloodshed, and even assassination. But gradually reason prevailed, order returned, and unity began to seem attainable.

These Five Tribes conspicuously exhibited the traits that prompted whites to give them the encomium of Civilized. Each constituted a "nation," with national boundaries, national constitution, and national political institutions rooted in American democracy but also reflecting Indian traditions. On fertile, well-watered lands blessed also with timber, coal, and other resources, the people took up individual homesteads. They farmed much like the white yeoman farmer, or in the manner of the Southern planter managed great plantations worked by black slaves, and for the most part they prospered. They set great store by classroom learning, and during the 1850s they developed public school systems surpassing in quality those in neighboring Arkansas and Missouri. They readily embraced Christianity and welcomed Methodist, Presbyterian, and Baptist missionaries, who became respected, influential members of the community. They looked for leadership to an extraordinarily gifted elite, native and mixed-blood alike, the latter usually descended from alliances between native women and English or Scotch traders—French, among the Choctaws—half a century and more earlier.

From their first appearance in the West, therefore, the Five Civilized Tribes moved willingly, even eagerly, in directions other tribes stubbornly resisted, and thus, in almost every tangible and intangible way, they set themselves apart from all other natives of the Trans-Mississippi West. They put down roots deep in a soil that could support them comfortably in the fashion of the white man. Because of the guarantees in the removal treaties, moreover, they held this soil more securely than other groups. For the Five Tribes the future seemed bright. As they were to discover, however, even these seeming advantages failed to provide strong enough defenses.[37]

In the 1850s the vast and varied wilderness that separated the settled Missouri border from the burgeoning settlements of Texas, New Mexico, and the Pacific Coast presented little incentive for reservation policies. The Mormons had staked out a tiny Zion in the Great Salt Lake Basin, but elsewhere only white travelers intruded on Indian domain. Their safety was the chief government concern, and it did not require the immediate compression of the Indians into reservations. The effort concentrated on the Great Plains, and on two major goals: to keep the Indians from molesting travelers on the Oregon-California and Santa Fe trails, and to end their time-honored custom of raiding southward into Texas and Mexico. The concern for Mexico grew out of a commitment, in the treaty ending the Mexican War, to keep U.S. Indians out of Mexico—a promise more easily made than kept.[38]

The man principally charged with carrying out this policy was already a living legend. Thomas Fitzpatrick—"Broken Hand" to the Indians, because a bursting rifle had carried away three fingers—knew the West and its Indians as few others did. Companion to Jed Smith, Kit Carson, and Jim Bridger, and guide to Fremont and Oregon emigrants, he was not only a master of wilderness skills but also possessed of a literacy, intellect, and depth of character not usually associated with the boisterous trapping fraternity. Fitzpatrick had served as a guide with General Kearny's army on its march to New Mexico. Returning eastward on the Santa Fe Trail in October 1846, he learned that he had been appointed U.S. Indian Agent for the Upper Platte and Arkansas Agency.[39]

A pragmatist, Fitzpatrick argued that no "big talks" should be held with the Plains Indians until they had been soundly thrashed by soldiers. Finally convinced that the army would never be given enough strength to make this a serious policy option, he set forth to have some "big talks." The first was held in a grassy valley near Fort Laramie, on the North Platte River, in September 1851. In color, animation, and sheer magnitude, no treaty council of the period surpassed it. Ten thousand Sioux, Cheyennes, Arapahos, Crows, Gros Ventres, Assiniboines, Arikaras, and Shoshonis mingled menacingly with one another and with 270 tense soldiers. They ended by signing a treaty and joyously sharing in the mountain of presents that lay enticingly nearby as a spur to the deliberations. Two years later Fitzpatrick worked out a similar accord with Kiowas, Comanches, and Plains Apaches at Fort Atkinson, on the Arkansas River.

In the Fort Laramie and Fort Atkinson treaties the Plains groups promised to dwell forever in peace with the white man and with one another and to allow the white man to build roads and forts in their country (he already had). The Fort Atkinson Treaty bound its signatories not to raid in Mexico. The Fort Laramie Treaty marked off tribal boundaries, a provision designed to cool the warfare among tribes that posed a threat to white travelers. These tribal "territories" were not called reservations and were not, as elsewhere, intended as instruments for the control and civilization of the Indians. But they laid the foundations for future reservations, as the Indians themselves may have sensed. "You have split my land and I don't like it," declared a Sioux chief at Fort Laramie. "These lands once belonged to the Kiowas and the Crows, but we whipped these nations out of them, and in this we did what the white men do when they want the lands of the Indians."[40]

The treaties did not end intertribal warfare, or even diminish the raids of Kiowas and Comanches in Texas and Mexico. For a time whites traveled the trails in comparative safety, although not necessarily because of the treaties. In fact, Kiowas and Comanches enjoyed the best of two worlds: peace with whites on the Arkansas and war with Texans to the south. Each year on the Arkansas they received $10,000 worth of presents, including guns and ammunition, and each year they killed and plundered in Texas as they had always done. As Texas Agent Robert Neighbors complained in 1855, $10,000 would not pay for the property these same Indians had stolen in Texas during the preceding three months.

Even along the Arkansas and the Platte, the peace did not last long. Near Fort Laramie, in 1854, an impetuous young army officer charged forth to punish the Sioux for butchering a strayed cow belonging to a passing emigrant and got himself and his command wiped out. This brought on a war with the Sioux in 1855, followed by one with the Cheyennes in 1857. To the south the continuing hostilities in Texas finally spread

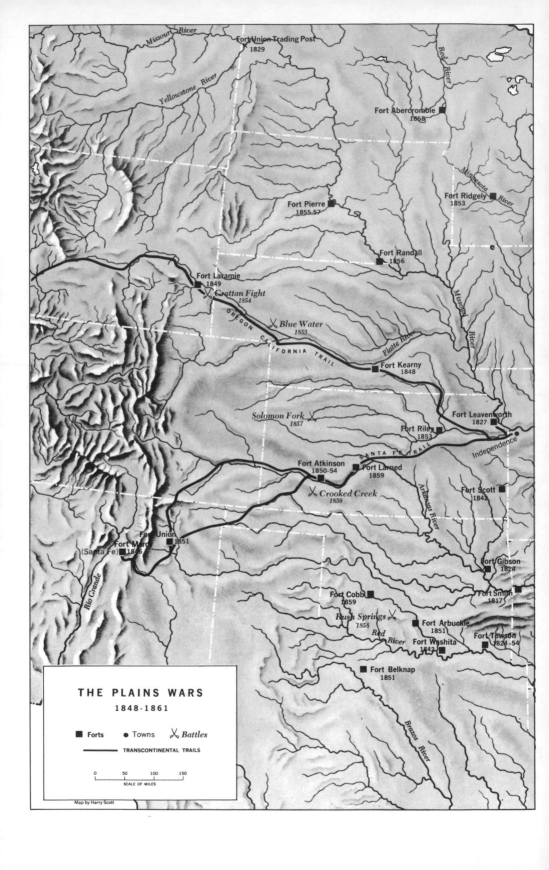

Missouri River

Fort Union Trading Post
1829

Yellowstone River

Red River

Fort Abercrombie
1858

Minnesota River

Fort Ridgely
1853

Fort Pierre
1855-57

Fort Randall
1856

Missouri River

Fort Laramie
1849
Grattan Fight
1854

Blue Water
1855

OREGON CALIFORNIA TRAIL

Platte River

Fort Kearny
1848

Solomon Fork
1857

Fort Leavenworth
1827

Fort Riley
1853

SANTA FE TRAIL

Independence

Fort Atkinson
1850-54

Fort Larned
1859

Fort Scott
1842

Crooked Creek
1859

Arkansas River

Fort Union 1851

Fort Marcy
(Santa Fe) 1846

Fort Gibson
1824

Rio Grande

Fort Cobb
1859

Fort Smith
1817

Rush Springs
1858

Fort Arbuckle
1851

Red River

Fort Washita
1842

Fort Towson
1824-54

Fort Belknap
1851

Brazos River

THE PLAINS WARS
1848-1861

■ Forts   ● Towns   ✗ Battles

━━━━━ TRANSCONTINENTAL TRAILS

0   50   100   150
SCALE OF MILES

Map by Harry Scott

north to the Arkansas and prompted sporadic campaigns against the Kiowas and Comanches from 1858 through 1860.

By the close of the decade, then, the military approach favored by Tom Fitzpatrick had come to dominate relations with the Plains Indians. But because of the military weakness that he had repeatedly and outspokenly decried, this approach gained no more success than the diplomatic. Broken Hand was not around to voice reproach; he had died in 1854, not in the adventurous style of his life, but of pneumonia, in bed, in the national capital far from his beloved West.

For U.S. Indian policy, the decade of the 1850s was a time of major innovation and testing made necessary by the collapse of the Permanent Indian Frontier in the wake of the Mexican War. Commissioner Medill's proposal of 1848 for Indian "colonies" evolved swiftly into the reservation program, the scheme by which Indian land titles were to be abrogated and the Indians settled on well-defined tracts where they could be kept from bothering whites, taught to support themselves by farming, insulated from white vices, and uplifted by white virtues. By 1860 this idealization of the reservation had become the foundation stone of federal Indian policy.

The experience of the 1850s, however, tended to confirm the warnings of Tom Fitzpatrick. Indians could not be induced to stay on reservations until they had been whipped, either by the army or by invading settlers. In California and the Pacific Northwest, Indians had accepted reservations only after heavy-handed violence. In Texas and New Mexico and on the Great Plains, efforts to corral tribes on reservations faltered or failed altogether as warfare flashed spasmodically or dragged on inconclusively. And even where reservations had been established, their potential as instruments of control and acculturation remained to be demonstrated.

As early as 1853 Fitzpatrick had branded the reservation system "the legalized murder of a whole nation . . . expensive, vicious, inhumane,"[41] and the history of the Indian frontier for the next half-century was to be largely a record of Indian resistance to it. But neither in objectives nor in execution were whites to challenge it seriously until well into the twentieth century.

3

When the White People Fought Each Other, 1861–1865

Mangas Coloradas (Red Sleeves) and Cochise towered above all other Apache leaders. Tall, muscular, gifted with uncommon intellect, and dynamic and forceful leaders possessed of warrior skills honed to perfection in countless raids on Mexican settlements, they held unchallenged dominion over their people. Mangas Coloradas and his Mimbres Apaches lived in southern New Mexico, ranging southward from densely forested mountains around the head of the Gila River across deserts studded with barren peaks and dry salt lakes, and into Mexico. Cochise and his Chiricahua Apaches occupied rocky mountain chains immediately to the west, in what would soon become the southeastern corner of the Territory of Arizona.

If Mangas Coloradas and Cochise did not themselves watch the strange actions of the American soldiers as the summer's furnace heat pounded the deserts in July 1861, some of their followers assuredly did, for few activities of the white people went unobserved by the Apaches. At Forts Buchanan and Breckinridge in Cochise's domain and Fort McLane in Mangas's, the soldiers burned the buildings along with all the stores they could not carry and marched eastward to Fort Fillmore, on the Rio Grande. The chiefs drew the obvious conclusion. They had whipped the soldiers and driven them from the country.

For these two chiefs, war had come but recently. Throughout the 1850s, as other Apaches fought the American newcomers, Mimbres and Chiricahuas gave them little trouble. Occasionally a small party might rob or kill in the settlements scattered down the Rio Grande Valley and clustered around the adobe village of Tucson, but these were nothing compared with the devastation unrelentingly visited on Mexicans in Chihuahua and Sonora. The Apaches allowed travelers to move in relative safety on the road between the Rio Grande and Tucson and offered no opposition to the Butterfield stagecoaches that appeared on this road in 1858. Cochise and his followers even supplied firewood to the stage station in Apache Pass.

The uncertain peace ended abruptly in 1860–61. For both chiefs the cause was intensely personal. In May 1860 prospectors discovered gold near the old Spanish copper mines at the southern edge of the Mimbres Mountains, the heart of Mangas Coloradas's homeland. By autumn the teeming camp of Pinos Altos claimed seven hundred miners. Mangas Coloradas went among them—in a spirit of friendship, said the Indians, to deceive them into going elsewhere, said the whites, somewhat lamely. Whichever, as an Apache later described it, "The White Eyes bound him to a tree and lashed him with ox goads until his back was striped with deep cuts. He crept away like a wounded animal to let his wounds heal. . . . Never before had anyone struck him, and there is no humiliation worse than that of a whip."[1]

For Cochise the collision occurred in February 1861, when a party of soldiers arrived in Apache Pass and asked to talk with him. He went into the soldier chief's tent. Through an interpreter the young officer, Lieutenant George N. Bascom, accused him of a raid on a ranch near Fort Buchanan, in which he had allegedly stolen stock and kidnapped a boy. Cochise explained that Coyotero Apaches had done this, not Chiricahuas. The officer would not believe him. Finally he declared that Cochise was under arrest. Enraged, the chief drew a knife, slashed his way through the tent wall, and sprinted to safety amid a volley of musket balls. At the same time, however, the soldiers seized five of his relatives who had been waiting outside the tent. In turn, Cochise seized a Butterfield station attendant and two travelers on the road through Apache Pass. These he tried to exchange for his relatives. The officer refused. Cochise struck back. His men massacred the drovers of a small freight train making its way through the pass, waylaid but failed to stop a stagecoach, and attacked soldiers watering stock at Apache Springs. After a week's standoff, Cochise cut out for Mexico, leaving beside the road in the pass the horribly butchered remains of the white hostages. In retaliation, the soldiers hanged their hostages from the limbs of a scrub oak tree. The bodies dangled there for months afterward.[2]

Mimbres and Chiricahua lashed back at the whites. The withdrawal of the soldiers inspired them to even greater aggression. Both travelers and settlers suffered. Pinos Altos withstood a direct assault, and then a siege that flushed most of the miners out of the country. The handful of Confederate soldiers that trooped across the desert to occupy Tucson made no attempt to fight back. The raiders easily eluded the "Arizona Rangers" mobilized by the miners in self-defense.

Then in June 1862, as summer again dried the desert water holes, the Apaches saw soldiers coming from the west in great numbers. The Confederates hastily retreated to the Rio Grande. Cochise and Mangas Coloradas gathered their warriors on the slopes of Apache Pass to ambush the invaders. The first contingent reached the pass on July 15. Thrown back by rifle fire, the soldiers regrouped and fought their way through the pass to Apache Springs. The Indians posted themselves behind rocks on the slopes above to keep them from the vital water. But the soldiers wheeled up big guns and opened fire. Explosions that filled the air with deadly flying metal scattered the Apaches. Next day they tried again, only to be driven off again by bursting shells. "We would have done well enough," one later told an officer, "if you had not fired wagons at us."[3]

The mettle of these new soldiers became even clearer the following winter. Mangas Coloradas had been shot in the Apache Pass fight. His men had borne him southward to Janos, Chihuahua, and forced a Mexican doctor to dig the bullet out of his chest. Soon he was again leading his men against the Pinos Altos miners. On January 17, 1863, however, he allowed himself to be lured by a white flag to a parley with a soldier chief, who promptly seized him as a prisoner. That night, as he tried to sleep next to a campfire, the guards heated bayonets and touched them to his feet. Rising in angry protest, he was instantly cut down by a volley of musket balls—killed, reported his captors, while attempting to escape.[4]

Like Mangas Coloradas and Cochise, Indians all over the West in 1861 watched the curious spectacle of white soldiers marching away to the east. In Texas, Indian Territory, and southern New Mexico the soldiers pulled out altogether. Elsewhere they left a few of their number behind to hold the forts. Some of the Indians joined the Apaches in supposing that they had frightened the white soldiers away. Others knew more or less about the white people's quarrel that, like their own wars, had grown so intense that they had begun to fight among themselves. Soon, however, these people also discovered, with Mangas and Cochise, that a new day had not dawned. Soldiers came back in greater numbers than ever. And as the fate of Mangas Coloradas demonstrated, they approached their task with uncharacteristic directness, vigor, and combativeness.

The firing on Fort Sumter in April 1861 had immediately drained the West of all the regulars who could be spared, and for a time the frontier

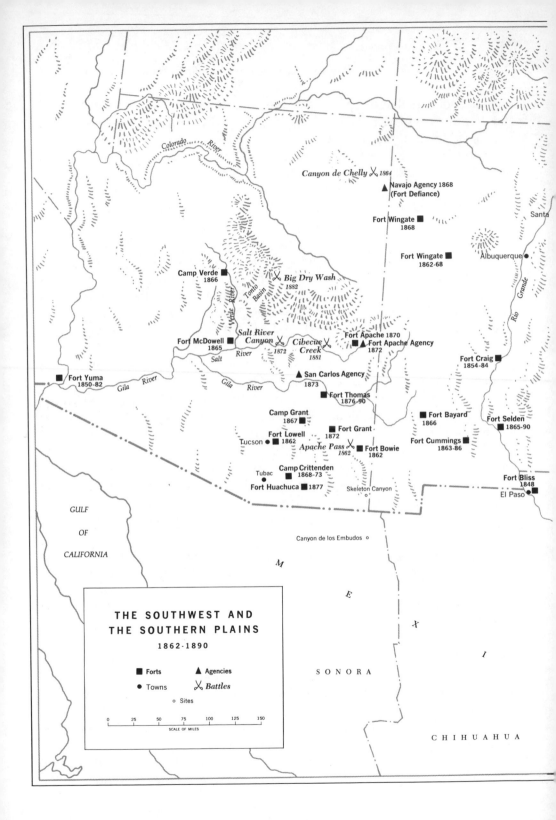

Colorado ···· River

Canyon de Chelly ✕ 1864

▲ Navajo Agency 1868
(Fort Defiance)

Fort Wingate ■
1868

Fort Wingate ■
1862-68

Santa

Albuquerque ●

Camp Verde ■
1866

✕ Big Dry Wash
1882

Tonto
Basin

Verde River

Salt River
Canyon ✕ Cibecue ✕
1872   Creek
1881

Fort Apache 1870
■ ▲ Fort Apache Agency
1872

Fort McDowell ■
1865

Salt   River

▲ San Carlos Agency
1873

Fort Craig ■
1854-84

Rio Grande

Fort Yuma ■
1850-82

Gila   River

Gila   River

Fort Thomas ■
1876-90

Fort Bayard ■
1866

Fort Selden
■ 1865-90

Camp Grant ■
1867

■ Fort Grant
1872

Fort Lowell ■
1862

Fort Cummings ■
1863-86

Tucson ●

Apache Pass ✕
1862

■ Fort Bowie
1862

Camp Crittenden ■
1868-73

Tubac ●

Fort Huachuca ■ 1877

Skeleton Canyon

Fort Bliss
■ 1848
El Paso ●

GULF

OF

CALIFORNIA

Canyon de los Embudos ○

M

E

X

I

SONORA

THE SOUTHWEST AND
THE SOUTHERN PLAINS

1862-1890

■ Forts   ▲ Agencies

● Towns   ✕ Battles

○ Sites

0   25   50   75   100   125   150

SCALE OF MILES

CHIHUAHUA

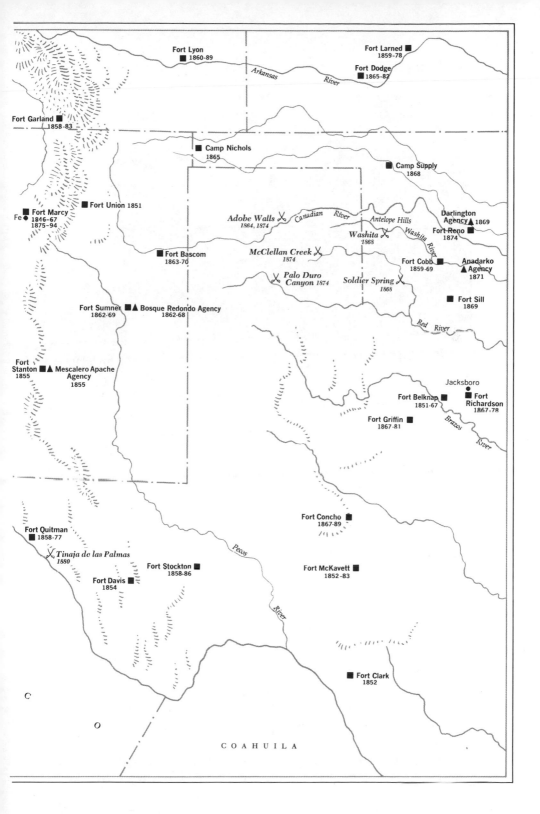

Fort Lyon
1860-89

Fort Larned
1859-78

Fort Dodge
1865-82

Arkansas   River

Fort Garland
1858-83

Camp Nichols
1865

Camp Supply
1868

Fort Union 1851

Fe Fort Marcy
1846-67
1875-94

Adobe Walls
1864, 1874

Canadian   River

Antelope Hills

Darlington
Agency   1869
Fort Reno
1874

Washita
1868

Washita River

Fort Bascom
1863-70

McClellan Creek
1874

Fort Cobb
1859-69

Anadarko
Agency
1871

Palo Duro
Canyon 1874

Soldier Spring
1868

Fort Sill
1869

Fort Sumner
1862-69

Bosque Redondo Agency
1862-68

Red   River

Fort
Stanton
1855

Mescalero Apache
Agency
1855

Jacksboro

Fort
Richardson
1867-78

Fort Belknap
1851-67

Fort Griffin
1867-81

Brazos

River

Fort Concho
1867-89

Fort Quitman
1858-77

Pecos

Tinaja de las Palmas
1880

Fort Stockton
1858-86

Fort McKavett
1852-83

Fort Davis
1854

River

C

O

Fort Clark
1852

C O A H U I L A

69

The Civil War depleted the West of soldiers only momentarily. Volunteer regiments replaced the regulars in greater numbers than ever, and throughout the war years Indian policy was chiefly a military policy. Here officers of the Eleventh Ohio Cavalry pose on the porch of Fort Laramie's "Old Bedlam" in 1864. *National Archives.*

settlements and travel routes lay perilously exposed to Indian attack. At once, however, the federal government mobilized for the war against the Confederacy. Between 1861 and 1865 two million men sprang to the defense of the Union. The overwhelming majority served in volunteer regiments rather than the regular army, which shrank to a feeble skeleton. Many of these men discovered that they had volunteered for duty against enemies clad in breechclout and feathers rather than Confederate gray. By 1865 almost twenty thousand soldiers, mostly volunteers, served in the West, about double the 1860 figure. In Texas, settlers looked to Confederate units numbering between one and two thousand for frontier defense.

The volunteers made effective fighters. They tended to be better educated and more energetic than the regulars; they wanted to get the job finished and go home. Those from the western states and territories brought to their task a harsh, uncompromising view of the Indian and usually preferred extermination to negotiation. They followed some tough and aggressive generals. Steely eyed "General Jimmy" Carleton and the fiery Irishman Patrick Edward Connor went about Indian fighting with gusto, persistence, and little compassion for the enemy. Henry H. Sibley, Alfred Sully, and the veteran George Wright all displayed notable leadership.

It was Carleton who led the "California Column," eighteen hundred strong, across the Southwest in 1862, his mission to head off a Confederate invasion of New Mexico. By the time he reached the Rio Grande, Colorado Volunteers had driven back the Confederates, and Carleton's California and New Mexico Volunteers spent the war years fighting Apaches and Navajos. It was the advance guard of Carleton's army that clashed with Mangas Coloradas and Cochise in Apache Pass in July 1862. It was Carleton's subordinates, too, who in January 1863 saw to it that Mangas Coloradas would never again interfere with the development of the Pinos Altos mines.

Connor, Carleton's fellow Californian, also led California units eastward, to garrison the central overland route and to war with Indians who threatened California's tenuous link with the East. On the frozen battlefield of Bear River, Utah, he showed himself a practitioner of Carleton's no-nonsense brand of Indian fighting. Here, in January 1863, Connor and his men smashed the village of Shoshoni Chief Bear Hunter and left the snowy ground littered with the bodies of the chief and more than two hundred of his people. From headquarters in Salt Lake City, Connor passed the remaining war years in similarly ruthless operations against Indians of Utah, Nevada, and Idaho, and he found time in addition to wage a vituperative feud with Brigham Young and the Mormon hierarchy.

The diversion of such military strength to the West when troops were so desperately wanted in the South revealed the measure of Abraham Lincoln's need for western gold and silver and western political support for the prosecution of the war. It also dramatized how little the war slowed the pace of the westward movement.

The West's mineral wealth continued to attract fortune-seekers. The Cherry Creek strikes of 1858 triggered the Pike's Peak rush and led to the founding of Denver and a proliferation of camps in the front range of the Rockies. On the eastern flank of the Sierra Nevada, discovery of the Comstock Lode in 1859 set off a rush that carried into the 1860s, gave rise to Virginia City, and sent prospectors north and south along the Sierra foothills. In the Pacific Northwest, the Colville strikes of 1855 were followed in 1858 by the Fraser River rush. In 1860 goldseekers pushed into the Nez Perce country and found color in the Clearwater River. Others who followed opened mines on the Salmon, the Boise, and the tributaries of the Snake River heading in Oregon. Beginning in 1861, prospectors turned up riches on the headwaters of the Missouri River, loosing an influx that built another Virginia City and swelled Montana's population to nearly thirty thousand by 1864. Gold deposits brought miners flocking to the lower Colorado River and the mountains bordering it on the east.

As population grew and spread, so did the transportation and communication network. The telegraph linked California to the Union in October 1861. Denied its southern route by the secession of Texas, the Butterfield Overland Mail moved northward, paralleling the telegraph wire on the central route. In 1862 Ben Holladay bought the enterprise and ultimately built a stagecoach empire that spanned the West and tapped the mining camps on each side of the trunk line as well. Stage lines also reached out from Leavenworth to Santa Fe and up the Smoky Hill to Denver. And with the opening of the Montana mines, steamboats in growing numbers ascended the Missouri River to Fort Benton, the head of navigation.

The political map of the West responded to the surge of activity: Dakota, Colorado, and Nevada territories were created in 1861, Idaho and Arizona territories in 1863, and Montana Territory in 1864. Silver-rich Nevada gained statehood in 1864.

For the Indians, the mounting tempo of westward expansion, the invasion of new areas of their homeland, the unsettling effect of the white man's Civil War, and the sudden appearance of a larger and more warlike military force combined to create new tensions and fears and new situations fraught with explosive potential. With the coming of the Civil War, many of the tribes entered a new and more traumatic phase of their relations with the white people.

No Indians experienced more trauma than the Five Civilized Tribes of Indian Territory. Many of these people owned slaves and felt a natural affinity for southerners. Also, geographical proximity gave the Confederacy an edge over the Union. The Choctaws and Chickasaws went overwhelmingly with the South. The Cherokees, Creeks, and Seminoles split, shattering the unity so painstakingly restored since the internal conflicts of the removal period. For all, the Civil War proved a calamity of far-reaching, long-lasting consequence.

The Confederate government moved swiftly in the spring of 1861 to embroil the populous Five Tribes in the conflict with the North. Albert Pike, Arkansas' noted poet-politician, appeared in Indian Territory as Confederate commissioner charged with concluding treaties and enlisting the various Indian groups in the war. Holding forth more liberal treaties than the United States had ever offered, Pike signed up Choctaws, Chickasaws, Seminoles, and Creeks. The last two agreed less than unanimously. Such chiefs as Chilly and Daniel McIntosh and Motey Canard led most of the Creeks into the pro-Confederate "United Nations of Indian Territory." But the respected Opothleyahola organized several thousand Union Creeks and Seminoles, and a scattering of like-minded people from other tribes, to stand firm for the North.

In the Cherokee Nation, the wise and able John Ross, long the Principal Chief, spoke eloquently for neutrality. "I am—the Cherokees are—your friends," Ross told Confederate proselytizers, "but we do not wish to be brought into the feuds between yourselves and your Northern Brethren. Our wish is for peace. Peace at home and Peace among you."[5] War among the whites distressed Ross, but war at home tormented him with visions of strife within and devastation from without should his people take sides. Yet he was helpless to stave off a revival of the old removal factionalism in which he himself had figured so prominently. Those who had opposed removal now lined up behind Ross's rivals, chief of whom was Stand Watie. Not only did Watie agitate for Cherokee adherence to the Confederacy; he also raised a Cherokee regiment for service in the Confederate army.

At last, despite his strong convictions, Ross had to give in. In August 1861 the Confederate victory at Wilson's Creek, Missouri, gave the South strength and prestige in this part of the country and made it unlikely that the North could back the Cherokees meaningfully even if they remained loyal. Moreover, the Confederate victory greatly enhanced Watie's position in the tribe, for he and his Indian troops had fought well in the battle. Fearing a Cherokee civil war if he held out longer, less than two weeks after Wilson's Creek Ross sorrowfully brought the Cherokees into alliance with the Confederacy.

Ross's defection stunned Opothleyahola and left him and his Union followers isolated. The civil conflict that Ross had feared occurred as Indian troops in Confederate service went after them. In three armed clashes,

John Ross. Principal Chief of the Cherokees in Georgia and later in Indian Territory, Ross gave statesmanlike leadership to his people for almost half a century before his death in 1866. Head of the faction opposing removal to the West, he became embroiled in the intratribal strife that so occupied the Cherokees, especially during the Civil War years. *Thomas Gilcrease Institute of American History and Art, Tulsa, Okla..*

in November and December 1861, they inflicted heavy casualties and scattered the loyalists, bereft of their stock, wagons, and other possessions, across a frozen, snow-covered land. Later the refugees reassembled in Kansas, to live precariously on government charity and to furnish recruits for federal regiments.

In Indian Territory, the bright hope offered by the Confederates began to dim. All the tribes contributed troops—three Choctaw-Chickasaw regiments, a Creek regiment, a Creek-Seminole regiment, and two Cherokee regiments, including Stand Watie's. They fought at Pea Ridge, Arkansas, in March 1862, where both sides accused all but Watie's men of undisciplined excesses. The Union victory at Pea Ridge, moreover, opened the way for a Union drive into Indian Territory from Kansas. Cherokees, betraying their true sentiments, defected by the hundreds. But Ross's high sense of honor kept him firmly in the Confederate camp until Unionists settled the question by taking him prisoner. For the rest of the war, from a base in Philadelphia, he served his nation well as head of the government in exile and as emissary to the U.S. government. In Washington he formed a close friendship, based on mutual respect, with Abraham Lincoln.

At home the war dragged on, the fortunes of the Confederates and their Indian allies now in decline. In July 1863 the Battle of Honey Springs dealt them a decisive defeat. Confederate Cherokees, Creeks, and Seminoles fled southward to the Choctaw-Chickasaw country and even to Texas, forming camps of suffering refugees matching those of the loyalists in Kansas. Everywhere desolation reigned—fields untended, stock running loose, homes empty or burned, and Indian fighting Indian as Cherokee, Creek, and Seminole pursued civil wars of their own. Each of these nations had two governments, one Union and one Confederate, with each claiming legitimacy. After Ross's departure, Stand Watie set up a rival Cherokee government with himself as chief. Watie also continued to compile a war record that won high praise from Confederate authorities but also drew allegations of guerrilla atrocities. In 1864 the Confederates made him a brigadier general, the only Indian to hold such high rank, and in 1865, more than two months after Appomattox, he was the last Confederate general to surrender his forces.

With war's end the Five Tribes faced a disheartening prospect. Like white southerners, the people had to rebuild their homes and eke out a living. They had to repair the divisions of war, compose the differences that had set them violently one against another, and suppress the bitter factionalism that the war had revived and so disastrously aggravated.

And they had to brace themselves for the retribution an outraged North would be sure to loose upon them as punishment for siding with the Confederacy.

The Eastern Sioux of Minnesota grew hungrier and angrier as July and August 1862 slipped by without the annual distribution of their annuities. The agency warehouse contained stores of food and other goods, but the agent would not make the issue until the cash portion of the annuity arrived too. This made no sense to the Indians, especially as the traders would claim most of it to satisfy credit they said, and nobody could disprove, had already been extended.

Little Crow argued with the white officials. The leading chief, he was a man of oratorical ability and persuasive power, although his authority had come under increasing challenge from more militant chiefs who regarded him as a tool of the whites, a charge given substance by his part in the treaties that had compressed the Eastern Sioux into a ten-mile-wide reservation extending 150 miles up the south side of the Minnesota River. Even Little Crow, the friend of the whites, could not get the warehouse doors opened. The attitude of the whites was conveyed in a remark by trader Andrew Myrick that, summing up the grievances of a decade, furnished a rallying cry for revolt: "So far as I am concerned," said Myrick, "if they are hungry let them eat grass or their own dung."[6]

The Eastern Sioux—Mdewakanton, Wahpekute, Wahpeton, and Sisseton—had once roamed the expanse of forest and lake drained by the upper Mississippi River, sharing its bounty with Winnebagos and contesting it fiercely with Chippewas. In the 1840s, however, the white frontier of settlement crept up the Mississippi. Minnesota became a territory in 1849. The census of 1850 showed a population of six thousand whites and more than twice as many Indians. By 1858 whites numbered more than 150,000 and Minnesota gained statehood. Methodically, treaty commissioners negotiated with the tribes of Wisconsin and Minnesota for cession of the lands into which lumbermen and farmers were moving. For the Sioux, treaties in 1851 and 1858 extinguished title to 28 million acres in exchange for annual annuities and the reservation on the Minnesota River. Little Crow played a prominent role in persuading the Sioux to accept these treaties.

Reservation life had not been happy. Some Indians, including Little Crow, cut their hair, moved into log cabins, and tried to learn farming. Others did not. Discontent deepened as more and more whites, mostly German and Scandanavian immigrants, surrounded the reservation and

Ta-oyate-duta_
Little Crow_

Little Crow. The Santee Sioux of Minnesota thought Little Crow too much a tool of the whites, but when they demanded that he lead them in the uprising of 1862, he reluctantly agreed. After the collapse of Indian resistance, he escaped to Canada. Back in Minnesota a year later, he was shot down by a settler while picking berries. Painting by T. W. Wood, *Minnesota Historical Society*.

as less and less of the annuities promised in the treaties found their way to the Indians. By one means or another, the money due the Sioux always seemed to end up in the pockets of traders and other claimants. More than any other factor, this pattern, repeated year after year, kindled in the Sioux a dangerously volatile temper.

In fact, Minnesota in the 1850s afforded a classic example of the corruption of the federal Indian system, especially after statehood provided voting representation in the Congress. Senators and representatives dictated the appointment of their friends and supporters to the Indian Bureau's field posts back home and exerted their influence to keep federal appropriations flowing to the reservations back home. The local officials, in league with traders and contractors, plundered the annuities and other appropriations to the personal enrichment of all. Profits and patronage also oiled local party machinery and forwarded the political fortunes of candidates for state and national office.[7]

Minnesota's leading public figures came out of this tradition. Among the negotiators of the Sioux treaty of 1851 were Agent Alexander Ramsey and trader Henry H. Sibley. Of $475,000 the Indians were to receive when they moved to their new reservation, Sibley claimed $145,000 as overpayments his firm had made to them for furs. Agent Ramsey allowed this and other claims amounting to two-thirds of the total due the Sioux. Again, in 1858, Sibley and other traders entered claims against the $266,880 the Sioux were to get for selling half their Minnesota Valley reservation, and only $100,000 found its way to the Indians. Sibley became the state's first governor, Ramsey the second.

Critics condemned the system and cried in vain for reform. In 1860, urging reform on President James Buchanan, Minnesota's Episcopal Bishop Henry B. Whipple warned that "A nation which sowed robbery would reap a harvest of blood."[8] Exemplifying all the evils of the Indian system, Minnesota provided the setting for the fulfillment of the bishop's prophecy.

On August 17, 1862, four Sioux youths hunting north of Redwood Agency murdered five white settlers. The deed had not been planned. One had dared another to prove his courage. But for the Sioux the issue of whether or not to stand behind the boys provoked a stormy scene in which the gathering wrath of a decade boiled over. Militant chiefs, bolstered by a riotous mob of young men shouting for blood, won the pledge of a reluctant Little Crow to lead them in war against the whites.

At dawn on the next day Indians swept through Redwood Agency,

Innocent of frontier skills, Minnesota farmers fell by the score as angry Sioux swept through the settlements in 1862. Of twenty-eight here waylaid on Sacred Heart Creek, only one got through to Fort Ridgely. This scene is typical of many. *Minnesota Historical Society.*

killed the men, took the women and children captive, and put the buildings to the torch. In wide-ranging parties they spread over the countryside, killing, raping, pillaging, and burning. Surprised, unequipped for defense, unversed in frontier life, the farmers fell by the score, dispatched with a savagery rarely equalled in the history of Indian uprisings. By evening some four hundred whites had been slain, and hundreds more flew in panic toward Fort Ridgely.

Nothing, it seemed, could prevent the onslaught from engulfing St. Paul itself. But divided counsel overtook the Indians. Little Crow and part of the rebels attacked Fort Ridgely. The rest of the Sioux rode against the town of New Ulm. In desperate fighting at both places, the defenders turned back the assaults.

Governor Ramsey called on his old associate Henry Sibley to organize

Henry H. Sibley. Pioneer Indian trader, first governor of Minnesota, and savior of the Minnesota frontier in 1862, Sibley was a major figure in Indian relations of Minnesota and Dakota. He is shown here as a brigadier general of volunteers, about 1863. *Minnesota Historical Society.*

the relief. Commissioned colonel in the state militia, Sibley led some fifteen hundred men up the Minnesota River against the foe. "My heart is steeled against them," he told Governor Ramsey, "and if I have the means, and can catch them, I will sweep them with the besom of death."[9] The scenes of carnage and desolation along the march only intensified the spirit of revenge. At Redwood Agency Andrew Myrick's mutilated corpse lay outside his store, mouth stuffed with blood-caked grass in gruesome rejoinder to his callous remark about hungry Sioux.

Their leaders quarreling among themselves, the Sioux fell back before Sibley's advance. On September 23 they rallied enough to stage an ambush at Wood Lake. Sibley's troops easily drove them from the field in an action that proved decisive. After Wood Lake many of the fugitives scattered westward into Dakota and northward into the British possessions. Some two thousand, however, fell captive or surrendered to military patrols scouring the countryside. With no more battlefields to sweep with the besom of death, Sibley turned to the courtroom. A military commission found 303 Sioux guilty of various offenses, most on the flimsiest of evidence, and condemned them to die by hanging. President Lincoln called for the trial records, however, and over the vehement protests of Minnesota authorities reduced the list to thirty-eight. On a frosty December day they died on the gallows.

The Minnesota bloodbath cost the Sioux their reservation—and the innocent Winnebagos theirs, too—for Lincoln could not resist the demand of Minnesotans for their removal westward to new homes in Dakota Territory. Some settled on a reservation on the Missouri River. Others scattered over the Dakota prairies or mingled with the Teton Sioux. Picking berries on a farm near Hutchinson, Minnesota, the following summer, Little Crow was gunned down by the owner. The state legislature voted him a $500 reward.

The coming of the Civil War heightened the complexity of the Navajos' relationship with one another and with the Hispanic population of New Mexico. Indians and New Mexicans had always alternated raid and counterraid with friendly intercourse and trade. In 1861, with the departure of the regulars, New Mexicans donned blue uniforms and took their places in the forts, thus adding to the usual ambiguity of the war-peace relationship.

Compounding the ambiguity, most Navajos fell into one of two categories, *ladrone* or *rico*, the former poor in sheep and other possessions by which the latter measured their wealth. The raiders who preyed on New Mexican settlements usually came from the ranks of the ladrones, while New Mexican retaliation usually fell on the peaceably disposed ricos, whose abundance of sheep, horses, and orchards made them more tempting as well as more convenient targets. As the tempo of military activity in the Navajo country quickened in the late 1850s, rico and ladrone became synonymous with peace party and war party. Progressive impoverishment by Hispanic raiders transformed ricos into ladrones, proportionately swelling the war party and shrinking the peace party.[10]

As the bluecoats abandoned their forts and concentrated to meet the graycoats, Navajo raiders struck fiercely at New Mexican settlements. By the middle of 1862, however, the Confederates had been repulsed and new bluecoats had come from the west to join with the New Mexicans in fighting Indians. They built a new fort, Wingate, at the edge of the Nav-

Twin scourges of the southwestern Indians during the Civil War, Brigadier General James H. Carleton (left) commanded the Department of New Mexico and Colonel Kit Carson (right) led the First New Mexico Volunteer Cavalry. Under Carleton's direction, Carson conquered the Mescalero Apaches and the Navajos, and Carleton had them settled on the Bosque Redondo Reservation for an experiment with "civilization" that ended in failure and tragedy. *Museum of New Mexico.*

ajo country. Word came that they were badly whipping the Mescalero Apaches east of the Rio Grande.

Worried, eighteen Navajo ricos journeyed to Santa Fe in December 1862 to talk with the new soldier chief. He dealt with them brusquely, without the ceremony usual for such meetings. He told them to go home and to tell their people he would need more than mere words before he would grant peace.

Actually, General Carleton's lack of specificity reflected his current preoccupation with the Mescalero Apaches, even then verging on collapse. Leading his troops in the field was an old friend—mountain man, fur trapper, scout, and now colonel of New Mexico Volunteers, Kit Carson. By the spring of 1863 most of the Mescaleros had surrendered to Carson's

columns. Carleton had them moved from their mountain homeland to a barren stretch of the Pecos River Valley in eastern New Mexico called Bosque Redondo, "round grove of trees." Here he built Fort Sumner to watch over them. Now he was ready for the Navajos.

In April 1863 two peace chiefs, Barboncito and Delgadito, met with General Carleton near the edge of their home country. Again he talked bluntly. All Navajos who wanted to be friends, he said, must go live at Bosque Redondo. Stunned, the chiefs said no, but two months later he repeated his ultimatum in unmistakable terms. "Tell them," he directed the commander of Fort Wingate, "they can have until the twentieth day of July of this year to come in—they and all those who belong to what they call the peace party; *that after that day every Navajo that is seen will be considered as hostile and treated accordingly*; that after that day the door now open will be closed."[11]

This was no idle threat. The Navajos suddenly discovered Kit Carson and his soldiers thrusting deep into their homeland—north around Canyon de Chelly, west to the Hopi mesas, and south to the Little Colorado. On each sweep the troops killed Indians whenever they could, but mainly they seized stock and destroyed crops. Other Indians—Utes, Pueblos from Jemez and Zuñi, and even the normally mild Hopis—scented plunder and joined the fray, as did the ubiquitous citizen units that had always used Indian defense as a cloak for private gain. By the close of 1863, the Navajos had lost 78 people killed and 40 wounded and at least 5,000 head of sheep, goats, and mules.

The final blow, in January 1864, was Carson's defiant march the length of Canyon de Chelly, long the most forbidding Navajo citadel. As shouting, cursing Indians rained arrows from the rims of the sheer red sandstone walls, the troops, negotiating the sandy bottoms far below, corralled two hundred sheep and methodically destroyed fruit orchards. Sixty Navajos promptly surrendered with the admission, as Carson informed Carleton, that "owing to the operations of my command they are in a complete state of starvation, and that many of their women and children have already died from this cause."

These were harbingers of a flood of Navajos driven by hunger and demoralization to surrender. By the middle of March 1864, six thousand camped around Forts Canby and Wingate awaiting the threatened deportation. The soldiers organized a Long Walk, the eastward equivalent of the Trail of Tears by which Cherokees and others had journeyed westward to the Permanent Indian Frontier a generation earlier. In contingents of hundreds, the Navajos made their painful, sometimes fatal way under the guns of the soldiers across the territory to the Bosque Redondo. By late 1864 more than eight thousand people, three-fourths of the tribe, had been moved to their new home on the arid Pecos bottom. "The exodus of this whole people," observed an officer, "men, women, and children, with their flocks and herds, leaving forever the land of their fathers, was an interesting but a touching sight."

Carleton looked on Bosque Redondo as a testing ground for the reservation policy, and, employing his wartime powers to the limit, he set forth to show the Indian Bureau how the army could make it work. Far from their homes, he believed, the Navajos could be taught to farm, their children instructed in reading and writing, and all given "the truths of Christianity." Gradually the old people would die off, taking with them "all latent longings for murdering and robbing." The young would replace them without such longings. In ten years the Navajos would form

Bosque Redondo. For the Navajos, the four-year exile on the Pecos River, 1864–68, remains the central event of tribal memory. Hunger, disease, suffering, and death spelled failure for government policy but tragedy for the Indians. They returned to their homeland in 1868 determined never again to war with the white people. Here Navajos gather in front of a newly erected building at Fort Sumner, the post that watched over the reservation, in 1864 or 1865. *Museum of New Mexico.*

"the happiest and most delightfully located pueblo of Indians in New Mexico—perhaps in the United States." The Navajo Wars would be a thing of the past.

For the Navajos, life at Bosque Redondo turned out to be not so idyllic. There was not enough tillable land for so many Indians, and the crops they did grow fell victim to flood, drought, hail, and insects. The sheep and goats could not find enough grass, and Kiowas and Comanches from the plains to the east raided the herds. Government rations barely held off starvation. Government clothing did not hold off the winter cold. Weakened by malnutrition and exposure, the Indians succumbed to pneumonia, measles, and other diseases. They quarreled endlessly with their old enemies, the Mescalero Apaches, who shared the reservation with them, until the Mescaleros stampeded back to their mountain homes late in 1865.

Despite overwhelming evidence, Carleton refused to admit failure. And of one result he could boast: he had ended the Navajo Wars. Symbolizing this reality, in September 1866 Manuelito finally surrendered. Since 1855 this young spokesman for peace, on whom had fallen the mantle of Zarcillos Largos at the Laguna Negra council, had matured into the foremost Navajo war leader. With a diehard remnant of the tribe, he had withdrawn far to the west rather than yield to Carleton. His surrender marked the final triumph of the military campaign, and en route to Bosque Redondo Carleton had him paraded as a prisoner through the streets of Santa Fe.

Gentle, wise, wrinkled by sixty plains winters, Black Kettle personified the Cheyenne peace spirit. He believed accommodation with the whites more likely than war to preserve his people's freedom to follow the buffalo. War spirit fired the Cheyennes, too, especially the ever belligerent Dog Soldiers; and even in Black Kettle's own band, the young men now and then stole and killed along the Santa Fe Trail. Many, perhaps most, Cheyennes thought him too willing to do the white man's bidding, but enough shared his basic viewpoint to keep him constantly in the top ranks of tribal leadership.[12]

Not surprisingly, then, Black Kettle's name headed the list of Cheyenne chiefs who, along with a handful of Arapahos, signed the Fort Wise Treaty of 1861. This treaty addressed the perennial issue of Indian land "title." The Cheyennes and Arapahos ranged the High Plains approaches to the Rocky Mountains, now teeming with "Pike's Peakers" seeking fortunes in gold, and thus occupied a considerable portion of the newly created Territory of Colorado. At Fort Wise the chiefs agreed to a reservation south of the Arkansas River in exchange for all other lands identified as theirs in the Fort Laramie Treaty of 1851.

The compact suffered the defects of most such treaties. The Indians did not understand what they had promised. Only a handful of Southern Cheyenne and Southern Arapaho chiefs had signed. The document bore the mark of not a single Dog Soldier, most powerful of the Southern Cheyenne divisions, nor that of any representative of the Northern Cheyennes and Northern Arapahos, whose occupancy of this country also drew sanction, in the white scheme of things, from the Treaty of 1851. Territorial Governor John Evans labored diligently but vainly to sign up these other Indians, a tacit admission that the Fort Wise Treaty, despite official rhetoric, had not freed eastern Colorado of Indian title. In seeming vindication of his pacific course, Black Kettle and his band continued to wander the plains, occasionally pausing at the Upper Arkansas Agency to receive annuities from an agent more occupied with graft than with treaties and land titles.[13]

The failure of the Indians to grant a ready solution to Colorado's land problems sorely vexed Governor Evans. A conscientious and ambitious man, friend of President Lincoln, he nurtured a grand vision of Colorado's destiny and his own contribution to shaping it. The Indians stood in the way, maddeningly unresponsive to his efforts to gain land titles and settle them as farmers on the arid reservation defined in the Fort Wise Treaty. In the Indians' lack of cooperation Evans perceived sinister intent, and he readily credited reports that the tribes planned to go to war in the spring of 1864.

These reports drew plausibility from events on the northern Plains. Shock waves from the Minnesota uprising of 1862 rolled westward. In the summer of 1863 Generals Henry H. Sibley and Alfred Sully had led armies into Dakota Territory against the Minnesota fugitives and had also collided with the Teton Sioux of the upper Missouri. The generals planned another combined offensive against the Sioux in the summer of 1864. Also, along the Platte and the Arkansas, other Indians perpetrated scattered outrages, hardly enough to presage war but enough to sustain Evans's fears. One of Colorado's two volunteer regiments kept busy guarding the Santa Fe Trail, but as a measure of the tranquillity in Colorado itself, the other, the First, had stagnated at Camp Weld, near Denver, since its triumph over invading Confederates in New Mexico in 1862.

Governor Evans drew like-minded support from the military commander in Colorado. A man of impressive physique as well as enormous ego and ambition, Colonel John M. Chivington had forsaken the Methodist ministry to earn fame as Colorado's "Fighting Parson" in the New Mexico campaign. Now, as Congress authorized Colorado to apply for statehood, he harbored political ambitions that further military exploits could be expected to promote.

Whether Evans and Chivington cynically provoked an Indian war to advance their personal ambitions or simply were so certain of one that expectation proved self-fulfilling, the result was the same. No alliance of tribes materialized, although as usual the spring grasses stirred youthful energies, and stock herds and other white property suffered. To these offenses, real and imagined, Chivington's soldiers responded with heavy-handed violence. "Burn villages and kill Cheyennes whenever and wherever found," ordered one of his field officers.

Like other Cheyennes, the war burst on Black Kettle with painful

Colonel John M. Chivington. Colorado's "Fighting Parson" earned fame in battle with Confederates but is still rightly stigmatized for his treacherous attack on
Black Kettle's Cheyennes at Sand Creek in 1864. *Colorado Historical Society*.

suddenness. He and Lean Bear with their people, about four hundred in
all, had spent the winter near Fort Larned, Kansas. Moving north in mid-
May to hunt buffalo, they encountered some of Chivington's soldiers on
the Smoky Hill River. Lean Bear rode out to show them papers given
him during a visit to Washington, signed by Abraham Lincoln, telling of
his friendly character. The soldiers shot him and his companion from
their ponies, then opened fire with howitzers. The Indians returned the
fire for a time until Black Kettle rode up. "He told us we must not fight
with the white people," recalled one, "so we stopped." The soldiers
retreated; twenty-eight Indians lay dead.[14]

The war anticipated by the Colorado officials had now broken over the
Platte and the Arkansas. It featured but a few scattered raids in June and
July, then built to a destructive peak in August. Fed by sensational news-

paper accounts that multiplied and magnified actual depredations, hysteria gripped Denverites throughout the summer. Few doubted the governor's repeated declarations to Washington that the alliance he had forecast in 1863 now threatened to wipe out the Colorado settlements.

Coloradoans had another preoccupation that summer of 1864, secondary to the Indian war but not unrelated. A fierce political battle raged between Republican champions of statehood and Democratic opponents. As Lincoln's appointee, Evans led the statehood forces and, in the event of victory, aspired to a seat in the U.S. Senate. Chivington sought election to the House of Representatives. The voters would decide on September 13. Meantime, the Indian question became a central issue in the confused and bitter campaign.

Evans appealed to Washington for authority to raise more troops for Indian duty, and at last, on August 13, he received permission to recruit another regiment, the Third Colorado Cavalry, to serve for one hundred days. Unlike the other two Colorado regiments, called into federal service by the demands of the Civil War, the "Hundred Dazers" had but one purpose—to fight Indians.

With winter approaching, however, the war ardor of the Indians began to cool. Late in August Black Kettle sensed the time auspicious for a peace feeler. Not all the chiefs favored this course. The whites had started the war, and the raids on the Platte and Arkansas, and against the isolated homesteads of eastern Kansas, continued to yield plunder and captives. But Black Kettle gambled that he could bring all into line. Mixed-bloods framed a letter for him that asked for peace talks and, as earnest of sincerity, offered the release of white captives. At great peril a small party of Indians rode south with this letter. Fortunately they fell into the hands of an unusually sensitive and compassionate officer, Major Edward W. Wynkoop, commander of Fort Lyon. Also at great peril, and with grave misgivings, Wynkoop and a small command set forth to test the Cheyenne initiative.

Against large odds, Black Kettle and Wynkoop came to terms. The confrontation of 130 scared soldiers with more than 500 shouting, well-armed Indians almost ended in violence before talks could get started, and several times thereafter mutual suspicion, taut nerves, and dissent in both camps came close to precipitating armed collision. But in the end the white major and the Cheyenne peace chief prevailed. Black Kettle turned over four white captives to the soldiers, and Wynkoop, on September 18, wrote jubilantly to Governor Evans that he was on his way to Denver with Black Kettle and other chiefs for peace talks.

Edward W. Wynkoop. As an officer of Colorado Volunteers, Wynkoop under-took the hazardous task of trying to end the Plains war of 1864. Later, in 1867, he served as agent to the Cheyennes and Arapahos, who knew him affectionately as "Tall Chief." *Denver Public Library, Western History Department.*

The news hardly elated the governor. Although the electorate had re-jected statehood on September 13, political considerations still ruled. The Third Regiment had been called up to fight Indians. The recruits expected to. The citizens expected them to. Washington officials and Chivington's superiors at Fort Leavenworth expected them to. After emitting cries of alarm all summer and finally winning authority to form the Third Regi-ment, Evans could not concede peace without severe loss of credibility in all quarters. Besides, the issue of peace or war lay chiefly with the army, as General Samuel R. Curtis, Chivington's superior, made clear on September 28. "I want no peace till the Indians suffer more," he telegraphed. "No peace must be made without my directions."

Yet here on this very day came Black Kettle, Bull Bear, White Antelope, and other Cheyenne and Arapaho chiefs, under escort of one of Chiv-

At the Camp Weld conference in September 1864, Colonel Chivington told the Cheyenne and Arapaho chiefs they could have peace by surrendering to Major Wynkoop at Fort Lyon. While in Denver the chiefs had their picture taken. Major Wynkoop squats with pistol on hip, partially concealing Black Kettle. Seated far left is the Arapaho Neva and next to him Bull Bear. White Antelope (killed in the first fire at Sand Creek) is to Black Kettle's left. Standing third from left is famed interpreter "Uncle John" Smith. *Colorado Historical Society.*

ington's own officers, to talk peace. It posed a genuine dilemma for both the governor and the military commander, and they met it with dissimulation. After hours of verbal sparring, Chivington declared: "My rule of fighting white men or Indians is to fight them until they lay down their arms and submit to military authority. They are nearer to Major Wynkoop than anyone else, and they can go to him when they get ready to do that." Whatever Chivington meant by that, if indeed it was anything more than an artful attempt to straddle the dilemma, Black Kettle and his fellow chiefs took it at face value. They could have peace by surrendering to Major Wynkoop.

With full trust in Wynkoop, Black Kettle and Little Raven moved swiftly to do just as Chivington had instructed. Little Raven and 113 lodges of

Arapahos arrived at Fort Lyon in mid-October, and Wynkoop issued them army rations. Early in November Black Kettle and a party of followers rode in, having left their village of 115 lodges on Sand Creek about thirty-five miles northeast of the fort. To his dismay, Black Kettle discovered "Tall Chief" Wynkoop about to leave. He had been summoned eastward to explain to General Curtis his curious behavior in feeding hostile Indians. Major Scott J. Anthony had taken his place. The two majors explained the situation to Black Kettle. The army lacked sufficient rations to feed so many Indians, and official permission to accept them as prisoners would have to be obtained. Meantime, the Arapahos should move out to hunt, and the Cheyennes should remain on Sand Creek and also hunt.

Through October and November 1864 Colonel Chivington bore mounting abuse from the Colorado press, which ridiculed him and the "Bloodless Third" for their inactivity. He considered leading an expedition to the upper Republican River, where plenty of indisputably hostile Sioux and other Indians camped. But this would be chancy at best, especially with the Third's hundred-day enlistment running out. In Chivington's mind the Cheyennes and Arapahos near Fort Lyon were equally guilty of outrages against whites, just as surely deserved punishment, and were technically still "hostile Indians." They were also much easier to get at. With great secrecy, he concentrated his troops at Fort Lyon, where he found an eagerly cooperative Major Anthony.

At daybreak on November 29, 1864, Chivington deployed his column of seven hundred men and charged into Black Kettle's sleeping camp, which sheltered about five hundred Indians. Black Kettle hoisted an American flag and a white flag over his lodge and tried to calm his startled people. White Antelope ran toward the soldiers waving his arms and was shot down in the first volley. Frantically the Cheyennes fled, seeking cover, as the cavalrymen cut them down. They had no chance to organize resistance, and for several hours after the opening charge the troopers ranged the village and surrounding country, honoring their colonel's intent that no prisoners be taken. Men, women, children, and even infants perished in the orgy of slaughter, their bodies then scalped and barbarously mutilated. At day's close some two hundred Cheyenne corpses, about two-thirds women and children, littered the valley of Sand Creek.

"Colorado soldiers have again covered themselves with glory," exulted the *Rocky Mountain News* as the victors of Sand Creek paraded triumphantly through Denver's streets to the cheers of her citizens. Theater patrons applauded a display of Cheyenne scalps, some of them of women's pubic hair, strung across the stage at intermission. The "Bloody Thirdsters," and Chivington too, were mustered out of the service acclaimed as heroes by their admiring fellow citizens.

By 1865 military force as the solution to the Indian problem had achieved virtually unchallenged supremacy. In Indian matters President Lincoln had shown himself a humanitarian, but the struggle with the Confederacy ruled his White House years and he left Indian affairs almost entirely to Congress and the Indian Bureau. Commissioner of Indian Affairs William P. Dole skillfully promoted traditional civil policies—reservations, Christianity, "civilization"—but the Civil War so consumed public and official attention that he made little headway. In the Congress he encountered Indian committees dominated by westerners. In the West his agents found themselves powerless against military potentates such as Carleton, Connor, Curtis, Sibley, and Sully. Backed by regiments full of warlike westerners, supported by western public opinion, and unrestrained by a national authority preoccupied with saving the Union, the generals almost by default had made U.S. Indian policy overwhelmingly a military policy.[15]

No general believed more fervently in the military solution, or held the civil agents in greater contempt, than John Pope. Pompous, bombastic, quarrelsome, and verbose, he had been exiled to Minnesota after losing the Battle of Second Manassas in 1862. In directing the operations of Generals Sibley and Sully on the northern Plains, however, Pope had done so well that, late in 1864, General Ulysses S. Grant placed him in charge of a huge new command extending from the ninety-fifth meridian to the Rocky Mountains and from Confederate Texas to the British possessions. As the spring of 1865 opened, Pope organized the biggest offensive ever mounted against the Plains Indians.

Pope and his officers classed all the Plains Indians as hostile. Many in fact were, thanks in no small part to Colonel Chivington. Predictably, Sand Creek had touched off an explosion. As the survivors of Chivington's strike straggled into the other Cheyenne camps on the Smoky Hill, runners bore war pipes to all the Sioux, Cheyenne, and Arapaho bands of the central Plains. Throughout January and February 1865, they spread death and destruction along the overland route, burning virtually every ranch and stage station on the South Platte, twice sacking the town of Julesburg, ripping up miles of telegraph wire, plundering wagon trains,

John Pope. Exiled to the Plains after failing on Civil War battlefields, Pope performed ably as a frontier commander and also emerged as a noisy self-appointed expert on Indian policy. His views, sometimes thoughtful and sometimes silly, strongly influenced federal policy makers. This portrait dates from the 1870s, when he commanded on the southern Plains from Fort Leavenworth. *National Archives*.

running off cattle herds, and completely cutting off Denver from the East. Then, abruptly, the war ended. In council the chiefs had decided to cast their fortunes with their brethren to the north. Troops struggling desperately through snow and mud to confront the raiders found them all moving rapidly northward.

On the northern Plains, Teton Sioux, Northern Cheyennes, and Northern Arapahos had not been as directly provoked as the kinsmen who came among them with stories of Sand Creek. But some had fought General Sully on the upper Missouri the previous summer, and all were distressed by the growing traffic of whites to the Montana mines. Some of the goldseekers went by steamboat up the Missouri River. Others, more ominously, traveled overland by an increasingly popular route that ran northwest from Fort Laramie. Known as the Bozeman Trail, it cut through the very heart of the Sioux buffalo ranges in the Powder River country.

South of the Arkansas River, the Kiowas and Comanches were also classed as hostile. In the summer of 1864 they had endangered the Santa Fe Trail, the supply line to General Carleton's army in New Mexico. He had reacted with customary vigor by sending Colonel Kit Carson to deal with these tribes as he had with Apaches and Navajos. On November 25, 1864, at Adobe Walls in the Texas Panhandle, Carson and his New Mexico Volunteers had a hard fight with Kiowas. The Indians suffered losses, but Carson escaped disaster only under cover of artillery fire. Although the Kiowas and Comanches may not have regarded the conflicts of 1864 as placing them among the hostiles of 1865, General Pope and his campaign planners did.

Pope's Plains operations of 1865 represented the most extensive test ever of the military solution. In regiments and brigades rather than in companies and battalions, the army marched against the Indians. In all, six thousand troops took the offensive, while thousands more defended the travel routes and settlements. South of the Arkansas, General James H. Ford tried to bring the Kiowas and Comanches to battle. In the north General Sully campaigned once again on the upper Missouri, and General Connor launched three heavy columns into the Powder River country.

The offensive dramatized the limitations of the military solution and ended in a failure so complete that the generals could not gloss it over. They discovered that big columns operating in an inhospitable country far from their bases required massive logistical support and had to devote themselves almost entirely simply to keeping themselves provisioned. Some of Connor's units came close to disaster when bad weather wiped out horse and mule herds weakened by starvation and almost did the same to soldiers in similar condition. Also, big columns trailing long supply trains moved so ponderously that only the most careless Indians failed to get out of the way. In addition to such obstacles inherent in large-scale operations, the generals confronted other difficulties. Appomattox had ended the Civil War. The volunteers, hitherto such aggressive fighters, wanted to go home. Sent instead to chase Indians, they approached their task sullenly, even mutinously. Whole units melted away in desertion. Supply costs skyrocketed, moreover, at the very time the public demand for drastic curtailment of military expenditures hit the War Department. At the close of the season, the armies dissolved, beaten not by the Indians but by terrain, distance, weather, logistics, morale, and the miscalculations of the generals.

But the generals had also fallen victim to forces beyond the purely military, for the armies had marched against a rising tide of peace sentiment. Sand Creek had momentarily distracted public attention from the Civil War and sent waves of revulsion across the land. Three separate official investigations got under way, although civilian immunity now shielded Chivington and his lieutenants. In this climate voices of peace, hitherto drowned by the clash of arms, could be heard again. Before adjourning in the spring of 1865, Congress created a joint committee to investigate "the condition of the Indian tribes and their treatment by the civil and military authorities of the United States" and also authorized a treaty commission to approach the Sioux of the upper Missouri. These two commissions, beaming peace signals at the Plains Indians in the midst of a military offensive, contributed to the array of setbacks that dashed the hopes of the military strategists.

The two congressional enactments of March 1865 marked the first tentative steps toward a different kind of Indian policy, one that when fully matured would be described as "conquest by kindness." Both efforts reflected uncertainty among most civil and military authorities over what approach to take; war and peace factions had yet to polarize. Both efforts, too, reflected a pattern of motivation that would increasingly characterize federal measures toward the Indians, a pattern that rooted Indian policy in a strange mixture of genuine humanitarianism and crass self-interest.

The Dakota project rested on a large measure of self-interest. It germinated in the fertile brain of Territorial Governor Newton Edmunds. In Dakota, curiously, politicians and newspapers damned the generals and called on Congress to make peace. Actually, Dakotans had not suddenly acquired a sympathy for the Indians. For one thing, they were outraged that General Pope's quartermasters bought supplies for General Sully's expeditions in Sioux City, Iowa, rather than Yankton, Dakota. But the principal explanation for the new pacifism lay in the public image of Dakota as a war-torn territory; not only had immigration ceased, but settlers were packing up and leaving. So people had to be shown that they did not risk their scalps by settling in Dakota. In October 1865 the Edmunds Commission journeyed to the upper Missouri, signed up some chiefs of the "stay-around-the-fort" bands, and proclaimed peace. It was a brazenly cynical tactic, for as the governor and his associates well knew, not a single chief of the Sioux with whom Generals Sully and Sibley had been fighting for three years had even talked with the commissioners, much less touched the pen to their treaty. Yet the public perception fostered by the Edmunds Commission made it an influential force in the evolution of a peace policy.[16]

A similar contribution to policy sprang from a treaty negotiated at the same time with the Kiowas and Comanches on the Little Arkansas River in Kansas. This treaty owed much to Senator James R. Doolittle, chairman of the Senate Committee on Indian Affairs and author of the measure that sent three congressional groups to the West in the summer of 1865 to inquire into "the condition of the Indian tribes." Doolittle and two colleagues made up one of the groups. In Kansas, working with Kiowa-Comanche Agent Jesse H. Leavenworth, they successfully blocked General Pope's offensive against the Indians south of the Arkansas River and laid the groundwork for the peace initiative that culminated on the Little Arkansas in October. Throughout the tortured sequence of events that turned a military offensive into a peace offensive runs a mostly hidden thread of private gain. High officials in Washington as well as Kansas, both civil and military, had interests in the railroads that now, with the Civil War's end, would begin building across Kansas. Indian hostilities would scarcely promote either the financing or the settlement on which their progress depended. Although characterized by General Pope as "not worth the paper it is written on," the Little Arkansas Treaty, like the Edmunds Treaty, created the momentary illusion of peace and thus strenghtened the drive for an overall peace policy.[17]

The military debacle on the northern Plains in 1865 signaled the end of a distinct phase of U.S. relations with the western Indians. Although not repudiated, the purely military solution had been severely discredited. Now proponents of other approaches could at least gain a hearing. The autonomy enjoyed by frontier commanders during the war years vanished with the volunteer armies.

One who may have drawn satisfaction from helping to stimulate the peace sentiment among the white people was Black Kettle. Chivington thought he had killed the Cheyenne peace chief at Sand Creek. But, with other survivors of his band, he had fled to the Smoky Hill. When his fellow chiefs resolved to go north and enlist their brethren in the fight, Black Kettle led his people south of the Arkansas to escape the hostilities. Not surprisingly, in October 1865 he turned up with his band at the treaty council on the Little Arkansas.

With what emotions Black Kettle made his mark on the Little Arkansas Treaty can only be surmised. On the one hand, he surely saw a measure of vindication in its express repudiation of "the gross and wanton outrage" perpetrated by U.S. soldiers at Sand Creek. On the other hand, he may have puzzled over the reparation awarded him personally—a grant of 320 acres of patented land to be carved from a reservation in turn to be carved from those vast reaches of High Plains that he and other Cheyennes still looked upon as their birthright.

4

War and Peace: Indian Relations in Transition, 1865–1869

General Patrick Edward Connor's elaborate campaign of 1865 on the northern Plains stirred up a hornet's nest, and in white eyes the chief hornet was Red Cloud. Actually, the Teton Sioux in the Powder River country—mainly Oglala, Miniconjou, and Sans Arc—regarded Man-Afraid-of-His-Horse as their principal chief, but increasingly they looked to Red Cloud, an Oglala "Bad Face," for leadership in matters of war. About forty-three in 1865, ambitious, cunning, smart, somewhat enig matic even to his own people, Red Cloud had built an impressive reputation as a warrior and war leader in conflicts with Pawnees, Crows, and Shoshonis. He was not a chief, but rather a "shirt wearer," or head warrior, and his commanding influence among the Sioux rested on genuine merit.[1]

Red Cloud and his people, together with their Northern Cheyenne and Arapaho friends, ranged the plains rolling westward from the Black Hills to the Bighorn Mountains. In a decade or two of bitter fighting, they had taken this country away from the Crows, and now they behaved as if it were an ancestral homeland. The handful of white gold seekers who traveled over the Bozeman Trail to the Montana mines in 1864 unsettled these Indians; and General Connor's blue columns, lurching blindly about the Powder River country in 1865, infuriated them. Even so, the peace feelers put out by white officials in the spring of 1866 reached receptive people. An especially cold and hungry winter had brought them to the brink of destitution. The prospect of food and other presents that always warmed talks with the whites tempted Red Cloud, Man-Afraid-of-His-Horse, and other Powder River leaders to arrange a council with the whites.

The parley took place at Fort Laramie in June 1866. As expected, treaty commissioner E. B. Taylor had plenty of presents on hand to help persuade

99

Red Cloud. Although not a chief, Red Cloud amassed a war record that gave him great power among his people, the Oglala Sioux. He masterminded the Fetterman Massacre and Wagon Box Fight and forced the U.S. Government to abandon the Bozeman Trail as the price for the Treaty of 1868. On the reservation he pursued a precarious course between the demands of white officials and the demands of his people. Blind and nearly ninety, he died in 1909. *Oil painting by Henry Raschen, collection of David Blumberg.*

the chiefs to call off the war and subscribe to a treaty such as Governor Edmunds had concluded with the stay-around-the-fort people on the Missouri during the previous autumn. He made much of these presents and glossed over the key question of the Bozeman Trail. But all snapped into focus when, in the midst of the council, Colonel Henry B. Carrington and a battalion of regular infantry marched into Fort Laramie with orders to build forts on the Bozeman Trail and protect the emigration to Montana. Red Cloud made a stinging speech about white perfidy and, vowing to fight all invaders, angrily led the Sioux delegation back to the north. Taylor easily signed up the "Laramie Loafers" (more stay-around-the-fort people) and even the influential Spotted Tail, whose Brule Sioux ranged the Platte and Republican rivers and thus had little interest in the Powder. "Satisfactory treaty concluded," Taylor wired the Commissioner of Indian Affairs with a certain lack of candor. "Most cordial feeling prevails."[2]

Red Cloud's experience was symptomatic of an ambivalence that characterized the U.S. government's approach to the Indian problem over the next several years. After Appomattox the nation faced west. Emigrants crowded the transcontinental trails, streaming not only westward from the Missouri River but eastward from the Pacific shore, seeking wealth in gold or silver, cattle, timber, agriculture, commerce, or politics. Wells, Fargo and Company bought out Ben Holladay and others and consolidated all the stage lines west of the Missouri River. The firm's coaches mingled with freight caravans and emigrant wagons on the western trails. Twin rails of iron crept out onto the prairies of Kansas and Nebraska and assaulted the western rampart of the Sierra Nevada as Union Pacific and Central Pacific raced toward the union at Promontory Summit in 1869 that would span the continent. Other railroads—Southern Pacific, Santa Fe, Northern Pacific, Great Northern—launched parallel lines to the north and south. Steamboats plied the Missouri, the Columbia, and the Colorado.

It was a tumultuous and irresistible movement, one that the government could not deflect if it wanted, and certainly not out of respect for the rights—or even the existence—of a handful of Indians. As Senator John Sherman reminded his colleagues, "If the whole Army of the United States stood in the way, the wave of emigration would pass over it to seek the valley where gold was to be found."[3]

The big question, then, since the westward movement was a fact of life and beyond major governmental influence, was what to do with the Indians who stood in its way. As Red Cloud discovered, the government could not decide, and he would surely have agreed with the observation of an editor of the *Army and Navy Journal*. "We go to them Janus-faced," he wrote. "One of our hands holds the rifle and the other the peacepipe, and we blaze away with both instruments at the same time. The chief consequence is a great *smoke*—and there it ends."[4]

Such was the theme of Indian-white relations from 1865 through 1868. The rifle and the peace pipe contended in the councils of the Great Father. Championing the rifle were the heads of the postwar regular army called forth by the demands of the frontier West and the Reconstruction South, the idolized generals such as Grant, Sherman, and Sheridan who had put down the Southern Rebellion and their grimly formidable chief, Secretary of War Edwin M. Stanton. Spokesmen for the peace pipe were an able Secretary of the Interior, Orville H. Browning, and at least one force-ful head of the Indian Bureau, Nathaniel G. Taylor, together with two high–minded chairmen of the Senate Indian committee, James R. Doo-little and John B. Henderson. The clash of these two factions produced the obscuring smoke noted by the scribe for the *Army and Navy Journal,* but when it lifted early in 1869 it revealed an Indian policy that, what-ever its limitations in hindsight, at least at the time seemed rational, coherent, and cause for optimism.

Like Red Cloud, James R. Doolittle had his own memorable experience with the stresses between rifle and peace pipe. Impeccable in well-cut frock coat and neatly trimmed mustache and beard, he looked every inch a distinguished United States senator. With his associates of the joint con-gressional committee inquiring into "the condition of the Indian tribes," the Wisconsin Republican set in motion the movement that led to the Little Arkansas treaties, and then, in late July 1865, he arrived in Denver.

Here the congressional investigators found themselves in the midst of a population still distraught over Indian warfare. In the same opera house where the Cheyenne scalps taken at Sand Creek had been displayed to wild applause, Governor Evans introduced Senator Doolittle to a capac-ity crowd. Bravely, the senator spoke of the need to end costly wars and to find some other solution to the Indian problem. The question now presented itself, he said, whether the Indians should be placed on reser-vations and taught to support themselves or simply be exterminated. "There suddenly arose," he later recalled, "such a shout as is never heard unless upon some battle field;—a shout almost loud enough to raise the roof of the Opera House.—'Exterminate them! Exterminate them!' "[5]

Denver's rude rebuff of Senator Doolittle dramatized the polarization of East and West in the dispute over peace pipe or rifle. Sand Creek had horrified the East and given rise to a spreading peace sentiment, but as yet the cause of the Indian had inspired no organized movement that could influence policy or legislation. In the West, by contrast, public opinion remained resolutely antagonistic to such "sickly sentimentality." Animated by the spirit that produced and now justified Sand Creek, westerners overwhelmingly favored the rifle, and their newspapers cried for extermination.

As Doolittle also discovered, the issue opened a rift between the civil and military arms of the government. General Pope emerged as the noisi-est (and wordiest) champion of a new order. His scheme was elaborate

and, for the most part, politically unrealistic. But his proposal to put the
Indian Bureau back in the War Department made sense to a lot of people,
especially in the West. Not surprisingly, the transfer proposition offended
the nascent peace sentiment of the East and provoked heated opposition
from the Department of the Interior. It also presented itself as an issue
that Senator Doolittle and his joint congressional committee had to face.[6]

And finally, still closer to Doolittle's personal domain, peace pipe and
rifle pitted Senate against House of Representatives. Traditionally the Senate preferred the peace pipe and the House the rifle. These tendencies
had their roots largely in the mechanics of treaty ratification. The Senate
alone "consented" to the ratification of treaties, whether with Indians or
with foreign nations. House members bitterly resented the annual obligation of appropriating money to carry out the provisions of Indian treaties they had played no part in approving. The proposal to transfer the
Indian Bureau to the War Department deepened the split, as the House
listened sympathetically to the militarists and the Senate rebuffed them.

Part of the reason for the confusion in Indian policy lay in the preoccupation of legislators and government officials with more weighty concerns.
The Congress and the President's cabinet occasionally discussed the rifle
and the peace pipe, but their attention was otherwise almost entirely absorbed by the historic debates over Reconstruction of the conquered South
and the attendant constitutional struggle between President Andrew Johnson and the Congress. Senator Doolittle himself became so embroiled in
this fight that he took more than a year to draft the committee's findings
and recommendations—and, by then, his support of President Johnson
had cost him the nomination for another Senate term. Sand Creek faded
in public and official memory, and amid the fast-breaking and momentous events of Andrew Johnson's Washington, neither the condition of
the Indian tribes in general nor the Doolittle report in particular stood
much chance of gaining anyone's attention until another such spectacle
captured public attention.

It happened late in the Moon of Popping Trees—December 1866, as
the white people reckoned time. The cottonwoods in the Powder, Tongue,
and Bighorn valleys had dropped their bright autumn leaves. Snow spotted the brown hills and ridges. Heavy gray clouds warned of the deep
snows and bitter cold to come. Since summer, the Sioux, Cheyennes,
and Arapahos, now camped in the Tongue River Valley, had made good
Red Cloud's threat at Fort Laramie to fight all whites who tried to use
the Bozeman Trail. Not many did, but the soldiers worked busily to erect

Fetterman Massacre. Sioux decoys lured an overconfident detachment of troops out of the Bozeman Trail post of Fort Phil Kearny on December 21, 1866. Within moments after the trap sprang shut, all had been slain. The disaster touched off a strident debate over U.S. Indian policy. This pen drawing is by famed cowboy artist Charles M. Russell. *Whitney Gallery of Western Art, Cody, Wyoming.*

three guardian forts, and the Indians harassed them constantly. The biggest fort, where the top soldier chief lived, rose in stockaded defiance from the banks of Little Piney Creek, a tributary of the Tongue, with the snow-capped Bighorn Mountains forming a majestic backdrop.

For months Red Cloud and other Indian leaders had talked of striking a hard blow at this fort. Now, with construction almost finished and winter fast approaching, the moment seemed right. High-Back-Bone of the Miniconjous plotted the move and directed it, but Red Cloud and others surely gathered with the warrior force that massed just over the ridge from the hated fort. All were eager and full of confidence, for a "half-man" with holy powers had made an exciting prophecy. Four times he rode forth seeking a vision of how many soldiers might be brought to battle. Three times the assembled warriors rejected the counting as too few. On the fourth return, however, the holy person's hands held a hundred bluecoats, and the painted horde shouted in exuberant approval.

The Plains Indians greatly favored the decoy tactic: Send forth a small party to lure the enemy into ambush. That it almost never worked—anxious young men usually triggered the ambush prematurely—did not discourage its repeated employment. This time it worked. One decoy party attacked a wood train hauling timber to the post. Another, led by a youthful protégé of High-Back-Bone named Crazy Horse, rode boldly toward the fort itself. Soon soldiers came out from the fort—almost the hundred foretold. The decoys fell back tantalizingly. The soldiers followed, over the high ridge to the north and down the slope on the other side.

At just the right moment the trap sprang shut. Between fifteen hundred and two thousand warriors burst from hiding places in the ravines seaming the slope. Closing swiftly around the startled soldiers, they cut them down with clouds of arrows and then rode triumphantly over a last remnant that gathered near the crest of the ridge. Here two officers shot each other rather than face capture. As the victors raced about the hillside taking scalps and fearfully mutilating the corpses, a dog ran yelping up the slope toward the fort. "All are dead but the dog," shouted a Cheyenne; "let him carry the news back to the fort." "No," cried another. "Do not let even a dog get away." Another young man let fly an arrow, and the dog dropped before it could top the ridge.[7]

The news stunned the nation—Captain William J. Fetterman and eighty men slaughtered near Fort Phil Kearny, Colonel Carrington and his soldiers locked in their fort by plunging temperatures and great drifts of new-fallen snow, and the troops at Forts Reno and C. F. Smith similarly imprisoned. Like Sand Creek, the Fetterman Massacre propelled the Indian question into national prominence. Unlike Sand Creek, where right and wrong seemed plain, the Fetterman Massacre found no consensus. It thus served not only to gain attention for Indian policy but to intensify the debate over peace pipe or rifle.

"We must act with vindictive earnestness against the Sioux," exploded General William Tecumseh Sherman, the grizzled hero of Atlanta and the March to the Sea who now commanded all the troops on the Great Plains, "even to their extermination, men, women, and children."[8] As his subordinates worked on plans for summer operations, advocates of transferring the Indian Bureau to the War Department stepped up their campaign. Authorizing legislation enlisted enthusiastic proponents in the House of Representatives.

But the military offensive collided with a formidable peace offensive, given strength and direction by the long-deferred publication, in late January 1867, of the Doolittle report. The Doolittle committee found the Indians in a bad way, declining in population because of the loss of land and the growing scarcity of game, and progressively corrupted by whiskey, disease, and other white vices. Most Indian hostilities, the evidence showed, could be traced to white encroachment or white provocation. The reservation system offered the only sound basis for policy. Its success depended on people who could civilize the Indians and teach them to support themselves by farming. Military officers possessed neither the skills nor the inclination for such a task, and therefore the Indian Bureau should remain in the Interior Department. To oversee the civilization program and eradicate the evils of the existing system, the committee proposed five "boards of inspection," composed of high-ranking civilians and army officers, to operate in five inspection districts. A bill to authorize this, introduced by Doolittle, had passed the Senate in the previous session of Congress but had languished ever since in the House. The committee urged enactment of this legislation.[9]

Commissioner of Indian Affairs Lewis V. Bogy pitched headlong into the fight against the army. Endowed with more skill in vituperation than powers of intellect, he complained loudly of military blunders and accused the army of high-handed interference in the affairs of the Indian Bureau. Bogy proposed a somewhat vague plan to send fact-finding groups to all parts of the West to gather information and make recommendations. He also wanted to hold peace councils with the Plains Indians in the spring. Their chiefs were wise and intelligent men, he said, and if approached by able negotiators they would readily see the wisdom of settling on reservations.[10]

The Johnson administration plainly favored some kind of peaceful handling of Indian difficulties. In meetings of the President's cabinet throughout the early months of 1867, Secretary of War Stanton urged vigorous military retaliation for the Fetterman Massacre, and General Grant sometimes sat in to back him up. But Interior Secretary Browning always managed to line up most of the other department heads in opposition. Although he failed to sell Bogy's scheme either to the cabinet or the Congress, in February President Johnson agreed to send a commission to investigate the Fetterman Massacre, ascertain the temper of the northern Plains Indians, and find out if any of them could be induced to settle on reservations.[11]

Congress also came down on the side of peace—predictably through

Senator James R. Doolittle. Chairman of the Senate Committee on Indian Affairs in the Johnson presidency, the Wisconsin Republican headed a group that authored the congressional report on the "condition of the Indian tribes," a milestone in the unfolding of an Indian policy aimed at peaceful resolution of Indian difficulties. *Library of Congress.*

Senate rather than House action. In a cruelly ironic repudiation of Senator Doolittle (now a lame duck), the House amended his bill for the creation of boards of inspection, which the Senate had already passed, by striking out the entire body of the bill and substituting a measure for the transfer of the Indian Bureau to the War Department, and then promptly enacted it. The Senate refused to agree to such mutilation, and the session ended on March 3 without final action on either transfer or boards of inspection.[12]

Despite the preference in both the executive and legislative branches for peaceful approaches, the generals could not easily shrug off the humiliation of the Fetterman disaster. Not only did they rattle their sabers noisily, but in April, with Sherman's approval, General Winfield Scott Hancock took the field to awe the Cheyenne and other tribes of Kansas, whose behavior he judged to be menacing. As his column approached a large Cheyenne and Sioux village on Pawnee Fork, near Fort Larned, visions of Sand Creek suddenly seized the inhabitants, and they abandoned their lodges and fled in the night. Hancock sent in pursuit a cavalry force under the flamboyant "boy general" of Civil War fame, George Armstrong Custer, now lieutenant colonel of the Seventh Cavalry. The Indians easily eluded him, murdered and pillaged along the Smoky Hill road to Denver, and rode off to the High Plains of western Kansas. In retaliation, though without certain knowledge of which Indians had raided on the Smoky Hill, Hancock burned their village. Truly could Secretary Browning complain, after a cabinet meeting on May 28, "The War Department seems bent on a general war and will probably force all the Indians into it."[13]

Meantime, the commission to investigate the Fetterman Massacre, chaired by General Alfred Sully, came forth in early summer with some clear conclusions. All the Indians of the northern Plains wanted peace, the commissioners reported, and but for Hancock's aggressions in Kansas they themselves could have made peace. The course to follow now, they believed, was to abandon the Bozeman Trail as unneeded, confine military operations to defense of the Platte route, and set aside eighty thousand square miles of the Missouri and Yellowstone river basins for exclusive occupancy by the Indians. Also, the Indian Bureau should not be placed in the War Department but, rather, organized as a separate, cabinet-level department.

These views found ready acceptance in the Indian Bureau, where a new chief had taken office. The Senate liked neither the ethics nor the politics of Lewis Bogy and declined to confirm his appointment. President Johnson chose as the new bureau head an old Tennessee crony, Nathaniel G. Taylor. Former congressman, Methodist cleric, a man of ample proportions, florid speech, and generous gifts of certitude and rectitude, he speedily made the peace pipe the keystone of his administration. Two large reservations, he believed, should be set aside for the Plains Indians, one north of Nebraska and the other south of Kansas. Military operations should be placed under the "direction and control of the Indian department." Peace emissaries should be sent to the Plains at once, and similar approaches should be made to all other Indians.

While Taylor's pacifism discomfited the army, the findings of the Sully Commission badly rankled, penned as they were by one active and two former generals. To abandon the Bozeman Trail forts now, General Sherman responded tartly, "would invite the whole Sioux nation down to the main Platte road." Moreover, far from stirring hostilities, Hancock's timely operations had headed off a summer of general warfare. That said, Sherman had to admit that, however wrongheaded the means, Taylor sought the right end. Indeed, Sherman himself had advocated a goal similar to Taylor's in his annual report for 1866. By consolidating the Plains Indians north of the Platte and south of the Arkansas, he would rid the crucial belt of territory between these two rivers of all Indians. This would secure the principal emigrant thoroughfares, but most importantly it would open the way for completion of the Union Pacific and Kansas Pacific railroads. To them and others to come Sherman looked for the ultimate solution to the Indian problem, and he regarded no mission more urgent than affording protection to the construction workers.[14]

Fortified by the findings of the Sully Commission and the Doolittle committee, Taylor's recommendations won immediate congressional support. On July 16 Senator John B. Henderson, Doolittle's successor as chairman of the Committee on Indian Affairs, introduced legislation to authorize most of Taylor's program. After four days of debate and amendment, the bill passed both houses of Congress and at once received President Johnson's signature. The law directed the creation of still another peace commission, composed of Commissioner Taylor (as chairman), Senator Henderson, John B. Sanborn (lately a member of the Sully Commission), Samuel F. Tappan (prominent humanitarian crusader), and three army generals to be named by the President. The commission was to identify and remove the causes of hostility and attempt to consolidate all the Plains Indians on reservations.[15]

It was well that Sherman could find common ground with Commissioner Taylor, however narrow, for President Johnson promptly cast him in the uncharacteristic role of peacemaker. Together with Generals William S. Harney, Alfred H. Terry, and later Christopher C. Augur, Sherman found himself a member of the Taylor Peace Commission. The group's composition thus reflected the continuing tension between peace pipe and rifle as well as the intent of Congress, made explicit in the law, that if the commission could not negotiate a peace the army would be turned loose to conquer a peace.

By the end of the summer of 1867 Red Cloud enjoyed enormous prestige among the Powder River hostiles. Man-Afraid-of-His-Horse remained the principal chief, but Red Cloud wielded a power unusual for one not a chief. Throughout the summer his medicine had proved strong. After a great Sun Dance, the Sioux, Cheyennes, and Arapahos had decided to

William Tecumseh Sherman. Chief architect of the postwar regular army, General Sherman urged a hardline approach to Indian affairs but found himself a member of the Peace Commission of 1867–68. He headed the army during its final years of warfare with the western tribes and retired in 1883. *National Archives*

strike another blow at the soldiers. Typically they could not agree on which fort to attack, so they split into two forces and rode on both. Near one, under Red Cloud's leadership, they fell on a party of wood-cutters barricaded behind wagon boxes. Near the other they engaged hay-cutters in a log-and-thatch corral. In both fights they were driven off by resolute soldiers armed with new breech-loading rifles. The white people acclaimed the Wagon Box Fight at Fort Phil Kearny and the Hayfield Fight at Fort C. F. Smith smashing victories. But the Indians themselves rode away without any particular feelings of defeat. They had denied the Bozeman Trail to virtually all emigrant travel, bottled up the soldiers in their forts, forced army supply trains to fight their way through, and ended the summer with herds gratifyingly enlarged by stock stolen from the bluecoats.

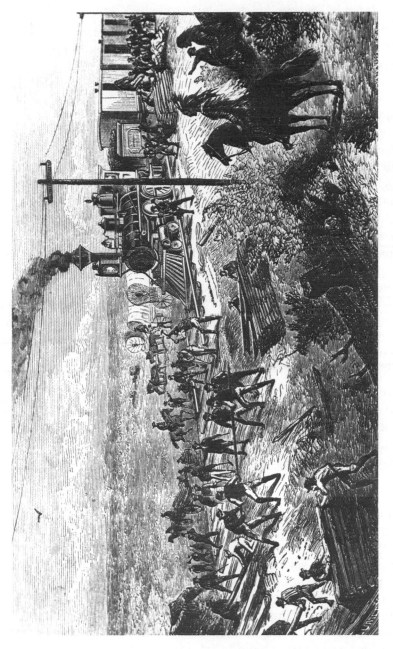

General Sherman looked to the railroads to solve the Indian problem, and he deployed the army to aid in every way possible their construction. The Union Pacific linked with the Central Pacific in 1869 to span the continent, and one after another others followed. Railroads sliced through the Indian homeland, bringing white settlers in their wake and fulfilling Sherman's prophecy. From Samuel Bowles, *Our New West*.

Thus the messengers who rode into the hostile camps with an invitation to come down to Laramie for peace talks rode back with word that Red Cloud was too busy preparing for the fall buffalo hunt to talk just now— perhaps next year.[16]

Among the Indians of the southern Plains, messengers from the Great Father's new peace talkers found greater receptivity, even though relations with the whites had been almost as stormy as in the north. Late in 1865 the Southern Cheyennes and Arapahos who had joined the Powder River Indians after Sand Creek came back home. Here they learned that Black Kettle had touched the pen on the Little Arkansas and given away the cherished Cheyenne hunting grounds in western Kansas. With only eighty lodges, Black Kettle had stressed to the commissioners that he could not speak for the two hundred lodges in the north, but he had yielded to the persuasion of the highly respected William Bent and to assurances that the other chiefs could sign later, when they returned.

But the other Cheyennes stoutly asserted their attachment to their hunting grounds. Buffalo beyond counting blackened the High Plains between the Platte and the Arkansas. South of the Arkansas, where the treaty said they should live, game ran less abundantly and the land belonged to the Kiowas and Comanches. But in 1866 another respected and persuasive white man came among them. This was their old friend "Tall Chief" Wynkoop, now out of the army and serving as agent for the Cheyennes and Arapahos. He managed to talk nearly all the leading chiefs into signing the treaty.

Chiefs might sign, but the hot-headed young men, especially among the Dog Soldiers, did not automatically obey. Not only did they resist yielding hunting grounds, they looked on the new Smoky Hill road to Denver in about the same light as Red Cloud viewed the Bozeman Trail. Emigrant wagons, freight caravans, and stagecoaches plied it regularly; soldiers built forts to guard it; and a railroad steadily shortened it while advancing ominously toward the heart of the buffalo range. The Cheyennes' antagonism to the Smoky Hill road prompted General Hancock's decision to intimidate them with a show of force. And that inept operation, in turn, tipped the balance of political power in the Cheyenne camps against the chiefs who had signed the Little Arkansas Treaty. Thus the summer of 1867 witnessed hostilities on the central Plains as well as the northern Plains, as raiding parties struck at stagecoaches, stage stations, and even military outposts, and led Custer's cavalry on an exhausting, summer-long chase through the buffalo ranges.[17]

Meantime, the Kiowas and Comanches continued to draw annuities

Satanta. Alternately ingratiating and insolent, this Kiowa chieftain baffled and exasperated white officials on the Arkansas River. In 1867, resplendent in a general's uniform, he ran off the mule herd at Fort Dodge. Imprisoned in the Texas penitentiary for his part in the Salt Creek Prairie Massacre of 1871, he was released as a peace offering only to be returned after the Red River War of 1874. Despairing, he threw himself from an upper window to his death. *Smithsonian Institution National Anthropological Archives.*

on the Arkansas and raid savagely southward into Texas and Mexico. In Texas bluecoats had replaced graycoats and manned a double chain of forts designed to shield the frontier of settlement all the way from Red River to the Rio Grande, a distance of five hundred miles. But the raiders easily slipped through the cordon to murder, plunder, and burn. Often they returned with captives, to be absorbed into the tribe or ransomed to the white officials on the Arkansas.[18]

With these whites on the Arkansas the Kiowas and Comanches enjoyed generally amicable relations. They ignored the stern rebukes about their Texas raids; they had always regarded Texans, like Mexicans, as a people distinct from Americans—a view reinforced by the recent Civil War. Also, the Kiowa and Comanche agent, Jesse H. Leavenworth, vied with his colleague Wynkoop in extolling the friendly and contented temper of his charges. The only discordant note issued from a big barrel-chested chief named Satanta, an uncommonly able fighter and shrewd leader given to insolence toward whites. He commanded the soldier chief at Fort Dodge to make the whites quit using his grass and shooting his game and, finally, to get out of his country altogether. Distracted by Cheyenne hostility, no one took Satanta very seriously until, resplendent in the dress uniform of a major general presented to him by General Hancock, he scooped up the mule herd at Fort Dodge, doffing his plumed hat in parting salute to his pursuers.[19]

Despite the hostilities of the summer of 1867, however, peace sentiment still flickered in all the southern Plains tribes. While Satanta blustered, the Kiowa peace leader Kicking Bird steadily gained adherents. Black Kettle and Little Raven spoke for peace among the Cheyennes and Arapahos. Thus the Peace Commission's messengers found sympathetic listeners when they rode south of the Arkansas in the autumn of 1867. Doubtless nudged by the prospect of presents and the approach of winter, the balance tilted back to the peace advocates.

The great treaty council took place in October 1867 in a pleasant valley of Medicine Lodge Creek about seventy miles south of Fort Larned. Five thousand Indians had assembled for the festive occasion. Their tipis by the hundreds crowded the valley, and their vast pony herds overflowed to the benches on either side. The white officials enlivened the scene still more when they arrived trailing an escort of two hundred soldiers, a squad of newsmen, and thirty wagons laden with a tempting variety of presents.

The Kiowas and Comanches took the lead in the talks, for the Cheyennes, still afflicted by internal stresses, hung back. Black Kettle and fifty lodges had appeared by the time the council opened, but most of the other Cheyennes, some two hundred lodges, camped on the Cimarron River thirty miles distant. They had a plausible excuse for procrastinating: they were engaged in the annual rite of renewing their sacred medicine arrows. Beyond this, however, they still felt angry over Hancock's torching of their village the previous spring, and they were nervous about talking with whites so soon after a season passed in killing whites. To the exasperation of the commissioners, the Cheyennes kept everyone in suspense until, late in the proceedings, they moved their tipis over to Medicine Lodge Valley and joined the talks.

A brush arbor erected in a grove of trees shaded the negotiators. It resounded with the eloquent and sometimes pointed oratory of the chiefs, resplendent in their best finery, and the labored explanations of the white

INDIAN LODGE AT MEDICINE CREEK, KANSAS—SCENE OF THE LATE INDIAN PEACE COUNCIL.—SKETCHED BY J. HOWLAND.—[SEE PAGE 725.]

COUNCIL AT MEDICINE CREEK LODGE WITH THE KIOWA AND COMANCHE INDIANS.—SKETCHED BY J. HOWLAND.—[SEE PAGE 725.]

On Medicine Lodge Creek, Kansas, in October 1867, the Peace Commission negotiated treaties with the southern Plains tribes. These accords, together with the treaties signed at Fort Laramie the following spring, were expected to bring peace to the Plains. Almost immediately, however, war broke out on the southern Plains and shattered the hopes of the peace advocates. Here *Harper's Weekly's* special artist sketched scenes at the Medicine Lodge council. *Library of Congress.*

peace talkers, also imposing in frock coats and full military uniforms. The chief commissioner, Taylor, bored everyone with tedious pontification. Senator Henderson got to the point more directly. One day the buffalo would all be gone, he warned, and "the Indian must change the road his father trod." That meant settling in a white-man house on a reservation and becoming a farmer. Old Ten Bears of the Comanches summed up the Indian reaction in one sentence: "I love the open prairie, and I wish you would not insist on putting us on a reservation."[20]

But insist the officials did, persistently, day after day. Always, talk about the good features seemed to get in the way of talk about the bad features. The Indians could continue to hunt anywhere south of the Arkansas River so long as the buffalo ran. They would receive annuities for thirty years. And stacked before their eyes, ready to be handed out once the chiefs signed, were bales of beads, buttons, bells, iron pans, tin cups, butcher knives, blankets, bolts of gaudy calico, pants, coats, hats, and, most enticingly, pistols and ammunition. All this tended to obscure the promise to yield all lands outside of the proposed reservations, to bury the hatchet and take up the plow, and to put their children in school. Such a life seemed remote and incomprehensible. Why worry now, when the treaty said they could continue to follow the buffalo?

So they signed, almost every chief of importance on the southern Plains: Satank, Satanta, and Kicking Bird of the Kiowas; Ten Bears, Horse Back, and Iron Mountain of the Comanches; Poor Bear of the Kiowa-Apaches; Little Raven of the Arapahos; Black Kettle, Tall Bull, and Little Robe of the Cheyennes. Even the belligerent old Dog Soldier Bull Bear at last signed, though with great reluctance and only after General Harney pointed out that the Great Father knew Bull Bear as a big chief and would not accept the treaty unless it bore his name. He made his mark, not by lightly touching the pen but by pressing down so hard he almost buried its head in the paper. The Great Father could not fail to see it.[21]

The Peace Commission had abundant lands from which to create new reservations for the Plains tribes—and, for that matter, any other tribes inconveniently located in Kansas or elsewhere. They lay in Indian Territory and came from the holdings of the Five Civilized Tribes, forfeited for a token compensation as part of their punishment for choosing the wrong side in the Civil War. The Kiowa and Comanche Reservation coincided with the old Leased District once owned by the Choctaws and Chickasaws. To the north, the Cheyenne and Arapaho Reservation had once made up the western lands of the Creeks and Seminoles. The Cherokees did not actually cede their western lands, but they agreed that other tribes could be settled in this so-called Cherokee Strip beyond the western boundary of the Cherokee Nation.

The Five Tribes and other Indian Territory groups ensnared by the Civil War got a taste of what was in store for them at a council convened at Fort Smith, Arkansas, in September 1865. Here Commissioner of Indian Affairs Dennis N. Cooley and other commissioners spoke harshly to the "Great Father's erring children" and spelled out the principles on which the treaties restoring peace would be based: surrender of western lands, abolition of slavery, granting of railroad rights-of-way, establishment of U.S. military posts, and measures directed toward a territorial government for Indian Territory. Most of the tribal spokesmen, former leaders of Confederate factions, ingratiatingly accepted Cooley's stern pronouncement.

Not so Cherokee Chief John Ross, who wisely perceived some of the implications of the treaties that escaped other leaders. He recognized that the move toward territorial government aimed at liquidating the tribal self-government so explicitly guaranteed in the removal treaties, and this more than any other provision he fought. He knew, too, that the railroad agents and Kansas land sharpers who had rushed to Fort Smith made it essential to scrutinize with infinite care all language relating to land. And he felt outrage that the Cherokees and others who had remained loyal should suffer for the actions of their wayward brothers. For himself, he had resisted the Confederacy as long as he could, and he had spent the three years since his liberation working closely with federal authorities in Washington, including President Lincoln himself. Now he heard Cooley denounce him as a traitor and declare him deposed from the office of Principal Chief to which he had been repeatedly elected for the past forty years.

Even so, and even though aged and broken in health, Ross persisted in his opposition while Cooley tried to treat exclusively with former Confederate Elias Boudinot, acting on behalf of Stand Watie. And Ross at length, by carrying the fight to President Johnson himself, staved off some of the more odious provisions that Cooley would have imposed. In the treaties of 1866 that reestablished relations with the United States, all the tribes fared better than they had expected, although, as Ross warned, provisions relating to land, railroads, and territorial government boded an amplitude of troubles in the years ahead. Bedridden, Ross did not sign for the Cherokees when their treaty at last, in July 1866, reached its final form. Less than two weeks later, he died.[22]

The Peace Commission's report of January 7, 1868, advanced the cause of peace and humanity still another notch, even though the chief who in the white perception most embodied Indian hostility remained aloof. After Medicine Lodge the commissioners had returned to Fort Laramie in hopes of talking with Red Cloud, but they had to content themselves instead with a handful of friendly Crows. Red Cloud and all the other hostile Sioux remained resolutely hostile in the Powder River country.

Even so, the Medicine Lodge treaties could be presented as corroborating the soundness of the peaceable approach. After all, they appeared to realize half the grand design of consolidating all the Plains Indians on two huge reservations out of the way of the principal travel routes. Written by erstwhile clergyman Taylor, the report read like an exhortation from the pulpit. It called for just and humane treatment of the Indians, a thorough overhaul of the Indian intercourse laws, and an intensive program to educate and civilize the Indians. Like the Sully Commission, the Taylor Commission straddled the volatile issue of where to put the Indian Bureau by recommending that it be established as a separate, cabinet-level department.[23]

Sherman and the other generals on the commission did not like the report, but they signed anyway. Actually, except for the evangelical and antimilitary tone, it contained little to which they could plausibly object. Also, they believed that time worked against the Indians. "The chief use of the Peace Commission," Sherman wrote Grant, "is to kill time which will do more to settle the Indians than anything we can do."[24]

The Peace Commission report also called for another effort at treaty-making. The commissioners had word from Laramie that Red Cloud would meet with them in the spring, and they sweetened the proposed treaty with a concession they felt sure would win his assent. The draft still contained provisions similar to the Medicine Lodge treaties; in particular, it provided for a large reservation north of Nebraska and west of the Missouri River (all of present western South Dakota). But now it also promised abandonment of the Bozeman Trail forts and designation of the Powder River country as "unceded Indian territory," closed to all whites. Red Cloud had won his war, although in point of fact the surrender was politically expedient only because the rapid advance of the Union Pacific Railroad opened better routes to the Montana mines farther west.

At the first sign of spring in 1868, runners arrived in the hostile Sioux camps in the Powder River country with invitations to come down to Laramie and talk with the Peace Commission. Some Sioux did show up

The Fort Laramie Treaty kept the Sioux relatively quiet for several years but also laid the groundwork for the great wars of 1876–81. Here commissioners meet with Sioux at Fort Laramie in the spring of 1868. Identifiable are Generals Harney (with bald head and white beard), Sherman (to Harney's left), Augur (with mutton chops), and Terry (to Augur's left), and (far right) Commissioner of Indian Affairs Taylor. *Smithsonian Institution National Anthropological Archives.*

to receive presents and sign the treaty, but, except for Spotted Tail's Brules from the Republican River country, they were mostly the same old stay-around-the-fort people who had signed earlier treaties. From Red Cloud came a message as unmistakable as it was humiliating to the Great Father's emissaries: "We are on the mountains looking down on the soldiers and the forts. When we see the soldiers moving away and the forts abandoned, then I will come down and talk."[25]

Other Sioux proved equally obdurate. These were mainly Hunkpapa and Blackfoot Sioux who lived north and east of the Powder River Sioux, on the upper Missouri and lower Yellowstone rivers. The Bozeman Trail did not bother them, and they had not been seriously threatened since General Sully invaded their domain in 1864. But their chiefs, Black Moon, Four Horns, and a rising leader of superior ability named Sitting Bull, rejected white overtures with all the firmness of Red Cloud. The respected "Black Robe," Father Pierre Jean De Smet, came among them to recruit a delegation for a council with the Peace Commission at Fort Rice, on the Missouri River. But even his description of the steamboat loaded with presents and docked at the Fort Rice landing failed to entice any important chief to return with him. Again, none of the Indians who signed the treaty at the close of the council in July could even pretend to speak for the hostile Sioux.

All that summer of 1868 messengers rode into the Sioux camps with pleas to come down to Laramie and sign the treaty, which had been left in the care of local authorities. From his mountains, Red Cloud watched. At last, at the end of July, he saw the soldiers march out of Fort C. F. Smith, the northernmost post, on the Bighorn River. Next day he and his men rode into the deserted fort and put it to the torch. A few days later the garrisons of the other two posts also withdrew, and Sioux burned Fort Phil Kearny. Now the messages from Laramie came frequently and temptingly, but still Red Cloud did not hurry. The Sioux would put in their winter's meat and then think about going down to Laramie.

In contrast to the Plains Indians, one group welcomed the Peace Commission almost as a providential gift. These were the Navajos. For four years, since their conquest by Kit Carson, they had endured the agonies of Bosque Redondo, the reservation General Carleton had established for them on the Pecos River of eastern New Mexico. Their sheep herds ravaged by Comanche raiders, their crops ravaged by drought, flood, and insects, their people ravaged by disease and malnutrition, they had led a miserable existence on paltry handouts grudgingly given by their keepers. Eagerly the Navajos looked to the peace commissioners for liberation. (After the Fort Laramie rebuff in May 1868, the commission divided; Sanborn remained at Laramie, Sherman and Tappan went to Bosque Redondo, and the others went to Fort Rice.) Sherman offered the Navajos a reservation in Indian Territory, to the east. But he quickly saw that only a return to their homeland to the west would end the soaring costs of Bosque Redondo without provoking the Navajos to a desperate last stand. Joyously the chiefs made their marks on the treaty, emotionally embraced the white general, and went home. Never again, despite ample cause, did they war with the whites.[26]

General Sherman's predictions about the workings of time proved accurate. Events of the summer and autumn of 1868 did not bode well for the cause espoused by Taylor and like-minded members of the Peace

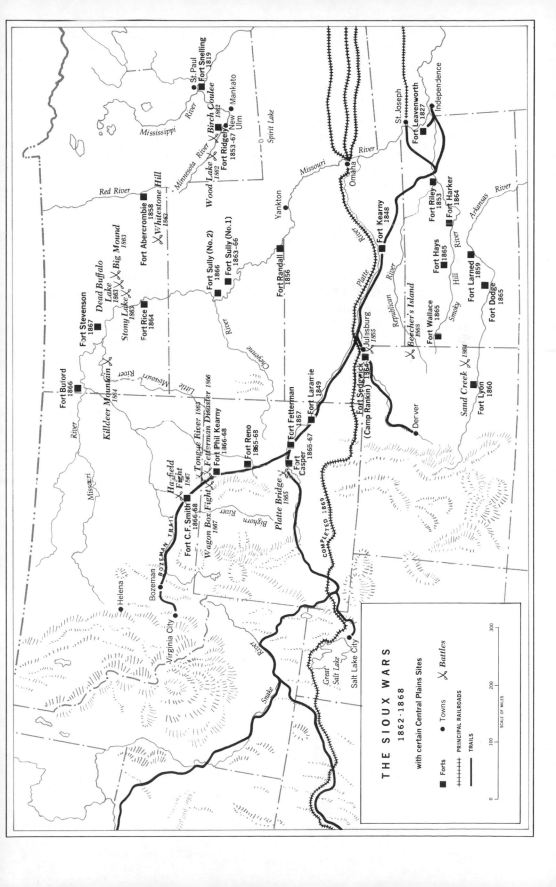

St. Paul
Fort Snelling
1819
Birch Coulee
1862
Mankato
New Ulm
Fort Ridgely
1853-67
Mississippi River
Minnesota River
Wood Lake
1862
Spirit Lake
Red River
Fort Abercrombie
1858
Whitestone Hill
1863
Yankton
Missouri River
St. Joseph
Fort Leavenworth
1827
Independence
Omaha
Fort Kearny
1848
Fort Riley
1853
Fort Harker
1864
Arkansas River
Big Mound
1863
Dead Buffalo Lake
1863
Fort Stevenson
1867
Stony Lake
1863
Fort Rice
1864
Fort Sully (No. 2)
1866
Fort Sully (No. 1)
1863-66
Fort Randall
1856
Fort Hays
1865
Smoky Hill River
Fort Larned
1859
Fort Dodge
1865
Fort Buford
1866
Killdeer Mountain
1864
Missouri River
Little Missouri River
Cheyenne River
Platte River
Republican River
Fort Wallace
1865
Beecher's Island
1868
Julesburg
1865
Fort Sedgwick
(Camp Rankin) *1864*
Denver
Sand Creek
1864
Fort Lyon
1860
Tongue River *1865*
Fetterman Disaster *1866*
Fort Phil Kearny
1866-68
Fort Reno
1865-68
Fort Fetterman
1867
Fort Laramie
1849
COMPLETED 1869
Hayfield Fight
1867
Fort C. F. Smith
1866-68
Wagon Box Fight
1867
Bighorn River
Platte Bridge
1865
Fort Casper
1865-67
BOZEMAN TRAIL
Bozeman
Helena
Virginia City
Great Salt Lake
Salt Lake City
Snake River

THE SIOUX WARS
1862-1868
with certain Central Plains Sites

■ Forts   ● Towns   ✕ *Battles*

++++++ PRINCIPAL RAILROADS

—— TRAILS

SCALE OF MILES

0   100   200   300

Commission. For one thing, the Congress handed the army an enormous advantage in its bureaucratic battle with the Indian Bureau. Preoccupied with the impeachment of President Johnson, national legislators had little time in the summer of 1868 for Indian matters. However, appropriating money to concentrate and feed the Indians covered by the Medicine Lodge and Fort Laramie treaties, they registered their lack of confidence in the civil agents by decreeing that the money be spent under the direction of General Sherman. He moved at once to create two military districts to coincide with the northern and southern reservations. To superintend the first he named General Harney, and to oversee the second, General William B. Hazen. Controlling "all issues and disbursements," these officers thus neatly displaced the civil agents, in fact if not in name.[27]

Far more detrimental to the cause of peace was the persistence of war. Indeed, Indian wars seemed to flare almost everywhere in the West. In southeastern Oregon and southwestern Idaho, General George Crook had campaigned for a year and a half against hostile Paiutes. In Arizona and New Mexico, the thin ranks of regulars contended ineffectually against Apache raids that devastated virtually every corner of the two territories. Apaches also preyed on the travel routes that connected the Texas frontier with El Paso, while the Kiowas and Comanches continued to enjoy their double standard of peace on the Arkansas and bloody war against the frontier settlers of Texas.

But developments in these far-off places did not much affect debates on Indian policy. Easterners seemed only dimly aware of hostilities beyond the Great Plains. Ever since Sand Creek, relations with the Plains Indians had almost alone shaped public opinion and government policy. The Doolittle committee, the Sully Commission, and the Taylor Commission all found their origins with the Plains Indians. Now, as the Peace Commission met for the last time in October 1868, the clash of arms elsewhere served only as a muted echo of the theme building to a crescendo on the Plains.

In July the Cheyennes had gathered around Fort Larned to receive their first annuity issue under the Medicine Lodge Treaty. They especially looked forward to the arms and ammunition they had been promised. But in June some Cheyennes had raided a Kaw Indian settlement, and Superintendent of Indian Affairs Thomas Murphy had decided not to let them have arms. Murphy finally relented, but not before a party of young men left for a raid against the Pawnees. En route, still in an ugly temper because of Murphy's ban, they ripped through the white settlements on the Saline and Solomon rivers of Kansas. In a two-day raid, they looted

When Ulysses S. Grant became President in 1868, he brought General Sherman to Washington to command the army. Philip H. Sheridan took his place as commander on the Great Plains. Here Sheridan and some of his officers were photographed in a Topeka studio in 1872. Left to right: George A. Custer, George A. Forsyth, Sheridan, M. V. Asche, Nelson B. Sweitzer, Michael V. Sheridan, and James W. Forsyth. George Forsyth had made the much-heralded stand at Beecher's Island in 1868, Custer would die at the Little Bighorn in 1876, and James Forsyth would command at Wounded Knee in 1890. *National Park Service, Custer Battlefield National Monument.*

and burned cabins, ran off stock, ravished five women, and killed fifteen men. "War is surely upon us," conceded Superintendent Murphy.[28]

General Sherman wasted no time in mounting a military response. He had a new commander in Kansas, General Philip H. Sheridan. With Sherman, the scrappy little Irishman believed in total war, as residents of Virginia's Shenandoah Valley had good reason to know. Sheridan set to work organizing a winter campaign. Meantime, his troops conducted a precarious holding operation as Cheyenne raiders ran wild across Kansas. The eastern press kept the public informed of scouts, patrols, expeditions, skirmishes, and one dramatic encounter, in September, in

Beecher's Island. With a company of experienced plainsmen enlisted as scouts, Major George A. Forsyth went looking for Cheyennes after the outbreak of August 1868. On September 17 hordes of warriors corraled him and his men on an island of the Arikara River and in a week-long siege almost wiped them out. This is *Harper's Weekly's* rendition. *Library of Congress.*

which massed Cheyenne warriors almost overran a company of scouts under Major George A. Forsyth entrenched on an island of the Arikara River near the Kansas-Colorado border.

Against this backdrop, the Peace Commission met in Chicago on October 7 and 8, 1868. All were present except Senator Henderson. Sitting in on the meeting too was the Republican nominee for President, Ulysses S. Grant, whom few doubted would win the White House in the November election. Fresh in the minds of all was Forsyth's bloody stand at Beecher's Island and a war that, in the white perception, the Cheyennes had begun without provocation. The Medicine Lodge Treaty seemed dead. And the Fort Laramie Treaty, though signed by a host of Sioux chiefs, still lacked the one signature that would give it validity. No longer, as in January, need the generals bow to Taylor.

For Taylor and Tappan, the meeting turned into a rout. In resolution after resolution, Generals Sherman, Harney, Terry, and Augur carried the vote. Thus the commission went on record as believing that the time had come to quit recognizing Indian tribes as "domestic dependent nations," except as necessitated by existing treaties, and henceforth to make Indians individually subject to U.S. laws. This meant, of course, an end to the negotiation of treaties. Another resolution declared that the recent outbreak in Kansas justified abrogation of the provision in the Medicine Lodge Treaty permitting the Indians to hunt outside the reservation as well as the use of military force to make the Indians move to their reservations. And, predictably, the Indian Bureau should be transferred to the War Department.[29]

With that, the Peace Commission adjourned, never to meet again. The error of the commission's old policy, Sherman explained to a reporter, had been plainly demonstrated. "Too many scalps have disappeared from the heads of their legitimate owners to make it safe to prolong this policy." And so there would be no doubt about where the presumptive next President of the United States stood, General Grant told the same reporter that the settlers and emigrants had to be protected even if it meant the extermination of every Indian tribe.[30] And so the rifle seemed to have triumphed decisively over the peace pipe, although, disconcertingly, only a month later Red Cloud and Man Afraid-of-His-Horse showed up at Fort Laramie and signed the treaty.[31] At the same time, on the southern Plains, General Sheridan's winter offensive got under way, with the dashing Custer, he of the long golden locks, heading the cavalry striking force. Throughout the nation, voters went to the polls and voted overwhelmingly to make as their next president the general who would obliterate every tribe if necessary to protect U.S. citizens.

In the Washita Valley of western Indian Territory, Cheyennes, Arapahos, Kiowas, and Comanches laid out their winter camps. At Fort Cobb, downstream, resided the soldier chief, General Hazen, detailed by General Sherman to superintend, for the time being, the new southern reservation set up under the Medicine Lodge treaties. All the peaceful Indians were to report to him while General Sheridan made war on the rest.

Black Kettle, of course, rode down to have a talk with this soldier chief. General Hazen informed him that he would have to make his peace with the "big war chief," Sheridan. Black Kettle confessed that, much as he wanted peace, he had a hard time keeping his young men under control. In fact, his young men rejoiced in Hazen's rebuff of Black Kettle. At the

Custer's dawn attack on Black Kettle's Cheyenne village on the Washita, November 27, 1868, was the high point of Sheridan's winter campaign against the southern Plains tribes. Black Kettle, eternal champion of peace, died in the charge. Charles Schreyvogel's "Early Dawn Attack" typifies a number of engagements like the Washita where troops caught Indians napping. *Library of Congress.*

very moment, some of them were returning from a raid against Kansas settlers. Sadly the peace chief went back to his village.

The returning war party left a trail across the snow-mantled prairies that led unerringly to Black Kettle's village. As the frigid dawn of November 27, 1868, broke over his tipis, the blare of a military band and the crash of carbines jolted him awake. Hastily he and his wife together leaped on a pony tethered outside the lodge and galloped for safety as the charging cavalrymen, pistols blazing and sabers swinging, crashed into the camp. At the river a bullet slammed into Black Kettle's back, and another struck his wife. Together they fell into the icy stream, dead.[32]

5

Grant's Peace Policy, 1869–1876

During the four-month interval between election day 1868 and inauguration day 1869, President elect Ulysses S. Grant continued to serve, somewhat uncomfortably, as General in Chief of the United States Army. He occupied a suite of offices in a small two-story residence at Seventeenth and F Streets NW, rather than in the War Department. In the parlorlike front room of this house, looking out on the Navy Department across the street, Grant held court to a procession of callers urging policies, projects, and special favors on his forthcoming administration.[1]

Among these callers, on January 25, 1869, was a delegation of Quakers, fresh from a national convention in Baltimore that had adopted resolutions favoring an Indian policy founded on peace and Christianity rather than on force of arms. The Friends urged Grant to embrace such a policy and, in filling agency posts, to appoint men of religious conviction. As enshrined in Quaker memory, the President-elect replied: "Gentlemen, your advice is good. I accept it. Now give me the names of some Friends for Indian agents and I will appoint them. If you can make Quakers out of the Indians it will take the fight out of them. Let us have peace."[2]

"Let us have peace!" As historians would one day recount it, that call rallied the nation's religious and philanthropic community, cemented it in alliance with the federal government, and gave birth to Grant's Peace Policy. Suddenly and inexplicably, the nation's preeminent warrior seemed to have gone over to the enemy. He who had so emphatically subscribed to the belligerent final resolutions of the Peace Commission in October could in February, on the eve of his inauguration, announce: "All Indians disposed to peace will find the new policy a peace-policy."[3]

Grant's vague promise of a "peace-policy" betokened no grand design for a fresh and humane approach to Indian relations. Indeed, in a warning that went generally unheard amid the applause for his proffer of peace,

129

he added: "Those who do not accept this policy will find the new administration ready for a sharp and severe war policy." In fact, at this point Grant held no very strong convictions about Indians. It is true that as a young officer on the Pacific Coast in 1852–54 he had seen Indians at first hand and had lamented their condition. It is unlikely, though, as some biographers would have it, that he had then vowed to obliterate the evils of the Indian system if ever he got the chance, or even that the Peace Policy owed much debt to this early experience. Before 1865 the Civil War dominated Grant totally. After 1865 the Reconstruction struggle left him little time for Indians. When he had to deal with the subject, he simply fell into step with his trusted lieutenant, Sherman, but without any special emotional or intellectual commitment of his own.

Thus Grant remained as pragmatically open minded on Indian policy as he did on other issues confronting his administration. He did not consciously craft the Peace Policy as an instrument of radical change. At first it was little more than a platitude. Later, measures took shape that gave it recognizable definition. Springing from diverse origins, these measures fell together circumstantially, almost randomly, and collectively they took on the label Peace Policy. Grant embraced them as they came before him, and he made conspicuous use of the label as a slogan of his presidency.[4]

A combination of forces prompted the new administration and congressional leaders to turn so emphatically toward peace. The Doolittle committee and the Taylor Peace Commission had laid firm groundwork, both in the substantive content of their reports and in their effect on public opinion. General Sheridan's winter offensive of 1868–69 handed peace propagandists volatile ammunition just as the new administration took shape. Agent Edward W. Wynkoop—the "Tall Chief" of Cheyenne affections—had resigned in protest and filled the eastern press with denunciations of General Custer's destruction of Black Kettle and his hapless people at the Washita.

Among the strongest forces giving direction to the thinking of the new President and key members of his administration was a man almost constantly at his side since Vicksburg. A big, powerfully built figure whose long black hair and dark, swarthy countenance betrayed his racial origins, Colonel Ely S. Parker had excelled in both Indian and white worlds—as chief of the Senecas and Grand Sachem of the Iroquois Confederacy, and as lawyer, engineer, and soldier for the United States. He had loyally served his chief as adjutant, military secretary, and aide-de-camp; it was he at Appomattox who, as Grant dictated, wrote out the surrender terms

Ely S. Parker. A full-blooded Seneca Indian and intimate of President Grant, the acculturated Parker represented the ideal of reformers. As Grant's secretary in the weeks before the inauguration, Parker laid important groundwork for what later became Grant's Peace Policy. Grant named him Commissioner of Indian Affairs, but conflict with the Board of Indian Commissioners forced his early resignation. *Library of Congress.*

for Lee's army. From 1865 to 1869 the General in Chief relied more and more on his advice in Indian matters. In 1867 Parker drew up a comprehensive plan of Indian management, including transfer of the Indian Bureau to the War Department, that won strong support in the Congress. He served as a thoughtful and conscientious member of the Sully Commission investigating the Fetterman Massacre. For Grant, he probably personified the acculturated ideal toward which all Indians should be pushed, and during the critical months before the inauguration he had the President-elect's ear nearly continually. After the inauguration, in a historic first, Grant appointed Parker Commissioner of Indian Affairs.[5]

Most significant of all influences, peace sentiment at last crystallized in organized lobbying activity. The major religious denominations, long involved in missionary work, began to launch attempts to influence policy, as the Quaker call on Grant demonstrated. The most compelling pressures, however, came from an association recently formed to work for "the protection and elevation of the Indians." Misleadingly styled the United States Indian Commission, its organizers included some of the nation's most powerful and respected citizens, notably industrialist Peter Cooper, clergyman Henry Ward Beecher, and merchant William E. Dodge. In 1868 the commission had shown that it could sway legislators; in 1869–70, by urging reform measures on the President and Congress, it played a key role in the formation of Grant's Peace Policy.

Beyond the dedication to "conquest by kindness," most of the aims of the Peace Policy were hardly original. For years reformers and policy makers had called for "concentration" of the Indians on reservations, for their "civilization" through education, Christianity, and agricultural self-support, for a cleansing of the Indian Bureau of corruption and inefficiency, and for replacement of the treaty system with something better suited to the actual status of the Indian. Both the Doolittle and Taylor groups had recommended some version of all these measures. Now, however, they would be conscientiously attempted as administration policy.

Saliently marking the Peace Policy was the Board of Indian Commissioners. As early as 1862 Bishop Henry B. Whipple had advocated a panel of unpaid humanitarians to aid in formulating and administering Indian policy. The Doolittle committee had proposed "boards of inspection," and after the inauguration some of the prominent philanthropists involved with the U.S. Indian Commission urged Grant to organize a body to serve the interests of the Indians in much the same fashion as the quasi-official U.S. Christian Commission had served the interests of Union soldiers during the Civil War. Congress proved receptive.

Thus the Indian Appropriations Act of April 10, 1869, empowered the President to appoint ten men "eminent for their intelligence and philanthropy" to serve without pay and to "exercise joint control with the Secretary of the Interior over the appropriations made by this act." The charter of the commissioners from President Grant went much further; they were also to concern themselves with the whole range of policy, especially with civilizing the Indians, and with evaluating the performance of superintendents and agents.[6]

The most conspicuous feature of the Peace Policy was church nomination of Indian agents. Grant's challenge to the Quakers to send him some names at first disconcerted them, but they hesitantly responded. Two superintendencies on the Plains, the Northern and Central, fell entirely to Quaker administration. So identified with the Friends did this mode of appointment become that it took on its own nomenclature—the Quaker Policy.

In the Quaker experiment Grant bowed to the urgings of his Indian friend and aide Ely Parker, but he had no intention of extending the practice. Reflecting Sherman's influence and his own military background, he still looked to the army to play a central role in Indian affairs. While naming eighteen Quakers to posts of superintendent and agent on the Plains, he appointed sixty-eight army officers to similar posts elsewhere. He saw no inconsistency in entrusting the Peace Policy to army officers. Nor had he changed his mind about the wisdom of placing the Indian Bureau in the War Department.

Grant's appointments struck at the heart of the old Indian system—the patronage prerogatives of members of Congress. They could not well openly oppose the religious appointments, but the military appointments were another matter, especially in view of the administration's proclaimed devotion to peace. As had happened with Sand Creek, the Fetterman Massacre, and the Washita, a violent episode out West helped produce decisive political consequences in the East. On January 23, 1870, Major Edward M. Baker and a squadron of cavalry charged into a Piegan village on Montana's Marias River and slaughtered 173 Indians, mostly women and children, many prostrated by smallpox. A spasm of outrage electrified the country and jolted the Congress. A bill for the transfer of the Indian Bureau to the War Department that had every prospect of passage failed, and disgruntled lawmakers seized on the affair to go a step further and outlaw the appointment of army officers to any civil post.[7]

The stubborn man in the White House, however, had not made his reputation by retreating. To the spoilsmen, as General Sherman reported it, Grant rejoined: "Gentlemen, you have defeated my plan of Indian management; but you shall not succeed in *your* purpose, for I will divide these appointments up among the religious churches, with which you dare not contend."[8] Already reformers had advocated this move, most notably the energetic secretary of the Board of Indian Commissioners, Vincent Colyer. Now Grant bowed to them. By 1872 seventy-three agencies had been apportioned among the nation's principal denominations, and good religious men set forth to elevate the Indians, in Commissioner Parker's words, "toward that healthy Christian civilization in which are embraced the elements of material wealth and intellectual and moral development."[9] Thus did grubby politics and high altruism spawn the intimate, often contentious, constitutionally dubious alliance between church and state that would so prominently characterize Grant's Peace Policy.

Still another hallmark of the Peace Policy was the abandonment of the treaty system. Grant favored this course, which had long been championed by reformers and military leaders alike, most recently by the Taylor Peace Commission. But in the end it came out of the long-standing feud between the Senate and House of Representatives over Indian affairs. Each year an increasingly rebellious House, resentful of the Senate's exclusive role of advice and consent, imperiled the Indian appropriations bill. Finally the two chambers compromised their differences. Tucked away in an obscure corner of the Indian Appropriations Act of March 3, 1871, was the historic proviso that demolished John Marshall's concept of "domestic dependent nations" and, while affirming the obligations of all treaties then in force, barred the United States from ever again negotiating an Indian treaty.[10]

Such were the particulars of Grant's Peace Policy. Beyond the measures and institutions that gave it definition, however, the Peace Policy was essentially, as a leading authority has pointed out, "a state of mind, a determination that since the old ways of dealing with the Indians had not worked, new ways which emphasized kindness and justice must be tried."[11] The new ways were in truth not so new. What was new was their official adoption and the serious attempt to make them work.

The new look in Indian policy presented new opportunities but also intensified old dilemmas. The emphasis on kindness and justice alone created all sorts of possibilities where Indians genuinely desired accommodation with the whites. But the heightened interaction induced and directed by the new spirit of harmony also multiplied the chances for misunderstanding and discord. However sincere the intent on either side, formidable cultural barriers still prevented both Indians and whites from truly understanding the motivations, purposes, and ways of thinking of the other. Proclaiming high-sounding principles and worthy objectives in Washington was one thing, making them work out on the frontier another. Nowhere did the obstacles find more disheartening or exasperating illustration than in the war-wracked Southwest.

For a decade New Mexico and Arizona had suffered ravages begotten of military treachery. The Bascom affair and the slaying of Mangas Coloradas under a white flag had loosed outraged Chiricahua and Mimbres Apaches across the land. From the Rio Grande to Tucson and deep into Mexico, stockmen and settlers lived under virtual siege; all lost property, and many their lives. A growing population of miners in the Pinos Altos country, where new chloride strikes had given birth to what would become Silver City, bore the brunt of the raids. Travelers fell frequent casualty to lurking marauders. "They kill all they can," complained a postal official.[12] No agent had dealt with these Indians for years. Now they seemed prime candidates for the new Peace Policy. Paradoxically, the first agent to approach them was an army officer, Lieutenant Charles E. Drew, one of the sixty-eight Grant named to the Indian Service before Congress demurred. He was an idealistic young man, thoroughly in accord with Grant's Peace Policy.

Fortuitously, these very Indians had begun to tire of hostilities. Many of their young men had been slain or injured. Raids provided only the barest and most uncertain subsistence. The people lacked food, blankets, and clothing. They lived in constant dread of Indian-hunting "posses" from the mining towns, and of bands of scalp hunters ranging up from Mexico in search of scalps—any would do, so long as Indian—that could be redeemed for pesos with the governor in Chihuahua City. Cochise of the Chiricahuas wanted peace. Among the Mimbres of southwestern New Mexico, Loco and Victorio had emerged as the principal heirs of Mangas Coloradas. The young, hot-blooded Victorio remained distrustful of any dealings with the whites, but the older Loco felt more optimistic. When word came in August 1869 that an officer at Fort McRae wanted to talk peace, Loco reacted at once.

With four men and three women, Loco rode boldly into Fort McRae, a rude post on the Rio Grande at the northern end of the Jornada del Muerto. Victorio and the rest of the people kept to the hills, wary and apprehensive, expecting treachery. But all went well. Loco liked the officer and came away feeling he could be trusted. He wanted peace, Loco declared through interpreters, a good peace, "and no lie;" and so did all the other Apaches. He wanted to plant corn on Cuchillo Negro Creek as in the old days, before the war. He wanted to hunt west to the Mimbres Mountains and east to the Sierra Caballo, on the east side of the Rio Grande. He wanted the soldiers at Fort McRae to protect him from bad whites. In reply, the soldier-agent talked good words, but cautioned that he would have to get permission from the Great Father before any promises could be made. Loco said he would wait where he was for a month, and he went away contented.

The next meeting took place on the edge of Cañada Alamosa, a largely Hispanic village about twenty-five miles northwest of Fort McRae. The Indians felt comfortable there because nearly every resident traded whis-

Victorio (left) and Loco. As these two Mimbres Apache chieftains discovered, Grant's Peace Policy was often more rhetoric than action. Loco never gave up hope of making peace. Victorio did, and the Victorio War of 1879–80 followed. It ended with Victorio's death in battle with Mexican troops. *Smithsonian Institution National Anthropological Archives* and *School of American Research Collections, Museum of New Mexico.*

key and other goods to them for the plunder seized in raids. A "posse" from Silver City searching for Apaches camped ominously nearby, but after Lieutenant Drew coaxed them into moving on, Loco ventured in with forty well-armed and alert followers. Even the suspicious Victorio came along. A large force of Mogollon Apaches also seeking peace proved less trusting; mounted on sleek horses, rifles and lances at the ready, they dotted the nearby hilltops. The Mimbres, Mogollon, and Gila all stood ready to settle on a reservation, said Loco; they wanted one extending down Alamosa River from the present site. They also had to have food and clothing. The officer explained repeatedly that word had not come yet from the Great Father, and so he still could not make any promises. Loco and his chiefs could not understand why it took so long.

Winter approached, and they badly needed blankets and rations. They would remain near Cañada Alamosa a while longer, but word must come soon. They were hungry and ill-clothed, and with "posses" and scalp hunters roaming the countryside it was dangerous to stay very long in one place.

And so it went all winter. Loco, Victorio, and the Mimbres moved camp every now and then, but they kept within reach of Cañada Alamosa. They liked and trusted Agent Drew. He gave them a scant ration of corn and beef, but otherwise he had to admit that no word had yet come from the Great Father. From the west, Loco heard that Cochise wanted peace too. If only the government would treat the Chiricahuas as well as the Navajos, Cochise promised, he would bring them in and settle down. Even this encouraging information, however, failed to bring a reply from the Great Father. Victorio grew restive, and the people sank more and more into destitution, but still Loco urged them to have patience and faith in Drew.

For his part, all that winter of 1869–70 Lieutenant Drew grew more and more exasperated and discouraged. He believed in the Peace Policy, and he believed that peace with the two most hostile Apache groups lay within his grasp if only the government would act quickly. Repeatedly he implored his superiors to decide the matter swiftly and to rush the supplies that would keep the Indians in place until the location of a reservation could be fixed. In December his immediate superior, the territorial Indian superintendent, let him have $2,800 to buy corn and beef, but this did not provide three hundred Indians much food for very long. His inability to make Loco understand the difficulty of communicating with the Great Father badly disturbed him, but his own inability to break through to the Great Father enraged him. An Indian-hating population opposed him at every turn, and traders with their own interests to serve sought his dismissal. He felt his credibility with the Indians slipping away along with the chance to secure peace. Yet he labored on, striving to calm Loco and his people on the one hand and pleading with his superiors on the other, all to no apparent avail.

Early in June 1870, as summer came to the bare mountains bordering the Jornada del Muerto south of Fort McRae, a Mescalero raiding party ran off some stock near the fort. Drew accompanied the pursuing force. Water grew scarce, and Drew started back to the fort with five soldiers. Four made it. The lieutenant and another perished of heat and thirst. Three years later Victorio would ask for an agent "like the first one they had."[13]

The thwarted attempt of Loco and Drew to fashion a peace revealed many of the obstructions the Peace Policy encountered throughout the West. The sheer bureaucratic complexity of translating Washington policy into field decision and action—of getting responsive guidance out of the Great Father—confounded the persistent efforts of agents. A part of the local citizenry invariably hated Indians of whatever variety or disposition, opposed any policy but extermination, and often threatened to take matters into their own hands. Another part had vested commercial interests in the old system, exploited political connections to override or even remove agents, and kept the Indians stirred up and mistrustful of government officials. And on top of all, that great chasm between cultures made every exchange between agent and Indian a welter of words that failed to achieve genuine comprehension.

The enterprise begun by Drew and Loco dragged on for years. Loco and Victorio heard a succession of well-meaning agents, military and civilian, say the same things as the good agent Drew. They remained poor, badly clothed, and hungry, kept from starvation by occasional dole from army warehouses. The Great Father at last sent word that they could not have a reservation near Cañada Alamosa; it would cost too much to buy out the citizens who lived in the valley. Instead, the Apaches must move some fifty miles to the west, to the high basin of the Tularosa, and there settle on a reservation. They resisted, in some part at least because of the influence of the trading families at Cañada Alamosa. But at last they went. Life at Tularosa proved fully as unhappy as expected. Disgruntled young men took to raiding again. Friction and chronic bad feeling between agent and charges kept relations in turmoil. The government also discovered drawbacks to Tularosa; freight costs to the remote agency soared. Ojo Caliente, a few miles upstream from Cañada Alamosa, would be much better. By 1874 the spirit of accord and impulse toward peace that had animated Loco and Drew had gone sour, and each side looked upon the other with anger, frustration, and distrust.

The officials who dealt with Loco and Victorio also set their sights on the elusive Cochise. Emissaries came to his rocky stronghold in Arizona's Dragoon Mountains. They wanted him to settle with the Mimbres Apaches in New Mexico. He himself liked the idea, but his people preferred their traditional mountain homeland. Cochise remained noncommittal, suspicious not so much of the government agents as of angry citizens who wanted the Chiricahuas obliterated. Only recently, in April 1871, a band of Pinal and Aravaipa Apaches had paid a terrible price for settling on a reserve near Camp Grant. At dawn a force of Tucson citizens had fallen on the sleeping camp and, under the very eyes of the military agent, slaughtered, raped, and mutilated scores of victims and carried twenty-nine children into slavery.[14] From the New Mexico mining towns came threats of similar direct action. Cochise wanted no Camp Grant Massacre to befall his people. By the autumn of 1871, however, this threat had so far receded as to allow him to spend the winter with his Mimbres kinsmen near Cañada Alamosa. Officials tried to convince him to visit Washington, but he resisted. As the forced move to Tularosa approached in the spring of 1872, Cochise and his people once again returned to their Arizona haunts.

Perhaps symptomatic of flaws in the normal administrative machinery, the really decisive moves, for better or worse, came from high-ranking functionaries working directly out of Washington. One was Vincent

Colyer, a professional humanitarian of high ideals and inexhaustible zeal who served as secretary of the Board of Indian Commissioners. Colyer cut through the red tape that had withheld food from hungry Apaches when it was so crucial to the peace movement. He went directly to President Grant and got a signed order to the army to issue military rations. This kept the Apaches in a negotiating stance until the Indian Bureau could regularize issues.

Colyer also, in the autumn of 1871, armed himself with a presidential commission and careened about the Southwest laying out reservations with supreme disdain for the plans of local officials and coaxing Indians to come in to make peace. He infuriated citizens—"Vincent the Good," this "sanctimonious old humbug"—and made some bad decisions, but he also laid the groundwork for the reservation system of the Southwest and introduced many Apache groups to it for the first, though scarcely the last, time.[15]

Another presidential emissary was Oliver O. Howard, the army's one-armed "praying general," whose humanitarian credentials surpassed even Colyer's and who enjoyed a bright reputation as friend and benefactor of the recently freed slaves. Howard followed Colyer to the Southwest in 1872. He made some refinements in Colyer's reservations and, like Colyer, left a trail of confusion to confound and annoy local agents. But his great achievement was to make peace with Cochise. His published story of the ride into the heart of Cochise's Stronghold in the Dragoon Mountains, and the tense negotiations that ended in peace and a reservation in the Chiricahua Mountains, is suspenseful adventure, made the more heroic by the absence of any mention of the peace talkers who preceded him or of Cochise's sojourn at Cañada Alamosa during the previous winter. Although the danger to the general may have been exaggerated, the feat was nonetheless significant. For the first time since Lieutenant Bascom's blunder in 1861, Cochise's warriors posed no danger to settlers.[16]

Despite Howard's achievement, peace had not come to the Southwest. Other Apaches remained at large, engaged in traditional martial pursuits. Some presently at peace, or ostensibly so, such as Victorio and his increasingly militant followers, would sooner or later return to the warpath. Here, as elsewhere, the Peace Policy had a long way to go before success could be claimed.

The Fort Sill Agency in Indian Territory formed a crucible in which Grant's Peace Policy encountered perhaps its severest test. Here Kiowas

General Oliver Otis Howard. In 1872 the pious one-armed "praying general" rode boldly into the Cochise Stronghold of Arizona and negotiated an end to the decade-long Cochise War. In 1877 he pursued Chief Joseph and the Nez Perces from Idaho across the Rocky Mountains to Montana only to see victory fall to Nelson A. Miles. Howard's labors in behalf of Indian rights made him one of the army's handful of "humanitarian generals." *Oregon Historical Society*.

To Kiowas and Comanches, captives as well as plunder were the fruits of raids into Mexico. The captives were but one of the issues over which "Bald Head Agent" Lawrie Tatum contended with his charges at the Fort Sill agency. The Salt Creek Prairie Massacre of 1871 caused Tatum's Quaker principles to give way, and he was replaced by an agent of more orthodox pacifism. Tatum is shown here with a group of Mexican children freed from bondage. Photograph by William S. Soule, *Smithsonian Institution National Anthropological Archives.*

and Comanches confronted gentle Quakers bearing Christianity and civilization. People who exalted war and did exactly as they pleased matched wit and will with people divinely enjoined from violence in deed or thought. As in the Southwest, high-minded theory shattered on hard cultural reality.

Both sides boasted leaders of strong character and resolve. Lawrie Tatum, a beefy, balding Iowa farmer, took over as agent late in 1869. Although innocent of Indian experience and suffused with Quaker pacifism, he brought to his mission intelligence, honesty, common sense, and determination. Backing him from adjacent Fort Sill was that military rarity, a soldier completely in accord with the Peace Policy. Tall, heavy bearded Benjamin H. Grierson, colonel of the black Tenth Cavalry, worked closely with Tatum even at the sacrifice of the good opinion of fellow officers. On the other side, chiefs of force and authority pursued their own aims, most prominently a trio of powerful Kiowas: Lone Wolf, Kicking Bird, and Satanta. The first two contended for supremacy in the tribe, the one on a war platform and the other on a peace platform, while the third—erratic, violent, boastful—pursued an opportunistic self-interest.

Stubbornly the Kiowas and Comanches resisted Tatum's fine plans for their salvation. They lived distant from the agency, riding in every two weeks to draw the rations due them under the Medicine Lodge Treaty. They watched the agent's paid farmers plow and fence vegetable plots, but once planted the men declined even to send their women to tend them. They refused to place their children in the schoolhouse presided over by a good Quaker couple, who, in despair, filled it with more pliable Caddos. They continued the time-honored custom of raiding in Texas, offering their captives for ransom at the same time that they received their coffee, sugar, and beef. One especially daring raider, White Horse, even succeeded in stealing seventy-three mules from the fort's quartermaster corral. Grierson's soldiers, immobilized by the Peace Policy and not knowing whom to blame anyway, did nothing. Similarly, in Texas, raiders occasionally found soldiers on their trail, but they always stopped at Red River, the reservation boundary.

The Indians' behavior led to some stormy scenes with "Bald Head Agent." He implored them to give up their roving ways, plant crops, and put their children in school. He upbraided them for the Texas raids and attempted, with partial success, to end the practice of ransoming captives. For the most part the Indians simply laughed at his scolding, or tried to scare him by menacingly honing knives, flexing bow strings, or thumbing cartridges into rifle chambers. One chief insolently informed the agent that if the Great Father did not want young men to raid in Texas, then he must move Texas far away, where they could not find it. For a delegation of visiting officials, Satanta expressed the prevailing view: "He took hold of that part of the white man's road that was represented by the breech-loading gun, but did not like the ration of corn; it hurt his teeth."[17]

At last, in May 1871, the Indians went too far. Satanta led a hundred men on a routine raid into Texas. The party included some of the most prominent Kiowas: Big Tree, Eagle Heart, Big Bow, old Satank of the wispy mustache, and the medicine man Mamanti. They hid themselves in a favorite ambush, Salt Creek Prairie, an open stretch of the road between Forts Griffin and Richardson. A small train escorted by a handful of soldiers appeared. The raiders made ready to attack. But Mamanti stopped

Lone Wolf (left) and Kicking Bird. As with most tribes, intense factionalism divided the Kiowas. Lone Wolf led the war faction, Kicking Bird the peace faction. Kicking Bird kept many of his people out of the Red River War of 1874–75 but died shortly after its close, almost certainly of poison administered by a disgruntled fellow tribesman. Lone Wolf led the Kiowas in the Red River War, was imprisoned in Florida, and died in 1879, a year after his return home. Kicking Bird was photographed by William S. Soule at Fort Dodge, Kansas, in 1868, Lone Wolf by Alexander Gardner during a visit to Washington, D.C., in 1872. *Smithsonian Institution National Anthropological Archives*.

them; a far richer train would be along soon, he prophesied. And so it proved. Ten freight wagons manned by twelve teamsters came into view. The warriors swarmed to the attack. Five whites escaped, but the rest fell under the onslaught. The raiders mutilated the corpses, plundered and burned the wagons, and rode off with forty-one mules.

The wagons spared by Mamanti's vision, it turned out, carried none other than the General in Chief of the U.S. Army, come to see for himself whether Texan complaints had validity. William Tecumseh Sherman, top commander since Grant's inauguration to the presidency, had spent an evening hearing the testimony of Jacksboro citizens when a survivor

of the Salt Creek Massacre brought word of the butchery. Ordering cavalry in pursuit, Sherman stormed off to Fort Sill to seek out the Indians who had so nearly ended his inspection tour fatally. There he found a despondent Tatum, his Quaker pacifism sorely strained. Together they waited to confront the Kiowas.

On ration day Tatum summoned the Kiowa chiefs to his office and asked if any knew who had perpetrated the Salt Creek Massacre. "Yes," answered Satanta with his usual effrontery, "I led in that raid." He had not been given the arms and ammunition he had asked for, he said, nor had other requests been met: "You do not listen to my talk." The Kiowas had many grievances, and so they went off to raid in Texas. They found the mule train and attacked it. "Three of our men got killed, but we are willing to call it even." They would not do any more raiding around Fort

Satank (left) and Big Tree. Together with Satanta, these Kiowas played conspicuous roles in the Salt Creek Prairie Massacre of 1871. General Sherman had the three arrested at Fort Sill and sent to Texas for trial in the civil courts. On the outskirts of Fort Sill Satank, singing his death song, shucked off his manacles, leaped from the wagon, and was shot down by his guard. The other two were convicted of murder but later pardoned. Both were photographed by William S. Soule in 1870. *Smithsonian Institution National Anthropological Archives.*

Sill this summer, but they expected to raid in Texas. As for Salt Creek, Satanta concluded: "If any other Indian claims the honor of leading that party he will be lying to you. I led it myself."[18] Indignant, Tatum marched over to Colonel Grierson's quarters and, his Quaker principles dissolving, asked for the arrest of Satanta and the other leaders of the raid.

The arrest turned out to be a chaotic collision between U.S. and Kiowa power and authority. In a tense confrontation on Grierson's front porch, Sherman and Grierson faced Satanta, Kicking Bird, Lone Wolf, and other chiefs. Satanta repeated his boast. Sherman ordered him, Satank, and Big Tree arrested. Satanta threw off his blanket and went for his revolver as others drew weapons. Sherman signaled. Window shutters banged

open to reveal black troopers, carbines leveled, behind each window. "Don't shoot, don't shoot!" cried Satanta, flinging his arms upward. Later, as the two sides argued, tempers flared again. Stumbling Bear let fly an arrow at Sherman, but another Indian struck his arm and ruined his aim. Then Lone Wolf leveled his rifle at Sherman; before he could fire Grierson jumped on the chief and the two sprawled on the floor. When order returned, Satanta, Satank, and Big Tree found themselves lodged in the post lockup awaiting movement to Texas for civil trial. En route, though heavily manacled and guarded, Satank worked loose and tried to escape, only to be shot down by a guard. A cowboy jury in Jacksboro tried and convicted Satanta and Big Tree of murder, and the judge sentenced them to death by hanging.[19]

The stern treatment of Satanta and Big Tree earned hearty applause from opponents of "conquest by kindness," who saw it as signaling a new toughness in Indian management. It did not. If anything, Peace Policy visionaries renewed their dedication to nonviolence. The Kiowas and Comanches themselves furnished the example. Washington officials persuaded the governor of Texas to commute the sentence of Satanta and Big Tree to life imprisonment and, later, to pardon them altogether. Tatum's superiors made clear their disapproval of his retreat from conciliation. The trouble with the Kiowas, declared Superintendent Enoch Hoag, could be ascribed wholly to "influences irresistibly evil" emanating from the soldiers at Fort Sill. Accorded "full confidence and trust in their integrity," he predicted, the Indians would reciprocate in kind.[20] Undermined by his superiors, Tatum resigned in favor of an agent more mindful of the precepts of his faith. Instead of prompting a stiffening of the Peace Policy, the Jacksboro affair served chiefly as a demonstration of the futility of simplistic solutions.

Late in April 1870, a telegram from the commandant of Fort Fetterman, Wyoming, brought Washington officials startling news: Red Cloud wanted to come to Washington and talk with the Great Father about the Fort Laramie Treaty and the possibility of going to a reservation. Here was unexpected good fortune: a chance to apply the soothing balm of the Peace Policy directly to the best-known and most intransigent hostile of them all. Whether the Peace Policy actually brought about or simply coincided with peace with Red Cloud, never again did he take up arms against the whites. But peace with Red Cloud did not necessarily mean tranquillity. Before the old chief's death almost forty years later, many a government official must have wondered whether a hostile Red Cloud was not to be preferred to a peaceful Red Cloud.

The Washington visit mixed high carnival with serious purpose. The delegation numbered twenty-one, including Red Cloud's archrival Spotted Tail. Lodged at a Pennsylvania Avenue hotel, they were dragged about the city to be impressed by such spectacles as the Congress in session, the big coastal guns at the navy yard, and the splendors of a White House reception. All in all, they handled the marvels spread before them with as much dignity as the frock-coated and gowned denizens of the capital who gathered to gawk at them.

The official talks went less well. The chiefs met in endless conferences with the Great Father at the White House and with Secretary Jacob Cox and Commissioner Ely Parker at the Interior Department. These sessions featured a great deal of confusion, irrelevance, and misunderstanding,

Spotted Tail. Like his arch-rival Red Cloud, Spotted Tail of the Brule Sioux led his people on the tortuous path between Indian and white worlds. His murder by Crow Dog in 1883 not only produced a precedent-making case before the Supreme Court but left the Brules leaderless and strife-ridden. Alexander Gardner took this picture in Washington, D. C., in 1872. *Smithsonian Institution National Anthropological Archives*.

with not a little impatience and ill humor on both sides. Red Cloud voiced many complaints, some trivial and some cogent and eloquently presented. He had many wants—guns and ammunition and horses, most notably— but he seemed to have a poor understanding of the treaty that was supposed to be the subject of the meeting. He wanted especially to talk about restoring the trade near Fort Laramie, and indeed it seems clear now that he signed the treaty chiefly with that purpose in mind. Yet a major aim of the government was to get the Sioux off the Platte and on to the reservation specified by treaty. The talks, therefore, served mainly to show how far the two sides had to go to reach agreement. Baffled and exasperated, the white officials still doggedly pursued the Peace Policy precept of conquest by kindness. They had wrung almost no concessions from

Red Cloud, but they must have been greatly relieved when he and his associates finally left for New York City and a triumphant appearance before a capacity crowd at Cooper Union.

The visit to Washington seemed bereft of result, but the appearance was deceiving. However carefully he hid his reactions, Red Cloud had for the first time glimpsed the numbers and power of the white people. He had also learned much about how to deal with white officials. And he had won a public acclaim and sympathy that would continue to serve him well. The trip to Washington marked the beginning of a long and tempestuous relationship between Red Cloud and white officialdom, but always it was one of diplomacy and not war.

For the next three years a succession of agents—nominees of the Episcopal Church—wrestled with the formidable question of an agency for Red Cloud. Even Felix Brunot, chairman of the Board of Indian Commissioners, tried his hand at negotiating a solution, but Red Cloud bested him even in the eloquence of his appeal for divine guidance. Red Cloud intended to trade and draw his treaty rations and annuities at or near Fort Laramie, and the government, especially the generals, just as resolutely intended that the Sioux be cleared from the Platte and settled along the Missouri. Finally, in the true spirit of the Peace Policy, the government gave in. The compromise was an agency in northwestern Nebraska just outside the boundary of the Great Sioux Reservation. Here in 1873 the government built Red Cloud Agency for the Oglalas and Spotted Tail Agency for the Brules.

During the years of these tortuous negotiations, Red Cloud perfected his style of dealing with white officials. He gave in little by little and only after bedeviling his adversary through endless consultation with his fellow chiefs, irrelevant demands, bewildering changes of mind, qualified promises, theatrical bluster, and a host of niggling delaying tactics. Shrewdly he exploited the mindset enjoined on agents by the Peace Policy. What few of them perceived, however, was that he walked a narrow line between his white overseers and his own people. Concessions not widely supported by the Sioux, or not yielded without ostentatious resistance, weakened his leadership—a leadership, incidentally, that depended in part on his continuing ability to manipulate the whites. What appeared to whites as mindless obstruction, therefore, usually had a quite logical explanation hidden in the internal politics of the tribe. It is a tribute to his skill that, for more than three decades, Red Cloud picked his way along this precarious path without losing power with his people and without the whites ever truly knowing whether he was friend or foe.

Peace with Red Cloud seemed a major victory for the Peace Policy, and for a time so it could be portrayed. But the triumph dimmed in disorders that kept the agency constantly on the edge of violence. In 1874, in fact, violence forced the Indian Bureau to call for military help, and the army established Camp Robinson nearby. At the same time, Red Cloud Agency became the target of a highly publicized investigation into contracting frauds. And finally, no more enthusiastically than the Kiowas and Comanches did the Sioux embrace the civilization programs that lay at the heart of the Peace Policy; the agents, indeed, had their hands full in simply holding together their agencies and in dispensing annuities. By 1876 even the peace turned out to be largely illusory. Although Red Cloud himself stood fast, Oglalas by the hundreds flocked to the standard of Sitting Bull and Crazy Horse in the last great armed resistance of the Sioux.[21]

The Grant era lasted for eight years. By 1876 the Grant administration had all but collapsed in a shambles of corruption and ineptitude. President Grant himself remained a towering national hero, but multitudes that still venerated him as savior of the Union sadly pronounced his presidency an abysmal failure. Amid its wreckage, battered by public denunciation, lay the Peace Policy. All its major features, so grandly proclaimed in 1869–70, had been tested and, so it appeared, found wanting. In part, but only in part, the perception was valid.

The Board of Indian Commissioners, that long-proposed panacea that assumed successful businessmen to be repositories of wisdom in all matters, had run afoul of reality. The first chairman, Philadelphia merchant William Welsh, resigned after only a month in office when he discovered that the "joint control" with the Interior Department decreed by Congress did not really mean that. Pittsburgh steel magnate Felix R. Brunot carried on, but he and his associates collided head-on with the entrenched interests that fed on the old system. The commissioners ran the clumsy but honest Ely Parker out of office as head of the Indian Bureau, and the able Jacob Cox quit as Interior Secretary when the odor of scandal began to grow noticeable. Their successors turned out to be creatures of the old system, in deed if not in word at odds with the board on control of expenditures and selection of personnel. For a time the commissioners succeeded in partly reforming fiscal and contracting practices. Also, their annual meetings in Washington provided a forum in which churchmen, reformers, and federal officials reinforced their shared convictions on how best to save the Indian. Finally, the board played a significant role in mar-

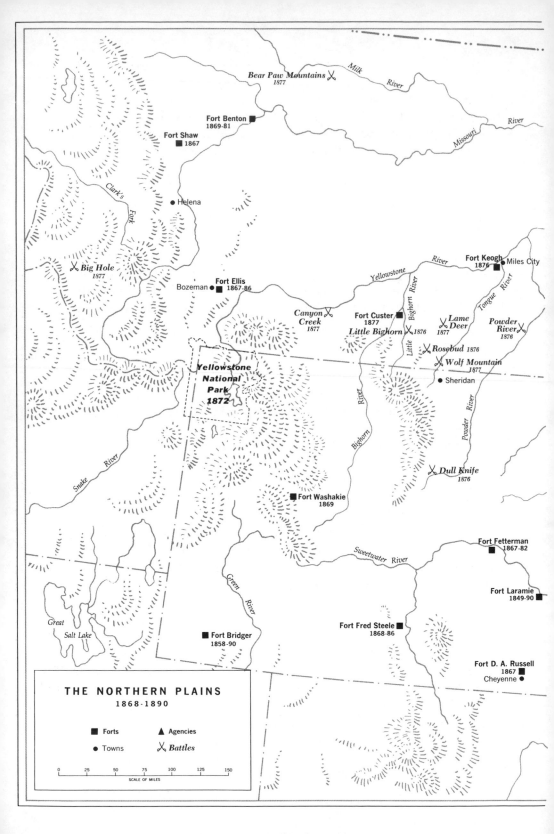

Bear Paw Mountains ✕
1877

Milk River

River

Missouri River

Fort Benton ■
1869-81

Fort Shaw
■ 1867

• Helena

Clark's Fork

Big Hole ✕
1877

Fort Ellis
Bozeman ● ■ 1867-86

Canyon Creek ✕
1877

Yellowstone River

Fort Keogh ■
1876 ● Miles City

Fort Custer ■
1877
Little Bighorn ✕ 1876

Bighorn River

Little River

Lame Deer ✕
1877

Tongue River

Powder River ✕
1876

Rosebud ✕ 1876

Wolf Mountain ✕
1877

● Sheridan

Yellowstone
National
Park
1872

Snake River

Bighorn River

Powder River

Dull Knife ✕
1876

Fort Washakie ■
1869

Sweetwater River

Fort Fetterman ■
1867-82

Green River

Fort Laramie ■
1849-90

Great
Salt Lake

Fort Bridger ■
1858-90

Fort Fred Steele ■
1868-86

Fort D. A. Russell ■
1867
Cheyenne ●

THE NORTHERN PLAINS
1868-1890

■ Forts   ▲ Agencies

● Towns   ✕ Battles

0   25   50   75   100   125   150
SCALE OF MILES

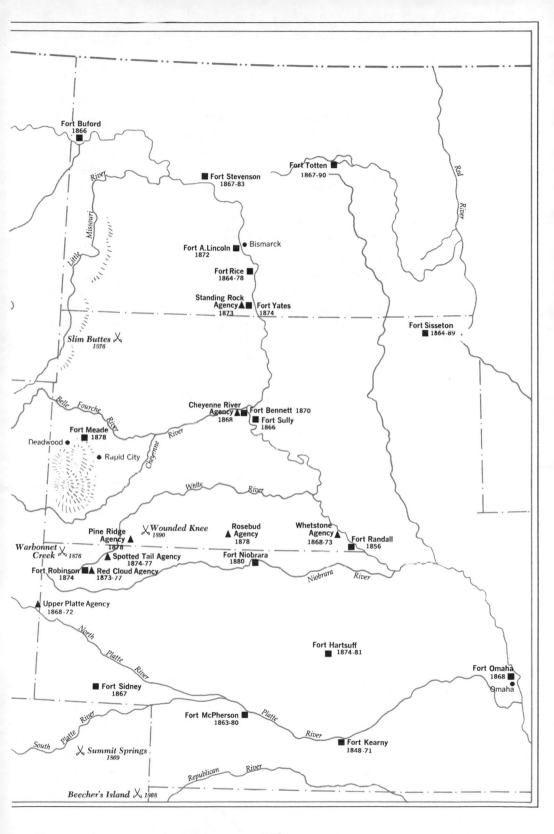

Fort Buford
1866

Fort Totten
1867-90

Fort Stevenson
1867-83

River

Little

Missouri

River

Red

River

Fort A. Lincoln
1872

Bismarck

Fort Rice
1864-78

Standing Rock
Agency ▲ ■ Fort Yates
1873   1874

Fort Sisseton
■ 1864-89

Slim Buttes ✗
1876

Belle   Fourche   River

Fort Meade
■ 1878

Deadwood

Rapid City

Cheyenne   River

Cheyenne River
Agency ▲ ■ Fort Bennett 1870
1868   ■ Fort Sully
1866

White   River

Wounded Knee ✗
1890

Rosebud
Agency ▲
1878

Whetstone
Agency ▲
1868-73

Fort Randall
■ 1856

Pine Ridge
Agency ▲
1878

Warbonnet
Creek ✗ 1876

▲ Spotted Tail Agency
1874-77

Fort Niobrara
■ 1880

Fort Robinson ▲▲ Red Cloud Agency
1874   1873-77

Niobrara   River

Upper Platte Agency
▲ 1868-72

North

Platte   River

Fort Hartsuff
■ 1874-81

Fort Omaha
1868
■

Omaha

Fort Sidney
■ 1867

Fort McPherson
■ 1863-80

Platte

River

Fort Kearny
■ 1848-71

South   Platte   River

✗ Summit Springs
1869

Beecher's Island ✗ 1868

Republican   River

shaling public opinion behind programs expressing these convictions. But the philanthropists still hungered for joint control, an ideal that, even if politically acceptable, would not have worked administratively. In 1874 the board resigned en masse, to be supplanted by a group equally dedicated but more aware of its true mission as advisor to the appointed federal authorities. Joint control, and the able and disinterested oversight it contemplated, expired with the old board.[22]

The end of the treaty system did not bring about the consequences that had been expected. True, it cured the ailment that occasioned it, for the House of Representatives now shared Indian responsibility fully with the Senate. But some other means had to be found to define relations with the Indians. "Agreements" emerged as the instrument. Identical to treaties in all but name and the exclusive Senate role in ratification, agreements did not get to the root of the main objection to treaties. Agreements as firmly as treaties reinforced tribal sovereignty, which in turn reinforced all the old ways deemed antagonistic to civilization.[23]

Nor did church nomination of agency personnel purify the Indian Service as hoped. In surprising numbers, the incompetent and even the corrupt slipped through the screen of the missionary associations. Worse, the government found itself embroiled in sectarian strife. Protestant and Catholic, Protestant and Protestant, and even factions within individual denominations waged un-Christian battle over territory. No scheme for apportioning agencies among denominations failed to antagonize more than placate. The Catholics, in particular, felt discriminated against; and rightly so, for Protestants overwhelmingly dominated the Indian reform movement. In 1874 the Catholic Church formed a lobbying bureau in Washington to fight for its fair share. Religious freedom was the rallying cry. The Indians had a constitutional right, Catholics asserted, "to the full enjoyment of liberty of conscience" and therefore must be allowed freedom to decide which *Christian* faith to embrace.[24] In Protestant eyes no less than in Catholic, liberty of conscience did not extend to the old Indian religion. Spoilsmen, of course, did not like church involvement in patronage, although, as Grant foresaw, they could not say so openly. They could quietly sabotage it, however, and by 1876 they had largely succeeded.

Fraud and corruption, a major target of the Peace Policy, most assuredly were not eliminated. On the contrary, despite the labors of the Board of Indian Commissioners and the churches, the rot that infected large segments of the Grant administration settled deeply in the Indian system. Scandal after scandal rocked agencies, bureau, and department. Three heads of the Indian Bureau, Ely Parker, Edward P. Smith, and John Q. Smith, left office under suspicion if not proof of wrongdoing, and Secretary of the Interior Columbus Delano resigned in the face of grave allegations. Under Grant, the old Indian system flourished in all its brazen immorality.

Even so, in terms of its objectives, the Peace Policy retained a life in 1876 largely unnoticed by the public. The Board of Indian Commissioners endured, playing a modest role in policy formulation well into the twentieth century. The churches did not withdraw from the reservations and continued to press on the Indians the Christian gospel regarded as crucial to the civilization program. And civilization remained a cornerstone of federal Indian policy until 1933, with the reservation as the hothouse for its germination.

But in essence Grant's Peace Policy was chiefly about peace, and peace it did not achieve. The public could thus hardly be faulted for failing to note the persistence of the Peace Policy when war so dominated the Indian news. Indeed, the era of the Peace Policy featured some of the bitterest warfare in the history of Indian relations.

6

Wars of the Peace Policy, 1869–1886

Second Lieutenant Walter S. Schuyler exemplified the qualities the army treasured in its junior officers. Scion of one of New York's most aristocratic families, he adapted swiftly to harsh frontier conditions. Short, stocky, and muscular, he combined ambition with intelligence, energy, imagination, and an unswerving devotion to his profession. Despite the hard frontier life, he remained cultured, literate, and possessed of social graces. Enlisted men and officers liked and respected him, and he quickly won the confidence of his superiors.

Graduating from West Point in 1870, Schuyler drew the toughest of assignments—the Fifth Cavalry in Arizona. "Perhaps no other of our frontier settlements ever presented so many obstacles to the pioneer," wrote a fellow officer of Arizona at this time. "Hostility appeared to be the normal condition of everybody and everything." Besides incredibly rugged terrain, punishing climate, vegetation covered with needle-sharp thorns, and rattlesnakes, centipedes, and scorpions, the Apache foes "were the most wily, shrewd and treacherous of all our native tribes." They required a special brand of warfare: "The campaigns in Arizona did not owe their ultimate success to any particular Waterloo-like victory, as much as they did to the covering of a great deal of ground by a comparatively small number of men, permitting the Indians no rest and rendering any and every hiding place insecure."[1]

This kind of campaigning depended on able junior officers, and Schuyler became one of the ablest. During his three years in Arizona he led dozens of such operations, usually with a handful of regulars, a contingent of Indian auxiliaries, and one or two white frontiersmen as scouts and guides. On ten occasions he saw combat, an extraordinary record in Indian campaigning. He owed his conspicuous success not only to his own

157

After the Civil War the army's network of frontier forts expanded, but most remained weakly manned. In major campaigns units had to be concentrated at strategically located posts before a strong expedition could be organized and sent into the field. Despite their deficiencies, the forts were a significant institution of the westward movement. Above is Fort Davis, Texas, a key outpost on the San Antonio-El Paso Road. Right, cavalry troops parade in front of officers' row at Fort Custer, Montana, erected in the heart of Sioux country after Custer's debacle at the Little Bighorn. *National Park Service* and *National Archives.*

ability but to the good fortune that awarded him the services of Arizona's premier scout and guide, Al Sieber. At the end of his tour, Schuyler's reward came in the form of appointment as aide to General George Crook.

One mission of the many led by Lieutenant Schuyler illustrates the kind of service Indian warfare demanded of the regular army in Arizona as well as, in varying degree, elsewhere on the Indian frontier. In 1872–73, in some of the hardest campaigning on record, General Crook had rounded up the Apaches of central Arizona and confined them to the reservations laid out by Vincent Colyer back in 1871. Not all stayed, however, and among those who had jumped the reservation was a particularly wily

159

and destructive chieftain named Delshay. Crook wanted him badly, and small-unit patrols combed the tangled mountains and gorges at the base of the Mogollon Rim in search. Lieutenant Schuyler led one out of Camp Verde on December 1, 1873.[2]

Schuyler's command, fairly typical of the searching columns, consisted of two veteran noncommissioned officers and nine cavalrymen, fourteen Apache scouts, and twenty-five pack mules with civilian packers. Al Sieber served as guide, along with another of Arizona's best, José de Leon, and his son. For four days, and at night too, they combed the mountains and valleys surrounding the Verde's east fork. Cold, wind, and deep snow in the high country made the march doubly exhausting. On the night of the fourth, José spied a campfire in the distance and, investigating, turned up two widely separated rancherías. The men had covered twenty-seven miles during the day, but now, since fires would betray their presence, they passed a brutal night tramping in circles through the snow to keep from freezing. Sending part of his men against the more distant camp, Schuyler and the bulk of the command headed for the nearest. In a swirling blizzard they charged into the surprised ranchería, cut down fifteen Apaches with carbines and pistols, and destroyed the wickiups. The firing alerted the other ranchería, whose inhabitants fled.

Day after disheartening day followed this success. Alternating rain and snow kept the men constantly wet and cold. Snow and mud made progress slow and fatiguing. An occasional deer relieved the tedium of hardtack and bacon. East of the Verde they probed, around the base of Turret Peak, and south toward the cactus-studded deserts of the Gila, seeking that small sign that would point toward a hidden Indian camp. At last, after more than two weeks of exhausting search, they spotted a telltale trail, and José and a few soldiers ran it back to eleven wickiups cleverly concealed under an overhang of a mesa on upper Cave Creek. Working stealthily into surrounding rocks during the night of December 22, at dawn they poured a rain of bullets into the camp and felled nine Indians. In the camp the attackers found several tons of mescal, the staple Apache food, and destroyed it.

Putting in for several days of rest at Camp McDowell, at the mouth of the Verde, Schuyler and his worn-out, tattered force set forth again on December 31 to scout the Verde and its shouldering mountains back up to their home station. Nine days later they sighted two Indians. Hoping they belonged to a mountaintop ranchería, the lieutenant laid over until midnight, then scaled the mountain. Dawn broke over a vacant summit, but a trail pointed down toward the East Verde, and off went the pursuers. José and his Indian scouts scurried in advance down the slopes for six miles and came up with the quarry on the river bank. In a sharp fight they killed four—a man, a woman, and two children. Others fell captive, while still others fled. José personally slew the man, who turned out to be Natotel, second only to Delshay among wanted fugitives.

For another two weeks the column scouted the water-soaked mountains and valleys, its progress slowed by bank-full streams. The Verde itself ran twenty-five feet above normal. On January 22, as the command neared the end of its ordeal, Schuyler sadly noted in his journal: "Jose and boy drowned at mouth of E. Fork." It was a tragic finale to a successful operation, one that combined perseverance and endurance with superior leadership and the ability, rare among army officers, to bring the elusive Apache to bay.

Most such scouts failed to overtake the foe or even to glimpse him. Except for the combat, however, this one of many Schuyler expeditions typified in its hardships and physical and mental demands the military experience in the Trans-Mississippi West. The big Indian campaigns and battles like Custer's legendary stand at the Little Bighorn dominate history, but they were not typical. Indeed, most soldiers never saw combat. The army's service in the Indian Wars was characterized not by the stirring charge of a hundred blueclad horsemen—bugles blaring, banners snapping, sabers waving—but by the punishing, unheroic, usually fruitless reconnaissance over hostile terrain, pounded by rain, snow, or scorching sun, searching for an invisible enemy.

For the Indians, the day they wiped out Custer was supremely exhilarating and memorable, the stuff of countless graphic paintings on tanned deerskins and of tales passed orally from generation to generation around smoky campfires. But it was scarcely representative of their conflict with the white people and their bluecoats. Much more characteristic was the raid by the small war-party intent on plunder, coups, scalps, and sometimes revenge. Illustrative was a raid into Texas led by Pago-to-goodle, a young Kiowa on the Fort Sill Reservation, in the summer of 1872.[3]

To the white mind, it seems an aimless journey that must have lasted most of the summer. Crossing Red River, the ten-man party wandered south and west into a virtually uninhabited country where few white targets could be expected. They ascended the caprock and came out on the great flat table of the Staked Plains stretching westward into New Mexico. Here they fell in with some Mescalero Apaches, traveled for a time with

The Indian Wars pitted Indian warrior against regular soldier. Man for man the warrior greatly excelled his opponent, but in an open fight the army's disciplined units usually prevailed. Here famed western artist Frederic Remington depicts a Cheyenne warrior (left) and a typical cavalry trooper (right). *Denver Public Library Western History Department* and *William Gardner Bell*.

them, and then, picking their way southward from one drying waterhole to another, dropped down from the caprock to a low peak called Mucha-que. Near here they came upon a lone white soldier, afoot, lost, and near death from thirst. They killed and scalped him and, having accomplished the purpose of the expedition, decided to head for home.

Again the Kiowas met up with some Apaches and invited them to join in a victory dance. Before it could be held, however, the party came across a recently abandoned Apache ranchería. Signs showed that it had been attacked by soldiers but that all the occupants had escaped unharmed. The Apaches invited the Kiowas to visit their village, but Pago-to-goodle declined, explaining that they had been out a long time and wanted to go home.

The party rested for ten days just south of Mucha-que, and then, with

a light rain falling, started for home. Pausing at a water hole, however, they suddenly discovered a column of soldiers following their trail. "Every man tie up his sheet and get ready to fight," ordered Pago-to-goodle. "We'll fight on foot, all except Set-maunte, who will stay mounted." Taking cover under a cutbank below the trail, the warriors waited. Soon about twenty horsemen came in view. One, on a black horse out in front, spotted fresh droppings from the Kiowa ponies and spurred his mount. "We had better get out of here," exclaimed Pago-to-goodle. "There are too many of them." But Hau-vah-te, proud owner of a repeating rifle and two revolvers, objected. "First let me shoot at them."

Approaching the cutbank, the soldier on the black horse spied the Indians lying in wait. Waving his pistol and hat in the air, he turned to urge his companions forward. Hau-vah-te fired. The bullet struck the soldier in the back, and he fell to the ground. The other soldiers wheeled and galloped in the opposite direction, firing their pistols back over their shoulders.

The Kiowas all scrambled to count coup on the fallen soldier. Setmaunte, mounted, won the race, but his pony suddenly reared and threw him off balance. Hau-vah-te counted first coup instead. The Indians chased the fleeing soldiers for a short distance, but turned back when more soldiers came up. The Kiowa party paused briefly again at the dead soldier. An-pay-kau-te (the narrator of this account) dismounted and scalped him. Beneath his raincoat, the Indian remembered, he wore blue pants with yellow stripes down the sides. As trophies, Mamay-day got the scalp, Hau-vah-te the army carbine, A-to-tainte the pistol, and An-pay-kau-te a watch and gold chain. An-pay-kau-te had never seen a watch and did not know what it was. "When we stopped for lunch, I examined my trophy. It was still alive! I could hear its heart ticking! So I smashed it between two rocks to kill it. Then I threw away the pieces; they were of no use to me."

Without further event of note, the war party made its way back to Red River and crossed into their reservation sanctuary. It had been a successful raid. Kiowas and Comanches conducted thousands like it between the middle of the eighteenth century and the end of their freedom in 1875.

However representative of the Indian Wars were the nearly unnoticed adventures of Lieutenant Schuyler and Pago-to-goodle, it was the big headline-grabbing uprisings that captured public attention and often decreed changes in the Indians' fortunes. One after another, such conflicts marked the years of the Peace Policy and dashed its bright hopes. In one sense, it is an irony that so many wars broke out under the mantle of the Peace Policy, but in another sense it is readily understandable. The Peace Policy aimed at placing all Indians on reservations, where they could be kept away from the settlements and travel routes and where ultimately they could be civilized. The Indians often had other ideas—if not at first, then after they had sampled the reality of life on the reservation. Virtually every major war of the two decades after Appomattox was fought to force Indians on to newly created reservations or to make them go back to reservations from which they had fled. From such perspective, it is not surprising that warfare characterized the Peace Policy.

As the years passed, moreover, the Peace Policy ceased to command the wide support it had at first. The army, in particular, grew more openly critical. Except for an occasional Lieutenant Drew or Colonel Grierson, officers scoffed at the notion of conquest by kindness, and they had little use for the idealistic yet often corrupt people and purposes of the Indian Bureau. As General Sheridan remarked simplistically in 1869, "If a white man commits murder or robs, we hang him or send him to the penitentiary; if an Indian does the same, we have been in the habit of giving him more blankets."[4] And as Lieutenant Schuyler observed at the Camp Verde Reservation, the Indians "can be governed for the present only with a hand of iron, which is a manner of governing totally unknown to the agents of the Indian Bureau, most of whom are afraid of the Indians and are willing to do anything to conciliate them."[5] Western sentiment, always militant, encouraged the army in its view of the Peace Policy. "Let sniveling quakers give place to bluff soldiers," ran a typical editorial comment.[6]

Who is friendly and who is not? military officers not unreasonably asked the civilian authorities. Those on the reservation were friendly and the exclusive responsibility of the Indian Bureau, came the answer; those off the reservation were hostile and the responsibility of the army. Superficially, it seemed a logical solution to a chronic dilemma. It drew a line that no one, including the Indians, could mistake. But as the record of the Fort Sill "city of refuge" demonstrated, a reservation could harbor a great many Indians of unfriendly disposition. Unfortunately, except for the rare Satanta who bragged of his exploits, their individual identities remained unknown or unprovable. Aggravating the army's frustration, garrisons on or near reservations had to watch helplessly while civilian corruption and mismanagement—or so it seemed to them—prodded Indians toward an armed hostility that would have to be suppressed at the risk of army lives. As General Sherman complained to a congressional committee in 1874: "The Indian Bureau keeps feeding and clothing the Indians, till they get fat and saucy, and then we are only notified that the Indians are troublesome, and are going to war, after it is too late to provide a remedy."[7]

Except by government decree, moreover, Indians off the reservation were not necessarily belligerent. They might be out hunting, or headed for a visit with friends in another tribe, or simply wandering about seeing the country. Even a whole band off the reservation did not automatically mean hostility. Indeed, few such could be clearly labeled friendly or hostile; ambiguity more accurately described their temper. Was Black Kettle's village on the Washita friendly or hostile? No chief and no band more diligently pursued peace. Yet it was the trail of a party of Black Kettle's young

The most innovative military leader was General George Crook, who matched the Indian's mobility with packmules rather than wagons and employed Indians against Indians. Here Crook sits astride his mule "Apache" at Fort Bowie, Arizona, in 1885, and (right) one of his Apache scout units poses for photographer at Fort Grant, Arizona, a year later. *Arizona Historical Society.*

men, their hands stained with the blood of Kansas settlers, that led Custer's cavalry to the luckless chief's winter lodges. The army never learned to discriminate between the guilty and the innocent simply because rarely was a group of Indians unmistakably one or the other.

The army did not pursue its Indian-fighting mission very creatively. Occasionally a General Crook recognized his foes as superb guerrilla fighters who called for techniques quite different than had Robert E. Lee's gray legions. Crook fought Indians like Indians and usually, in fact, with Indians. But the army as an institution never evolved a doctrine of Indian warfare, never taught its aspiring officers at West Point the difference between conventional and unconventional war, and never issued official guidance for troops in the field.

Lacking a formal doctrine of unconventional war, the army waged con-

ventional war. Heavy columns of infantry and cavalry, locked to slow-moving supply trains, crawled about the vast western distances in search of Indians who could scatter and vanish almost instantly. The conventional tactics of the Scott, Casey, and Upton manuals sometimes worked, by routing an adversary that had foolishly decided to stand and fight on the white soldiers' terms, by smashing a village whose inhabitants had grown careless, or by wearing down a quarry through persistent campaigning that made surrender preferable to constant fatigue and insecurity. But most such offensives merely broke down the grain-fed cavalry horses and ended with the troops devoting as much effort to keeping themselves supplied as to chasing Indians.

But when they worked, these offensives worked with a vengeance. They were a forerunner of "total war" against entire populations, as pi-

A Reconnaissance, by Frederic Remington. Whether employed in units such as General Crook organized or individually as scouts and guides, Indians played an important role in the army's operations against the western tribes. From *Century Magazine*.

oneered by Sherman and Sheridan against the Confederacy. Under the guidance and inspiration of these two leaders—the one now General in Chief of the army, the other heading the strategic Division of the Missouri, embracing all the Great Plains—the army set forth to find the enemy in their winter camps, to kill or drive them from their lodges, to destroy their ponies, food, and shelter, and to hound them mercilessly across a frigid landscape until they gave up. If women and children got hurt or killed, it was lamentable, but justified because it resolved the issue quickly and decisively, and thus more humanely. Although prosecuted along conventional lines and often an exercise in logistical futility, this approach yielded an occasional victory, such as the Washita, that saved it from serious challenge.[8]

No better than the army did the Indians adapt to new conditions. The westward surge of the white people after the Civil War confronted them with a crisis of apocalyptic implications, yet they met it, like the army, in the same old ways. Despite the common danger, tribal particularism and intertribal animosities remained as strong as ever. Sometimes tribes came together in alliance against an especially visible threat from the whites, but rarely did such an alliance hang together for very long. Even unity within a tribe proved elusive. Factions differed on how to deal with the white encroachment; some resisted, some accommodated, and some wavered and even oscillated between the two extremes. The highly individual character of tribal society inhibited the rise of leaders who could bring together diverse opinions, and, to make matters worse, the proliferation of "government chiefs" demoralized the traditional political organization. As one astute observer remarked, army officers, Indian superintendents and commissioners, and even agents had created so many chiefs that "Indian chiefs, like brevets in the army, are become so common they are not properly respected."[9]

Nor did fighting methods change. Indian culture still developed a superb fighting man. Warriors still practiced guerrilla tactics masterfully and made uncanny use of terrain, vegetation, and other natural conditions, all to the anguish of their military antagonists. But Indian culture also continued to emphasize the individual and withhold from any man the power of command, except through personal influence. Thus team discipline tended to collapse when opportunities for personal distinction or differing opinions on strategy or tactics arose. Man for man, the warrior far surpassed his blueclad adversary in virtually every test of military proficiency; but unit for unit—however great the numbers—the Indians could not come close to matching the discipline and organization of the army. When Indians made the mistake of standing and fighting on the army's terms, they usually lost.

In the end, however, the relative fighting qualities of the opponents made little difference. Despite all the wars of the Peace Policy, the Indians did not succumb to military conquest. The army contributed to the final collapse, of course, with "war houses" scattered all through the Indian country and with campaigns that hastened an outcome ordained by more significant forces. More than the army, railroads, settlements, and all the numbers, technology, and other trappings of an aggressive and highly organized society brought defeat to the Indians. Every white advance came at the expense of resources, especially wild game, essential to the Indian way of life. As the open land and its natural bounty shrank, the reservation offered the only alternative to extinction. For the Indians, General Sherman's jest held deadly portent: "I think it would be wise," he said of the Sioux insistence on hunting on the Republican River, "to invite all the sportsmen of England & America there this fall for a Grand Buffalo hunt, and make one grand sweep of them all."[10]

Yet the Indians' armed resistance to the westward movement, and the army's armed response, form dramatic and significant chapters in the history of both peoples and of the frontiers across which they faced each other. In the Trans-Mississippi West, the final and most intense phase coincided with the final phase of the westward migration and settlement of the whites and was a direct consequence of the Peace Policy's imperative to confine all Indians to reservations.

Kintpuash had tried the reservation and did not like it. An able, ambitious young man, he and other Modoc leaders had signed a treaty in 1864 ceding their homeland among the lake-dotted, lava-scored plateaus of southern Oregon and northern California and had agreed to live on a reservation with Klamaths and Snakes. Homesick, bullied by the more numerous Klamaths, some sixty to seventy families followed Kintpuash back to their old homes on Lost River, just south of the Oregon-California boundary. As more and more whites took up homesteads on the ceded lands, tensions rose. Officials of the Indian Bureau pressed Kintpuash—with other whites, they knew him as Captain Jack—to go back to the reservation. Persuasion failing, they asked the army to use force. That move provoked the Modoc War of 1872–73.

At dawn on November 29, 1872, cavalry attacked the village of Kintpuash. After an exchange of fire, the Indians fled, later crossing Tule Lake in boats. Another party of Modocs, under a leader the whites called Hooker

Jim, rode around the east side of the lake, killing settlers along the way. On the lake's southern shore they united in a wild expanse of black lava that nature had piled into a gigantic fortress. They knew its every fissure, cavern, and passageway. Patches of grass subsisted their cattle. Sagebrush and greasewood yielded fuel. Water came from Tule Lake. As the big army that quickly assembled discovered, it could not be penetrated by assault, reduced by artillery bombardment, or taken by siege. It swiftly drew national attention as "Captain Jack's Stronghold."

Kintpuash conducted the defense with great skill. For four months, with only about sixty fighting men, he held off an army whose numbers ultimately approached a thousand. Again the government decided to try diplomacy. A peace commission arrived and erected a lone tent on the plain outside the lava beds. Negotiations commenced. So did Kintpuash's troubles. Factionalism accomplished what an army could not. Hooker Jim and others challenged Kintpuash's course and taunted him for refusing to kill the peace commissioners in a bold stroke aimed at winning a reservation on Lost River. Ridiculed and humiliated, he finally agreed. On Good Friday, April 11, 1873, the Modoc leaders suddenly interrupted the peace talks, drew hidden weapons, and fell on the white negotiators. One escaped, but three were left on the ground shot, stabbed, and stripped. (Miraculously, one later recovered.)

The deed sealed the fate of the Modocs, for the head of the commission was none other than the commander of the military department, Edward R. S. Canby, who thus gained dubious distinction as the only regular army general slain by Indians in the entire history of the Indian Wars. (Others called general, such as Custer, held the rank by brevet or volunteer, not regular, commissions.) Foolishly the Modocs had called down upon themselves the wrath of an outraged nation. The army responded with more troops and better leadership at the same time that quarrels among the Modoc leadership intensified. Finally the Indians scattered from the lava beds and were run down, group by small group, by pursuing columns of soldiers. On June 1 a detachment found Kintpuash and his family hiding in a cave. His "legs had given out," he explained.

Against people who had treacherously murdered a popular war hero, the precepts of the Peace Policy could not be expected to govern. Kintpuash and three others involved in Canby's death died on the gallows; their heads were cut off and shipped to the Army Medical Museum in Washington. A furious General Sherman demanded that Kintpuash's followers, who had compiled such an extraordinary record of skill and courage in holding the lava beds, be scattered among other tribes "so

In the Modoc War of 1872–73 Captain Jack and a handful of Indians barricaded themselves in northern California's lava beds and thwarted all attempts to blast them out. In the end dissension among Modoc leaders brought defeat, and the assassination of General Edward R. S. Canby and other peace commissioners ensured swift and harsh retribution. Here (right) pickets watch for enemy movements among the sharp black rocks. *Library of Congress* (Canby) and *National Archives.*

that the name of Modoc should cease." In October 1873, 155 in number, they were resettled fifteen hundred miles to the east, in Indian Territory. The name did not cease, but their demand to live in their homeland ceased to be heard.[11]

The Modoc War—more accurately, the slaying of General Canby—badly crippled the Peace Policy. Newspapers everywhere saw it as dramatic evidence that Indians could not be trusted or reasoned with. Whether favoring extermination or civilization, editors judged Canby's death a grievous blow to the Peace Policy.[12] As always, however, events on the Great Plains more profoundly influenced public opinion and shaped policy than those elsewhere in the West. Throughout the 1870s, warfare with

the Plains Indians rose to a thunderous finale on the Little Bighorn in 1876 that was almost universally regarded as marking the demise of the Peace Policy. Like the Modoc War, the Plains wars centered chiefly on the issue of whether or not tribes were to live on reservations as demanded by the Peace Policy.

On the southern Plains, the big nomadic tribes had agreed to reservations in the Medicine Lodge treaties. They actually lived there—Kiowas and Comanches at Fort Sill, Cheyennes and Arapahos at Darlington—because General Sheridan's winter operations of 1868–69, especially Custer's persistent and wide-ranging marches, had made fugitive life tiring and insecure. But reservation life proved confining; clothing and ration issues scant, of poor quality, and badly selected for Indian wants; and the encroachments of white cattlemen, whiskey peddlers, horse

The Indian Wars attracted two fiercely competitive artists, Frederic Remington and Charles Schreyvogel. Remington's *Protecting a Wagon Train* (left) and Schreyvogel's *A Sharp Encounter* (right) are specimens. *Denver Public Library Western History Department* and *Library of Congress.*

thieves, and other opportunists unnerving, if not demoralizing. Particularly ominous to the Indians, white hunters slaughtered the buffalo for their hides alone, leaving carcasses by the hundreds of thousands to rot on the prairies. Kiowas and Comanches regularly raided in Texas and Mexico, as they always had, while Cheyennes and Arapahos raided less often in Kansas. Discontent and mutual aggression finally boiled over in the Red River War of 1874–75.

For a time, while Satanta and Big Tree languished in the Texas penitentiary and the government held 124 women and children seized in an attack on a fugitive Comanche village, reservation-based raiders had restrained themselves. But the release of these captives, in exchange for promises of good behavior, had removed the restraint. The spring and summer of 1874 found Indians raiding in Texas and Kansas with new ferocity. In particular, Comanches and Cheyennes attacked a camp of

white hide hunters at Adobe Walls in the Texas Panhandle, where Kit Carson had fought the Kiowas in 1864, and Kiowas under Lone Wolf ambushed a detachment of Texas Rangers near the site of the Salt Creek Massacre of 1871. These aggressions provoked the government to lift the ban against military operations on Indian reservations. Suddenly army officers at the Fort Sill and Darlington agencies were compiling lists of "friendly" Indians. Everyone else, sure to be classed as "hostiles," headed west, beyond the reservation boundaries. Some eighteen hundred Cheyennes, two thousand Comanches, and one thousand Kiowas moved in large encampments among the breaks surrounding the headwaters of the Washita River and the various forks of the Red, in the Texas Panhandle—hence the designation "Red River War."

Suddenly this country, hitherto so remote and secure, swarmed with soldiers. From north, east, south, and west, five columns converged. One

The postwar regular army included both cavalry and infantry regiments composed of black enlisted men and white officers. The black units compiled a record of hard and often notable service on the frontier. Frederick Remington's *A Study in Action* (left) portrays a typical black cavalryman, and Nick Eggenhofer's rendition of the Battle of Rattlesnake Springs, Texas (right), depicts a decisive action in the operations against Victorio's Apaches in 1880. *National Park Service.*

routed the Indians at the base of the caprock near the mouth of Palo Duro Canyon. Another fell on a Comanche village nestled deep in the canyon itself. August sun parched the land and dried the water holes. September brought days of rain, bank-full streams, prairies of mud, and an ordeal the Indians remembered as "the wrinkled-hand chase." Winter loosed blizzards and numbing cold. Through it all, the soldiers kept after the Indians. There were few clashes and little bloodshed, but gradually the exhaustion of the chase, the discomforts of weather and hunger, and, above all, the constant gnawing fear of soldiers storming into their camps at dawn wore them down. As early as October, some had tired and drifted back to the reservation. By the spring of 1875, all had returned.

At the agencies the Indians discovered white officials behaving with a sternness uncharacteristic of the Peace Policy. Throughout the winter, as parties straggled in from the west, army officers confined leaders who were somewhat capriciously judged guilty of particular "crimes" or simply of functioning as "ringleaders." Satanta found no disposition toward leniency; back he went to the Texas penitentiary, where three years later, in despair, he threw himself from an upper window to his death. As spring came to Fort Sill, soldiers herded seventy-four Indians, shackled and chained, aboard eight wagons. Among them were such noted chiefs as Gray Beard, Minimic, and Medicine Water of the Cheyennes; Lone Wolf, Woman's Heart, and White Horse of the Kiowas; and Black Horse of the Comanches. With women wailing their grief, the caravan moved out and headed for the railroad. After days of travel the Indians, so recently at large on the Staked Plains, found themselves enclosed by the thick walls and bastions of an ancient Spanish fortress on the Florida coast.

The army had gained a clear victory, not only over the Indians but over the more extreme proponents of the Peace Policy. From his Chicago headquarters General Sheridan had directed the strategy of convergence. Generals John Pope and Christopher C. Augur had overseen its execution. At least two field officers, Colonels Nelson A. Miles and Ranald S. Mackenzie, had won great distinction in carrying it out. Both had gained battlefield victories, Miles in the caprock fight, and Mackenzie in the celebrated charge into Palo Duro Canyon. But in the end it was not combat success but convergence, unremittingly prosecuted, that had won the war. Confinement of the "ringleaders" far from their homes and families helped ensure that another war would not occur. Never again did Kiowas, Comanches, Cheyennes, or Arapahos revolt against their reservation overlords. Never again did Texas and Kansas settlers suffer aggression from these tribes. Nor did Generals Sherman and Sheridan forget the lessons of the Red River War as they turned their attention to the northern Plains.[13]

Here, Sioux, Northern Cheyenne, and Northern Arapaho had yet to be finally brought within the reservation system. Oglalas and Brules drew rations at the Red Cloud and Spotted Tail agencies in northwestern Nebraska, where these two chiefs maneuvered tortuously between the opposing forces of white officialdom and their own people. Other Sioux formed tenuous connections with agencies along the Missouri River, the eastern border of the Great Sioux Reservation—Hunkpapas and Blackfeet at Grand River, Miniconjous and Sans Arc at Cheyenne River, and still others at Crow Creek and Lower Brule. Cheyennes and Arapahos mingled with Sioux at Red Cloud. In all, these agencies counted perhaps twenty-five thousand adherents.

But the strength of the adherence wavered with the seasons and the competing influence of rival chiefs, for off to the west roamed a hard core of kinsmen who had no intention of abandoning the free life of the chase for the dubious attractions of the reservation. They looked for leadership to a chief of surpassing influence. Of compelling countenance and commanding demeanor, quick of thought and emphatic of judgment, Sitting Bull held power not only as war and political chief but also as religious functionary. "He had a big brain and a good one," recalled an old warrior, "a strong heart and a generous one."[14] At the agency Indians he hurled a taunt: "You are fools to make yourselves slaves to a piece of

Sitting Bull. The Hunkpapa Sioux chieftain held great power among the hunting bands that refused to settle on the reservation and fashioned the mighty coalition of tribes that overwhelmed Custer at the Little Bighorn in 1876. Forced to surrender in 1881, he remained resolutely opposed to all features of the government's civilization program. Indian policemen shot and killed him during the Ghost Dance troubles of 1890. *National Archives.*

179

fat bacon, some hard-tack, and a little sugar and coffee."[15] And in fact, many did not. Nothing prevented them from sampling the old hunting life in the summer and the hardtack and coffee in winter. Back and forth they shuttled between the agencies and the camps of Sitting Bull and other "nontreaty" chiefs.

These "northern Indians" stirred up constant trouble. While on the reservation, they kept the agencies in turmoil, for they were ungovernable, a danger to white officials, and a bad influence on the agency Indians. While off the reservation, they did not always keep to the unceded hunting grounds guaranteed by the Treaty of 1868, but sometimes raided along the Platte and among the Montana settlements at the head of the Missouri and Yellowstone rivers.

That the whites called them hostiles and accused them of breaking the treaty while also enjoying its bounty did not bother these hunting bands. They could point to some treaty violations by the other side as well. For one thing, in 1873 surveyors laid out a route for the Northern Pacific Railroad along the northern margins of the unceded territory. For another, and most infuriating, in 1874 "Long Hair" Custer led his soldiers into the Black Hills, part of the Great Sioux Reservation itself, and there found gold. Miners swarmed into the Indian country, and the government, making only a token effort to keep them out, hesitantly broached the subject of buying the part of the reservation that contained the Black Hills. Then, late in 1875, runners arrived in the winter camps of the hunting bands with a stern message from the Great Father: Come to the agencies at once or be considered hostiles against whom the army would make war.[16]

They ignored the summons, and as spring turned to summer in 1876 they discovered blue columns converging on their hunting grounds. In March, one attacked an Oglala camp on Powder River but bungled the follow-up and retreated under assaults of bitter cold and deep snow. As the snow melted, the fugitive camps swelled. Worsening conditions at the agencies, the Black Hills issue, and the attempt to take away the freedom to roam the unceded territory set off an unusually large spring migration of agency Indians to the camps of the hunting bands. June found them coming together in a village that steadily expanded as it moved slowly westward across the streams flowing northward into the Yellowstone. These Indians were not looking for a fight, but, as never before, they were proud, confident, and at the height of their power. Chiefs of ability fortified the leadership of Sitting Bull—Black Moon, Gall, Hump, Lame Deer, Dirty Moccasins, Lame White Man, and the incomparable

A major cause of the Sioux War of 1876 was the invasion of the Black Hills, part of the Great Sioux Reservation set aside by the Treaty of 1868. The Custer Expedition of 1874 explored the Hills and discovered gold, which set off a stampede of miners. Here is Custer's wagon train in the Hills. *National Archives.*

Crazy Horse. Since his triumph as head of the party that decoyed Captain Fetterman out of Fort Phil Kearny ten years earlier, Crazy Horse had emerged as a splendid war leader and uncompromising foe of reservations.

By mid-June the Indians camped on a creek that ran into a river they knew as the Greasy Grass. Earlier, on the Rosebud, they had staged their annual Sun Dance. Sitting Bull had experienced a vision, in which he saw many dead soldiers "falling right into our camp." The people had thrilled to the image and the promise. Now scouts brought word of soldiers marching down the Rosebud. Crazy Horse led a large force to do battle. For six hours they fought, and after the Indians called off the fight the soldiers retreated.

George Armstrong Custer. The famed "boy general" of the Civil War achieved immortality at the Little Bighorn. This Brady portrait (left) shows him at 25, a major general of volunteers, in 1865. In group picture (right), Custer (third from left) poses with officers and ladies of the Seventh Cavalry at Fort Abraham Lincoln, Dakota Territory, in 1875, a year before many of them died at the Little Bighorn. At this time Custer's regular army rank was lieutenant colonel, but because of his brevet of major general he was usually addressed as "General Custer." *National Archives* and *National Park Service, Custer Battlefield National Monument.*

But this was not the triumph foretold by Sitting Bull. Soldiers had not fallen into their camp. Down to the Greasy Grass the village moved, and here the largest number yet of agency Indians joined the alliance. Six separate tribal circles—Hunkpapa, Oglala, Miniconjou, Sans Arc, Blackfoot, Northern Cheyenne—extended for three miles along the banks of the Greasy Grass. The village probably counted twelve hundred lodges and mustered almost two thousand fighting men.

True to Sitting Bull's prophecy, many soldiers were in fact about to fall into this village. As in the Red River War, General Sheridan had plotted a strategy of convergence. Advancing from the south, General Crook had struck the camp on Powder River on March 17 but had been driven back by winter. In May he sallied forth again, only to be stopped and turned back at the Battle of the Rosebud on June 17. Meantime, General Alfred

H. Terry approached from the east, and Colonel John Gibbon from the west. They joined on the Yellowstone at the mouth of the Rosebud. From here Terry launched a striking force of some six hundred cavalry, under the same Long Hair Custer who had invaded the Black Hills two years earlier. Custer followed the Indian trail up the Rosebud, across the Wolf Mountains, and down to the Greasy Grass, which his map labeled the Little Bighorn. The village there, because of the recent arrivals of agency Indians, contained about three times as many warriors as he had expected. On the scorching Sunday of June 25, 1876, his soldiers fell into it.

George Armstrong Custer presided over one of the most complete disasters in American military annals. A century later it still commanded public fascination and fueled heated controversy. More immediately, the Sioux and Cheyennes discovered what the Modocs had so painfully learned: the slaying of a big white chief could spell the doom of a people. Custer's Last Stand shocked and outraged Americans, shook the Peace Policy to the verge of collapse, brought a flood of soldiers to the Indian country, and afforded rationalization for forcing the agency chiefs, hitherto held back by the militant opposition of the northern Indians, to sell the Black Hills. An "agreement"—it resembled a treaty in all but name—legitimized the sale. For the Sioux and Cheyennes, final defeat lurked unseen in their soaring victory amid the brown hills overlooking the Greasy Grass.

Once again, winter combined with soldiers who could brave its blasts destroyed Indian resistance. Until the first snows the Sioux and Cheyennes, now fragmented in bands, easily eluded the big armies that ponderously gave chase. But winter, as usual, made them vulnerable. In the frigid, misty dawn of November 25, 1876, eleven hundred cavalrymen under Colonel Ranald S. Mackenzie burst into the Cheyenne village of Dull Knife and Little Wolf in a canyon of the Bighorn Mountains. Forty Cheyennes died, and the rest watched helplessly from the bluffs as the soldiers burned their tipis, clothing, and winter food supply. That night the temperature plunged to thirty below zero. Eleven babies froze to death at their mothers' breasts.

The suffering Cheyennes took refuge with Crazy Horse, but the soldiers tracked down these people too. In January 1877, on Tongue River, Sioux and Cheyenne warriors clashed with "walk-a-heap" bluecoats in a fight that petered out in a blinding blizzard. These soldiers had built a rude fort at the mouth of the Tongue, and they kept to the field all winter. Tired and discouraged, the Indians opened talks with the soldier chief at this fort. He wore a huge overcoat, and they called him "Bear's Coat."

The Battle of the Little Bighorn, June 25–26. 1876, as seen by the Sioux chief Red Horse. *National Park Service, Custer Battlefield National Monument.*

Colonel (Brevet Major General) Nelson A. Miles. "Bear's Coat" kept after the Sioux and Cheyennes throughout the winter of 1876–77, after the Custer disaster, and forced many to surrender the following spring. Here (right) Miles and staff pose in winter gear at Fort Keogh, Montana. Miles achieved great success in the Red River War of 1874–75, the Nez Perce operations of 1877, and the Apache War of 1886. He commanded all troops in the Ghost Dance troubles of 1890–91 and headed the army during the Spanish-American War. *Montana Historical Society* and *National Archives.*

He was the same Colonel Nelson A. Miles who had so resolutely pursued the southern Plains tribes in the Red River War.

Bear's Coat's combination of fight and talk, together with peace feelers put out from Red Cloud Agency through the agency chiefs, gradually strengthened the peace elements in the hostile camps. Spring saw the surrender of almost all the fugitives. On May 6, 1877, Crazy Horse led his Oglalas into Red Cloud Agency and threw his weapons on the ground in token of surrender. Four months later, amid circumstances that are still confusing, he died in a guardhouse scuffle, stabbed by either a soldier's bayonet or another Indian's knife. "It is good," said a fellow chief sadly, "he has looked for death and it has come."

The previous October, in a tense meeting between the lines, Sitting Bull told Bear's Coat that the Great Spirit had made him an Indian, and not an agency Indian. Rather than go to the reservation, he had led his people northward to the land of the "Great Mother." He got along well with her redcoats, but he and his people could not find enough food. Bear's Coat watched the boundary line like a hawk and prevented them from riding into Montana to hunt buffalo. Year after year, as they grew hungrier and hungrier, families and groups slipped away to surrender and go to the reservation. At last, in July 1881, Sitting Bull and about fifty families presented themselves at Fort Buford, Montana, the last vestige of the mighty alliance that had overwhelmed Long Hair Custer five years earlier. Sitting Bull handed his rifle to his eight-year-old son and told him to give it to the soldier chief. "I wish it to be remembered," he

Meeting Between the Lines. Frederic Remington portrays meeting between Nelson A. Miles and Sitting Bull in Montana in October 1876. The Great Spirit had made him an Indian, said the Sioux chief, and not an agency Indian. Sitting Bull and his people soon fled to Canada rather than surrender, but the growing scarcity of game there forced them to return and give up in 1881. *Library of Congress.*

Chief Joseph. Frank Jay Haynes photographed the famous Nez Perce chief in October 1877, immediately after his surrender at Bear Paw Mountain. *Smithsonian Institution National Anthropological Archives.*

said, "that I was the last man of my tribe to surrender my rifle, and this day have given it to you."[17]

More than most tribes, the Nez Perces divided into factions—"progressive" and "nonprogressive," Christian and "pagan," treaty and nontreaty. In 1855 the treaty Nez Perces, generally also Christian and "progressive," had agreed to a big reservation in Idaho, and in 1863, following gold discoveries within these boundaries, they consented to a much shrunken reservation surrounding the Clearwater River. The nontreaty people had agreed to neither reservation and made their homes elsewhere. One was White Bird, dwelling on the lower Salmon River south of the reservation. Another was Chief Joseph, living across the Snake River to the west, in Oregon's Wallowa Valley.

Like his namesake father, whose mantle he had inherited in 1871, Chief

Joseph displayed dignity, statesmanship, and a quietly effective leadership. Over and over he insisted that his father had never signed the Treaty of 1863 and had never sold the Wallowa Valley. At first the government agreed and set aside the valley as a reservation. But protests of Oregon settlers produced a swift change of policy. Instead, the authorities now declared, Joseph must go to the Idaho reservation to live, and, to hasten matters, they threw the Wallowa Valley open to settlement. After interminable conferences with stubborn commissioners, the nontreaty chiefs resignedly acquiesced in the government's ultimatum.

In June 1877, as the Nez Perces made their way slowly toward their new homes, three young men from White Bird's Salmon River band changed the decision of their chiefs. Fired by whiskey, they killed four white settlers. Fearful of swift retribution, the people took refuge among the deep gorges of the Salmon where White Bird's people lived. When cavalry and local militia, ignoring a flag of truce, came charging down the slopes toward their sanctuary, the Nez Perce warriors expertly turned the attack and sent the attackers scampering back up the hill in a demoralizing rout that left the line of retreat littered with dead soldiers.

The fight at White Bird Canyon made war inevitable. Eastward the Indians fled, to the twisted country around the south fork of the Clearwater. Behind them pushed a blue column about four hundred strong. They knew the soldier chief well, for he was one of the commissioners who had insisted that they move: the same one-armed "praying general" who had made peace with the Apache Cochise and now commanded all the troops in the Northwest. On a plateau above the Clearwater, General Howard caught up. For two days they battled, the Indians displaying a surprising talent for fighting in the way that the soldiers fought. Although the soldiers won the field, the Indians made good their escape.

On the night of July 15, as the people rested at a favorite camas ground called Weippe Prairie, the chiefs counseled. Joseph, his brother Ollokot, White Bird, old Toohoolhoolzote—none had a clear plan. Looking Glass did: he proposed a desperate flight across the Bitterroot Mountains to the buffalo plains of Montana. Here, he said, they could find safety with the Crows or, that failing, perhaps even with Sitting Bull in the land of the Great Mother. Some day the trouble would blow over and they could come back home. No one had a better idea, so next morning the cavalcade of eight hundred men, women, and children began the climb to the tortuous Lolo Trail by which, for generations, their people had surmounted the Bitterroots to reach the buffalo ranges beyond.

It was one of history's great—and tragic—odysseys. Across the mountains they trekked, ever mindful of the soldiers pressing up the trail from the rear. Once over the Bitterroots, on Montana's Big Hole River, Looking Glass said they must rest. It was a costly pause, for at daylight on August 9 two hundred soldiers attacked, drove them from their tipis, and felled eighty-nine people. Rallying, the warriors counterattacked, retook the village in savage fighting, and pinned down the soldiers for two days while their families escaped. On they pushed, across the Continental Divide and eastward into the wonderland at the source of the Yellowstone River. Other columns converged to cut them off, but skillfully Joseph and his fellow chiefs slipped around them and at length emerged on the plains of Montana, beating off pursuing cavalry at Canyon Creek.

With the soldiers in this last fight rode Crow Indian scouts. That discovery dashed all thought of sanctuary with the Crows. Sitting Bull remained the last hope. Northward toward the Canadian boundary raced the exhausted Nez Perces, General Howard still pushing hard behind them.

The flight of the Nez Perces, daily chronicled by the white people's newspapers, made the army look supremely inept. General Howard labored mightily to catch up but could never quite succeed. Colonel John Gibbon, marching from forts in western Montana, had taken such a bloody mauling at the Big Hole that he limped back to his stations. In the newly established Yellowstone National Park, the Nez Perces had almost snared a distinguished tourist—General Sherman. Leaving the park, they had outwitted Colonel Samuel D. Sturgis's cavalry column, and a few days later they had defeated him at Canyon Creek. All in all, the army had come off distinctly second to the chief whom the generals now, in embarrassed explanation, called the "red Napoleon." (Actually, Ollokot had more to do with managing the military aspects of the march.) Unless Howard could somehow overtake the fugitives, only one hope remained. A courier rode into Fort Keogh, the headquarters of Bear's Coat Miles, with an appeal from Howard to try to head them off before they reached the international border.

Again Looking Glass said the people had to rest, and again they slowed the journey. Again they paid the penalty, and this time a fatal one. On September 30, on Snake Creek, less than forty miles from Canada, Miles's soldiers attacked. Deadly fire from the Nez Perce rifles shattered the charge and dropped sixty horsemen, but the Indians found the way to safety blocked. For five days the besieged chiefs argued. White Bird and three hundred people slipped through the cordon and gained the Canadian haven, but on October 5, 1877, Chief Joseph faced Bear's Coat as Gen-

Surrender of Chief Joseph. In this painting by Frederic Remington, Joseph faces Colonel Nelson A. Miles while General Oliver O. Howard looks on. The surrender occurred in October 1877 after the defeat of the Nez Perces at Bear Paw Mountain, Montana. *Library of Congress.*

eral Howard looked on from behind. "I am tired of fighting," he said. "Our chiefs are killed. Looking Glass is dead. Toohoolhoolzote is dead. The old men are all dead. It is the young men who say yes or no. He who led the young men [Ollokot] is dead. It is cold and we have no blankets. The little children are freezing to death. . . . Hear me, my chiefs! I am tired. My heart is sick and sad. From where the sun now stands, I will fight no more forever."

Joseph had surrendered upon Miles's promise that he and his people would winter at Fort Keogh and then in the spring go back to the Idaho reservation. But the government repudiated the promise. Like the Modocs, the Nez Perces wound up in Indian Territory, far from their mountain homeland.[18]

Other mountain tribes, neighbors of the Nez Perces, met similar reverses. In 1878 friction with surrounding settlers provoked an outbreak of Bannocks and Paiutes. Again General Howard took the field and, after several engagements, drove the fugitives back to their reservations. A year later a handful of Sheepeater "renegades" collapsed under persistent campaigning by Howard's troops in the forbidding mountains cut by the Salmon River. Also in 1879, Utes of Colorado killed their agent, Nathan Meeker, and took the warpath. Here the stresses came from a fanatic and visionary agent, combined with the designs of whites on mineral deposits newly discovered on the Ute Reservation. The conflict brought forth a chief fully as statesmanlike and sympathetic as Joseph, Ouray, but he could only ease, not avoid, the inevitable collapse of resistance under military pressure.[19]

By 1881, when the surrender of Sitting Bull marked the close of the Plains wars, all tribes of the American West save one had been compelled by military force to go to, or return to, their reservations. Of them all, only the Apaches had not yet been made to face the truth that the reservation represented their only possible destiny. At one place or another in the Southwest, Apache warfare had been virtually continuous since Spanish colonial times. In the early 1870s General Crook had seemed to be on the verge of ending it permanently. His masterful Tonto Basin campaign of 1872–73 had brought about the collapse of the most troublesome Apache groups and their confinement on the reservations set up earlier by Vincent Colyer and General Howard. But Crook went north in 1875, to do less than brilliantly against the Sioux, and the iron military regime relaxed. At the same time the Indian Bureau decided to do away with the multiplicity of small reservations and to concentrate all Apaches west of the Rio Grande on a single reservation. A hot, barren, malarial

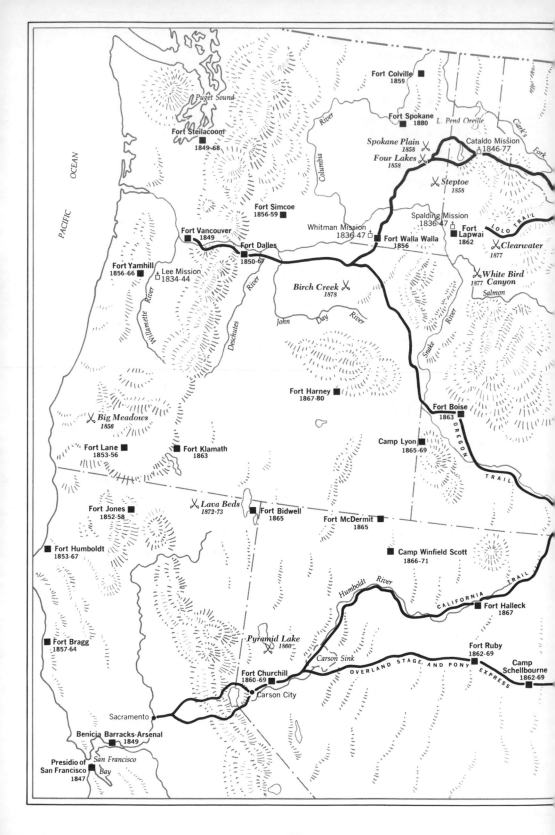

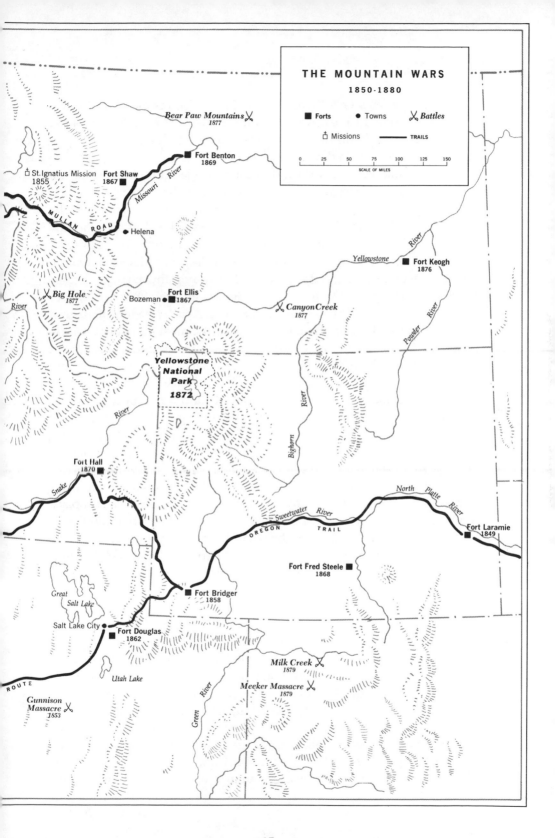

THE MOUNTAIN WARS
1850-1880

■ Forts   ● Towns   ✕ Battles

⌂ Missions   ▬▬▬ TRAILS

0   25   50   75   100   125   150
SCALE OF MILES

Bear Paw Mountains ✕
1877

■ Fort Benton
1869

⌂ St. Ignatius Mission   Fort Shaw
1855   1867 ■

Missouri River

MULLAN ROAD

● Helena

Yellowstone   ■ Fort Keogh
                   1876

✕ Big Hole   Fort Ellis
1877   ■
River   Bozeman ● 1867

✕ Canyon Creek
1877

Powder River

Yellowstone
National
Park
1872

Bighorn River

Fort Hall
1870 ■

Snake River

North Platte River

Sweetwater River

OREGON   TRAIL

Fort Laramie
1849 ■

Fort Fred Steele ■
1868

Great
Salt Lake

■ Fort Bridger
1858

Salt Lake City ●

Fort Douglas
1862 ■

ROUTE

Utah Lake

Green River

Milk Creek ✕
1879

Meeker Massacre ✕
1879

Gunnison
Massacre ✕
1853

flat along Arizona's Gila River, San Carlos was a terrible place to live. The final phases of Indian warfare in the United States grew out of the refusal of two powerful Apache leaders and their followers to settle permanently on the San Carlos Reservation.

These leaders were Victorio and Geronimo. Victorio, of the Mimbres, had learned his skills from the great Mangas Coloradas, whom he equaled in courage, stamina, cunning, and leadership. He wanted peace with the whites, and for a time, with Loco, he had pursued it. But soon he saw that few whites were as trustworthy as the good Lieutenant Drew, and the command to settle at San Carlos banished all such notions. Geronimo, of the Chiricahuas, emerged as a leader shortly after the death of Cochise in 1874. Short, thick, scowling, and ill-tempered, he exhibited few appealing traits, even to his own people. But of all Apache leaders, his cousin later remembered, "Geronimo seemed to be the most intelligent and resourceful as well as the most vigorous and farsighted. In times of danger he was a man to be relied upon."[20] No less than Victorio did Geronimo find the order to move to San Carlos in 1876 offensive.

For two years, 1877–79, Victorio tried to find a solution to the dilemma that the government's concentration program had thrust upon him. He even attempted to live at San Carlos. "That horrible summer!" recalled one of his followers. "There was nothing but cactus, rattlesnakes, heat, rocks, and insects. No game; no edible plants. Many, many of our people died of starvation."[21] Victorio also tried to live on his old reservation at Ojo Caliente, but the government had decided to close that place down. He tried to settle with the Mescaleros on the Fort Stanton Reservation, east of the Rio Grande, but that did not work. In fact, nothing worked, and on September 4, 1879, he and sixty warriors attacked a contingent of black cavalrymen near Ojo Caliente in the opening clash of the Victorio War.

In Texas, New Mexico, and Chihuahua, Victorio exacted a terrible price for the government's attempt to put him at San Carlos. With fresh numbers from the Mescalero Reservation, he counted between 125 and 150 warriors. Here and there they darted with lightning speed, cutting down isolated sheepherders and waylaying hapless travelers. Time and again they eluded the soldiers, both American and Mexican, who combed the mountains and deserts in an exhausting and mostly vain effort to destroy the marauders. In July 1880, in the hot, barren wastes of western Texas, Victorio found himself, for a change, thwarted by hard-riding units of black troopers who expertly kept him from the few waterholes and ultimately forced him into Mexico. Hungry, destitute, and low on ammunition, the raiders began to tire. Eastward they drifted, into the parched deserts of Chihuahua, seemingly without plan or purpose. By October 1880 they camped amid three low peaks rising sharply from the vast desert plain. Tres Castillos, the Mexicans called them.

At dawn on October 15 the Apaches awoke to the crash of gunfire and the shouts of Mexican soldiers and Tarahumara Indian allies. Their horse herd lost, the Indians scrambled up the boulder-strewn slope of one of the hills, and there they fought back. All day and into the night the two sides exchanged fire. In the dark the Indians tried to slip away, but failed. Singing the death chant, they turned to throwing up rock fortifications for a fight to the last. At daybreak they watched as the Mexicans began filtering upward among the boulders. The struggle was desperate and bloody and, in its final stages, hand-to-hand. When the smoke and dust cleared, seventy-eight Apaches lay dead among the rocks and another sixty-eight herded together as captives. Among the dead was Victorio.

At the time of Victorio's death, Geronimo was living, none too contentedly, at San Carlos. Besides its repugnant natural conditions, the reservation festered with intrigue, intertribal rivalries, incompetent and corrupt agents, and conflict between civil and military officials. White settlers pressed in on the reservation boundaries. Almost any spark could touch off an explosion. It came in August 1881. A medicine man had been preaching a new religion that whites regarded as incendiary. In an attempt to arrest him, the army got into a fight with his followers, shot and killed the prophet, and had to quell a mutiny among the Apache scouts. Frightened by the resulting military activity, Geronimo and other leaders, with seventy-four people, broke out and headed for Mexico.

An especially daring raid in the following spring drew attention to the deteriorating state of affairs in Arizona. Geronimo and others swooped down on San Carlos, killed the police chief, and forced old Loco and several hundred people to return to Mexico with them. That event prodded the government to decisive action. Early in September 1882 a familiar figure reappeared in Arizona—the "Gray Fox," General Crook. At once he clamped military rule on San Carlos. To keep the peace here and later to go after the "renegades" in Mexico, he recruited five companies of Apache scouts—"the wildest I could get"—and placed them under his brightest, most energetic young officers. Skilled packers organized efficient and sturdy mule trains. No cumbersome wagons would limit mobility.

The Sierra Madre of Mexico had always afforded Apaches an impregnable fortress. Its steep ridges, piled one on another toward towering peaks and perpetually shadowing plunging gorges and canyons walled

Geronimo. Most famous and feared of all Apache leaders, Geronimo and his Chiricahuas scourged settlements in Mexico as well as the United States. His surrender to General Miles in 1886 marked the end of the Indian Wars. A. Frank Randall made this portrait at San Carlos in 1884. Tombstone photographer C. S. Fly took the group picture (Geronimo at right) at the Canyon de los Embudos conference with General Crook in March 1886. *Museum of New Mexico* and *Smithsonian Institution National Anthropological Archives*.

in vertical rock, sheltered and protected these Indians and provided secure bases for raiding in all directions, on both sides of the international
border. One Chiricahua group, the Nednhis, had made this wilderness
their home for generations. Their chief, Juh, surpassed all others in power.
Geronimo, Nachez (son of Cochise), Chato, Chihuahua, Loco, Bonito,
battle-scarred old Nana (who had ridden with Victorio but had escaped
Tres Castillos), and others deferred to Juh. But one day Juh fell from a
cliffside trail to his death, and increasingly the captains of the Apaches
in the Sierra Madre looked to Geronimo for guidance. From their mountain lairs they continued to raid. In a foray of special ferocity, in March
1883 Chato and twenty-five warriors slashed across Arizona and New
Mexico, and then faded back into Mexico. In response, Crook marched.

A surprise attack by Apache scouts on Chato's camp high in the Sierra
Madre gave notice to all the fugitives that their fortress had been breached.

Where Mexican troops had never ventured, Americans had penetrated, and at the head of other Apaches. It came as enough of a shock that one by one the band leaders drifted in to talk with the Gray Fox. Geronimo, who had been raiding in Chihuahua, came last. Squatting around smoky campfires, the Indians listened to the harsh words of this general who so uncharacteristically wore a canvas suit and rode a mule. Surrender, he told them in a threat that he and all his listeners knew he could not carry out, or he would kill them all. At night, in long arguments among themselves, the chiefs debated what to do. Crook's success in reaching them in previously inaccessible refuges, combined with his ability to enlist their own people against them, tipped the balance. "We give ourselves up," Geronimo at last announced, "do with us as you please."

The surrender turned out to be only temporary. Back at San Carlos, tensions began building almost at once. A people accustomed to freedom found military rule irksome; the men especially bridled at the ban on beating their wives and on brewing the volatile intoxicant *tiswin.* In May 1885 off they went again, some 134 people, including Geronimo, Nachez, Chihuahua, and Nana. Once again they hid themselves deep in the Sierra Madre. Once again they discovered white officers leading their own people against them. And once again they quickly tired of keeping always on the run, always apprehensive of a sudden surprise attack. They sent word to the officer in charge of one of the scout units, Captain Emmet Crawford, that they wanted to talk. But before a meeting could be arranged, Mexican militia attacked the scouts, and the captain fell with a bullet in his brain. Later Geronimo and others met with Crawford's lieutenant, Marion P. Maus, and told him they wanted to talk with General Crook.

The meeting took place at Canyon de los Embudos, twelve miles south of the border, on March 25, 1886. Seated on the sides of a pleasantly shaded ravine, the general and the Apaches parleyed. As he had done two years earlier, Crook spoke sternly. Now the terms were harsher. The men with their families must go to a place of confinement in the East for two years, and only then could they return to San Carlos. Otherwise, Crook vowed, "I'll keep after you and kill the last one, if it takes fifty years." After two days of argument among themselves, the Apache chiefs accepted Crook's terms. While the general hastened north to telegraph the good news to his superiors, the Indians moved slowly toward the border. Along the way they found a whiskey peddler. In the midst of a drinking bout Geronimo and Nachez had second thoughts. With twenty men and thirteen women, they stampeded back to the Sierra Madre.

This development profoundly discouraged General Crook. Worse, it brought him into conflict with General Sheridan, who had succeeded Sherman as head of the army. Sheridan had never trusted the Apache scouts, and he thought Crook should use regulars instead. Now he issued orders that not only implicitly criticized Crook's methods but required him to break his word to the Indians who had not fled with Geronimo and Nachez. Rather than carry out such orders, Crook asked to be relieved. Sheridan lost no time in dispatching a replacement, Nelson A. Miles, now a brigadier general. It was a hard blow to the Gray Fox, for he and Miles had long been bitter rivals, personally as well as professionally. Bear's Coat welcomed the chance to succeed where Crook had failed.

Astutely, Miles made a great show of employing regular soldiers against the Apaches, but in the end he quietly adopted Crook's methods. Apache scouts combed the Sierra Madre, keeping the quarry on the run. As a special peace emissary, Miles sent Lieutenant Charles B. Gatewood, whom the Indians knew as a friend, to see if he could find and persuade them to give up. Ironically, Gatewood was a Crook protégé.

As in the past, the little band of fugitives soon tired of running. On August 24, 1886, they admitted Gatewood and two Indian companions to their camp. At considerable peril to his life, Gatewood stated the new terms: The Apaches must go to Florida and wait for the President to decide their ultimate fate. Geronimo said he and Nachez would give up, but only if they could return to San Carlos. Then Gatewood played his high card. At San Carlos Geronimo would find none of his kinsmen, only rival tribes. All the Chiricahuas, even those who had loyally served Crook as scouts, had been herded aboard railway cars and deported to Florida. Stunned, the Indians debated for a long time, but at last they told Gatewood that they would give up to General Miles personally. In Skeleton Canyon, just north of the border, Geronimo faced Miles and handed over his rifle.

A trainload of Apaches rattling across the Arizona desert toward far-off Florida signaled the end of armed resistance to the reservation system. Every important Indian war since 1870 had been essentially a war not of concentration but of rebellion—of Indians rebelling against reservations they had already accepted in theory if not in fact. Geronimo and his tiny band of followers were the last holdouts, and they only because the wilds of Mexico offered them a haven denied to most other tribes. Thus the wars of the Peace Policy, and indeed the Indian Wars of the United States, came to a close in Skeleton Canyon, Arizona, on September 4, 1886.

7

The Vision of the Reformers, 1865–1890

Mohonk House rambled in tiered splendor along the shore of Lake Mohonk, a glittering sheet of blue nestled in a satellite range of the Catskill Mountains less than a hundred miles up the Hudson River from New York City. Lichen-mottled gray cliffs capped by dark pines rose a hundred feet from the western edge of the lake, and a great chaos of boulders, fissures, caverns, and rock formations gave endless variety to the tumbled landscape. Hiking trails snaked through a wooded wilderness splashed with rail fences, towers, gazebos, and several score of rustic benches with thatched roofs, each named for a prominent guest of the resort. The hotel itself was a great and ever growing caravansary of native rock and wood, girdled on each floor by shaded porches with ornate railings, surmounted by shingled turrets and gables and tall brick chimneys, and everywhere ornamented with no end of the frilly gingerbread turned out so profusely by Victorian lathes. Inside, sleeping rooms and dining room yielded to the centerpiece, a spacious parlor furnished with upholstered couches and wicker chairs, writing desks bright with flowers fresh from the gardens, shelves full of books, and a patterned carpet.

The Lake Mohonk resort boasted a distinctive "spirit," induced and sustained by its owner-proprietors since its founding in 1869. The very embodiment of Quaker gentility, the twin brothers Albert and Alfred Smiley dispensed their own special brand of hospitality with their identical beaming countenances wreathed by neatly trimmed white beard and side whiskers. A "silent code" barred card playing, dancing, Sabbath breaking, and above all strong drink. The parlor contained a pulpit where, each Sunday morning, a guest clergyman or lay churchman preached a sermon. Experts warned that no resort could succeed without a bar, but summer after summer the Smileys filled their guest rooms with doctors,

The inspiration of Albert K. Smiley, right, member of the Board of Indian Commissioners and proprietor of a New York resort hotel, the Lake Mohonk conferences became a major forum for promoting the welfare and "civilization" of the Indians. Each year beginning in 1883 the "friends of the Indian" gathered at Mohonk, above and below, to debate reform measures and formulate the strategy that would win their adoption. *Keith Smiley, Mohonk Mountain House.*

lawyers, clergymen, educators, and public officials with their families—a clientele not of money but of well-bred and well-educated Protestant respectability. Jay Gould and Jim Fiske would not have felt comfortable with the "spirit of Mohonk."[1]

Beginning in October 1883, Lake Mohonk hosted the Indian reform establishment of the United States. Albert, named to the Board of Indian Commissioners in 1879 by President Rutherford B. Hayes, had found the board's January meetings in Washington too hurried and harried for the thoughtful contemplation of the Indian problem. His wife came up with the solution. "Albert," she said, "thee must call a hundred or more to meet at our house, as our guests, and with them organize the Mohonk Conference."[2] He did, and each autumn they came: spokesmen for the Indian Rights Association, the Women's National Indian Association, the

Thomas Jefferson Morgan. Baptist educator and Commissioner of Indian Affairs from 1889 to 1893, Morgan personified the purposes and style of the Mohonk reformers. *State Historical Society of Wisconsin*.

Boston Indian Citizenship Committee, the Ladies' National Indian League, and other reform organizations; members of the Board of Indian Commissioners; representatives of virtually all the Protestant religious press and some from the secular press as well; educators, missionaries, members of Congress, and federal officials. (Suggestively absent: anyone from the Bureau of Catholic Indian Missions, or from Dr. Thomas A. Bland's National Indian Defense Association, which fought for the Indian's right to be an Indian.) For four mornings and evenings the delegates read papers and discussed issues; in the afternoons they strolled the wooded paths or boated on the lake. Thus did Albert K. Smiley's invitation give birth to an institution destined to have decisive impact on United States Indian policy—the Lake Mohonk Conference of the Friends of the Indian.

At the 1889 conference the friends of the Indian glimpsed just how

powerful a force they had become. It was a well-attended gathering, numbering among the faithful former President Hayes and General Oliver O.
Howard. But the delegates especially looked forward to hearing what
the newly named Commissioner of Indian Affairs had to say. Of dignified bearing, bespectacled, bald-headed, with mutton-chop whiskers,
Thomas Jefferson Morgan enjoyed a distinguished reputation as Baptist
clergyman and expert on public education. He had also, in the Civil War,
served as an officer in a volunteer regiment commanded by Colonel Benjamin Harrison. "When President Harrison tendered me the Indian
Bureau," Morgan told the conferees, "he said, 'I wish you to administer
it in such a way as will satisfy the Christian philanthropic sentiment of
the country.' That was the only charge I received from him. I come here,'
where the Christian philanthropic sentiment of the country focuses itself,
to ask what will satisfy you."[3]

Actually, Morgan already knew what would satisfy them. He went on
to give them his own ideas about Indian policy, which, consistent with
his background, heavily emphasized education. But it surely came as no
surprise when his audience enthusiastically applauded his speech and
unanimously pledged their support. For differ as they might on means
and emphasis, these reformers stood solidly together on the basic goals,
and no important federal official ever differed with them on that score.
Morgan, no less than his predecessors back to Grant's presidency, embraced the conventional wisdom of the Indian reformers. Never could
the reformers override the spoils system to dictate appointments, but rarely
did a president appoint high officials of the Indian Bureau who did not
share their fundamental assumptions and aims. Lake Mohonk brought
together the people who had the agenda for the Indian's future as well
as the political power to impose it.

They had the political power in large part because of organization. The
reform movement reached back at least as far as 1867, when the Taylor
Peace Commission began to popularize "conquest by kindness" and the
radical notion that the Indian had rights that for humanity's sake ought
to be respected. But except for Peter Cooper's United States Indian
Commission, which demonstrated the power of organization in the beginnings of Grant's Peace Policy, the movement remained chiefly in the
custody of individual reformers. From lecture platform and pulpit, Wen-
dell Phillips, Lydia Maria Child, and eccentric old John Beeson trumpeted
their outrage over the iniquity of government and the barbarism of frontier whites. In 1874 Alfred B. Meacham joined their ranks. He spoke not
only with eloquence but with authority, for as Oregon Indian superinten-

dent a year earlier he had accompanied General Canby to the Modoc peace talks that ended in slaughter. Wounded almost to death, his scalp restored only with difficulty, Meacham became one of the most effective crusaders for Indian rights. Another who burned with indignation was author Helen Hunt Jackson. She hoped that *A Century of Dishonor*, published in 1881, would do for the Indians what *Uncle Tom's Cabin* had done for the slaves. Although falling short of that goal, her polemic—for the book was scarcely the "history" proclaimed—gained wide circulation and stirred the public conscience.[4]

Besides the individual reformers, other forces fertilized the soil in which the Indian reform organizations flourished. In particular, a new emphasis in Indian policy that marked the late 1870s yielded some controversies that captured public interest. In these years, parallel with the final stages of Indian warfare, policy makers carried the concept of consolidation beyond any previous lengths. In fact, Interior Secretary Columbus Delano and his Indian Commissioner John Q. Smith wanted to consolidate nearly all Indians in Indian Territory, with reservations in Minnesota and Washington to receive the rest.[5] Indian Territory, therefore, came to harbor a great many grievously unhappy Indians, sickening and dying in the unaccustomed climate and pining to return to distant homes.

Three events in particular aroused public sympathy and reinforced what the crusaders were saying. One was the dramatic four-year fight of the Ponca Indians to return to their Nebraska homes from Indian Territory. With the help of influential whites, in 1881 they finally succeeded. Another was the moving plea of Chief Joseph to be allowed to return to his homeland in the Northwest. His surrender at Bear Paw Mountain in 1877 had been conditioned on this, but the government had repudiated Colonel Miles's promise. Joseph's eloquence and persuasive logic touched the hearts of countless Americans but only partly succeeded in its objective. In 1883 and 1885 most of the exiled Nez Perces were allowed to go back to their Idaho reservation, but Chief Joseph had to be content with a home on the Colville Reservation in Washington. And finally, in 1878, in another tragic bid to escape Indian Territory, Dull Knife's and Little Wolf's Cheyennes fled northward toward their old homeland in Montana. For Dull Knife and his people the flight ended in midwinter confinement in unheated barracks at Fort Robinson and, finally, a suicidal attempt at escape in which soldiers gunned down fleeing, unarmed Indians.[6]

Against the backdrop of continuing Indian warfare, the Cheyenne tragedy highlighted the tension that still prevailed between the military and civil approaches to Indian affairs. Agitation for transfer of the Indian Bureau to the War Department rose and fell throughout the 1870s and almost succeeded in the aftermath of the Custer disaster in 1876. On this issue the reformers closed ranks. Ridiculing the army's pretensions as a civilizing agency, charging it with responsibility for most Indian hostilities, and branding soldiers as the source of "lingering, loathsome diseases" and other influences demoralizing to the Indians, they fought the advocates of transfer. Their rhetoric ignored the humanitarian activities of generals such as Howard, Crook, Miles, Grierson, and Pope, but it warded off transfer and helped awaken the conscience of the public on the Indian issue.[7]

From all these forces emerged not only a growing public interest in the Indian but the organization the Indian reform movement lacked. The Ponca controversy led directly to the formation, in 1879, of the Boston Indian Citizenship Committee, and one after another similar groups sprang up: the Women's National Indian Association, the Ladies' National Indian League, and the most powerful of all, the Indian Rights Association.

The Indian Rights Association all but belonged to Herbert Welsh. He created it, he nurtured it, and as its secretary he provided the energetic and efficient leadership that made it the dominant Indian reform group for two decades. A slim youth with thinning hair and neat mustache, scion of an aristocratic Philadelphia family, he drew his interest in Indian affairs from his uncle, William Welsh, first (but very briefly) chairman of the Board of Indian Commissioners and a stormy activist throughout the 1870s. In the summer of 1882 Herbert and a friend toured the Great Sioux Reservation of Dakota. They returned fired with zeal to civilize the Indians, and the following December, in Welsh's parlor, they called together some thirty kindred minds to give birth to the Indian Rights Association. Through an efficient fact-finding apparatus, an unceasing stream of publications, a network of local branches, a heavy schedule of lectures, connections to press and pulpit, and a paid Washington lobbyist, Welsh and the Indian Rights Association swiftly gained an ascendancy acknowledged by all the rest, and an influence that no Washington politician could ignore.[8]

And so the reformers brought to Mohonk not only a vision of the Indian's destiny but the organization to fight for it in congressional chambers and government offices. It was true, as western critics pointed out, that they were few in number and came almost entirely from New England and the Middle Atlantic states—far from the frontier and comfortably distant from real Indians. It was not true, as enemies such as Kansas Senator Preston B. Plumb charged, that their "barrels of tears, oceans of sympathy" flowed amid ignorance of the actual conditions and needs of the Indians.[9] Although based in the East, the reform groups sent investigators to the West to gather accurate, up-to-date information to guide their deliberations, to buttress their initiatives, and to turn against their opponents. They also formed constituencies throughout the nation—or at least that part of it on their side of the ninety-fifth meridian. Some were local chapters of their own societies, but most were church groups and other public-spirited organizations that would mobilize on the political battle lines when the reformers sounded the trumpet. To such organization the reformers owed one victory after another.

The men and women who gathered each autumn at Lake Mohonk to chart the Indian's future were basically the kind of people who made the Smiley brothers' resort a success—well-educated, comfortably well-off business and professional people, respected pillars of their communities, Protestant, deeply religious, practicing Christian living on a daily basis, moral, patriotic, in every way "Americans" in the conventional image of the 1880s. They were people like Clinton B. Fisk, founder of Fisk University for black freedmen and the Prohibition candidate for president in 1888, who authoritatively presided at the conferences; theologian Lyman Abbott, editor of the *Christian Union*, excelled by none in outspoken certitude; crusading Amelia Strong Quinton, lavishing great stores of energy both on the cause of the Indian and the cause of temperance; Massachusetts patrician Henry L. Dawes, a power in the U.S. Senate; Samuel C. Armstrong, founder and master of the pioneering black academy, Hampton Institute; and, of course, the virtuous Smiley brothers themselves. All brought to Mohonk a deep and abiding interest in the Indian and an inflexible commitment to giving him a bright future. They saw nothing worth saving from his past, and they had not the slightest doubt of the rightness and righteousness of their vision of his destiny.

This vision of the ideal Indian sharply delineated the dominant self-image of late nineteenth-century American society. It was a vision of an "Americanized" American Indian. By the 1880s and 1890s "Americanism" had come rather specifically, despite conventional platitudes about separation of church and state, to represent virtually a fusion of nationalism and Protestantism. A clergyman stated it explicitly to the Lake Mohonk conferees in 1890. "This Book," he said, speaking of the Bible, "furnishes the wheat out of which the bread of republics is made."[10] Mingling dogma as well as institutions, Americanism not only celebrated the nation's stirring history and the distinctive evangelical roots that ran deeply in its soil; it also rejected the "un-American" thought and ways and the predominantly Catholic religion of the immigrants now reaching American shores in numbers alarming to the older stock. The ideal American citizen lived a Christian life according to Protestant precepts, supported himself by labors propelled and guided by the Puritan work ethic, took the duties and privileges of citizenship with high seriousness, and loved his country and her institutions with uncritical patriotic fervor. The great melting pot that was America would cast the European immigrants in this form. American Indian policy would do likewise for the American Indian.[11]

In contrast to the immigrant, the American Indian presented a special challenge because of what the reformers saw as a legacy of savagery and heathenism that ran back to hazy antiquity. But consistent with the doctrine of progress still in vogue—and indeed validated by the perfection everywhere to be seen in American society—the Indian held the potential for swift advance. Even before the reform movement blossomed in the 1880s, this assumption had been scientifically questioned by no less an authority than Lewis Henry Morgan, the "father of American anthropology." Morgan accepted the idea of progress, but his studies of the American Indians led him to warn of its slow workings.[12] His skepticism went unheeded; impatiently, the reformers strove for quick results.

The agenda for attaining the reformers' vision contained little that was new. Most of the items figured importantly in Grant's Peace Policy, and some went back to colonial times. Civilization (that is, Americanism), agricultural self-support, education and Christianity (inseparable in reformist thinking), protection and punishment according to law (Anglo-Saxon law, not Indian law), and title to land in severalty—all fitted neatly into the reformers' blueprint. All interacted to reach for their vision in a two-stage process.

The first step was to "detribalize," or as also expressed to "individualize," the Indian: Break his tribal ties, dissolve his communal customs and thought patterns, and emphasize his family as the basic social and economic unit. Protestant evangelicalism demanded *individual* salvation. American citizenship demanded *individual* responsibility under the law. Agricultural self-support demanded *individual* labor according to the Puritan work ethic, on land *individually* owned. Between the Americanized American Indian and God, government, and the promise of worldly gain for honest toil, there was no place for the tribe.

Once the individual had broken free of his tribal heritage, the reformers' program would power the final stage, the leap into the mainstream of American life. No longer, as in the 1870s, did theorists think in terms of consolidating all Indians on a few big reservations but rather of getting rid of the reservations altogether, and as swiftly as possible. Now the Indian would be indistinguishable from all other Americans. Except for color, of course. But that was never mentioned. The reformers freely tossed about words like assimilation and absorption, but always in political, social, or economic terms. Like their predecessors in Grant's time and earlier, they ignored the racial implications of their program. Delicately, as befitted Victorian notions of propriety, they avoided talking about the mingling of red and white blood.

The reformers' agenda included still another item, one with a long history, mainly of futility. This was the effort to purify the administration of Indian affairs. If all went as designed, the reservations, and indeed even the Indian Bureau, would become self-liquidating. For the time being, however, they were necessary evils—"half-way houses" on the road to the ultimate state of grace. Therefore, the bureaucracy that manned them had to be purged of all the old evils of incompetence, corruption, and spoilsmanship. The better the administrators carried out the reservation programs, the sooner the whole apparatus could wither away, and the quicker all Indians could be submerged in the great body politic of America.[13]

In the Indian reform crusade of the 1880s, four issues overshadowed all others, both in their potential consequences for the Indians and in the zeal with which the reformers attacked them: land, education, law, and purification of the Indian Bureau. Give the Indian fee ownership in his own plot of land. Educate him in preparation for citizenship and self-support. Extend law for his protection against whites and other Indians. Upgrade reservation management in order to speed the civilization process and the ultimate dissolution of the reservations. On these measures the reformers deliberated and debated in a quest for the best design; behind them they mobilized the swelling public support they commanded among Americans increasingly conscience-smitten over their nation's treatment of the Indians.

Land in severalty spoke to many fine aspirations of the reformers. It would break down tribal loyalties and help to "individualize" the Indian. It would give him a firm base, secure against white aggression, for becoming self-supporting. Perhaps most important, it would provide him with the means and the incentive to better himself as he watched the fruits of his toil blossom each year in the soil. As Amherst President Merrill E. Gates observed at Lake Mohonk, the Indian had to be made "intelligently selfish," got "out of the blanket and into trousers,—and trousers with a pocket in them, and with a *pocket that aches to be filled with dollars!*"[14] The individual allotment afforded the ideal incubator for this process. And never lost sight of, even in reformist thinking, allotment would hasten the day when the reservation could be abolished altogether and the surplus land opened to white homesteaders. This argument appealed to almost everyone. "It is evident," observed the Board of Indian Commissioners in 1879, "that no 12,000,000 acres of the public domain whose hills are full of ores, and whose valleys are waiting for diligent hands to 'dress them and keep them,' in obedience to the divine command, can long be kept simply as a park, in which wild beasts are hunted by wilder men."[15]

The battle to win severalty legislation occupied the reformers in an ever more suspenseful crusade throughout the 1880s. Although severalty bills surfaced in the Congress in the 1870s, the movement gathered momentum with the introduction of legislation in 1880 by Texas Senator Richard Coke. But severalty came to be the unique cause and possession of Coke's successor as chairman of the Senate Indian Committee, Henry L. Dawes of Massachusetts, a yearly stalwart at the Lake Mohonk conferences and among all senators the special pleader for Indian rights. Severalty encountered a scattering of opposition, mainly from Senator Henry M. Teller of Colorado. "There is not a wild Indian living who knows what a fee-simple is," he declared, and he prophesied that "when thirty or forty years shall have passed and these Indians shall have parted with their title, they will curse the hand that was raised professedly in their defense to secure this kind of legislation."[16] But the Senate, as always anxious to do right by the Indians, ignored Teller's warning. The obstacles arose rather in the House of Representatives, and those were not of substantive opposition but rather amounted to a preoccupation with politically more pressing issues. At one point, for example, the House came breathtakingly close to a vote on severalty, only to turn suddenly to debate on the dairy farmers' plea for protection of butter against the insidious competition of oleomargarine. But at last the reformers had their victory. On February 8, 1887, President Grover Cleveland signed into law the Dawes General Allotment Act.

Hailed by reformers everywhere, the Dawes Act of 1887 seemed the key to the vision of the Indian citizen, blissfully freed of the reservation incubus, and dwelling happily and productively as a yeoman farmer on his western homestead. It authorized the President to cause the Indian reservations to be surveyed and classified for farming or grazing. Each head of family could receive 160 acres of farmland, each single male adult

Henry L. Dawes. Patrician senator from Massachusetts and Mohonk faithful, Dawes led the fight for severalty and gave his name to the Dawes General Allotment Act of 1887. Reformers acclaimed the act a triumph; history has judged it a tragedy. *Library of Congress*.

80, and each child 40; for lands suited mainly for grazing, the amounts could be doubled. The actual title would not be conveyed immediately but rather held in trust by the government for twenty-five years, this to prevent alienation to acquisitive whites until the civilization process equipped the Indian to make enlightened decisions. In anticipation of Indian resistance to the program, the law provided that, four years after allotment began on a reservation, the government could proceed to select lands for any Indian who had failed to make his own selection. After allotments, or before in the discretion of the Secretary of the Interior, the government could negotiate the purchase of surplus reservation lands and throw them open to white homesteading. The proceeds from the subsequent sale of these lands to whites would also be used for the Indian benefit. Finally, Indians who took allotments automatically became United States citizens, subject to both civil and criminal laws of the state or territory in which they lived.

For the most part the reformers were jubilant. A few wondered if the Indians were ready for homesteads and citizenship, but they wondered softly. More representative was the paean of the Indian Rights Association's Washington agent, who compared the Dawes Act to the Magna Charta, the Declaration of Independence, and the Emancipation Proclamation all rolled into one.[17] Senator Dawes saw the law as leading inexorably to the dissolution of the reservation system and to the assimilation of all Indians into American life. Answering some mildly expressed doubts at the 1887 Lake Mohonk conference, he declared: "It seems to me that this is a self-acting machine that we have set going, and if we only run it on the track it will work itself all out, and all these difficulties that have troubled my friend will pass away like snow in the springtime, and we will never know when they go: we will only know that they are gone."[18]

Side by side with severalty as a key plank in the reformers' platform went education. No reformer ever stated the goal of education better than one of the Indian pupils periodically put on display at Lake Mohonk. "I believe in education," said the boy, "because I believe it will kill the Indian that is in me and leave the man and citizen."[19] Besides instruction in the English language, the education program placed heavy emphasis on the manual skills—farming, carpentry, blacksmithing, and the like for boys, cooking, sewing, and cleaning for the girls. Indian education had two other major goals: Christianity and Americanism. "Civilization is a plant of exceedingly slow growth," observed Commissioner of Indian Affairs Hiram Price in 1882, "unless supplemented by Christian teaching and influences."[20] The school as well as the mission church provided an instrument for the inculcation of Christian virtues. Likewise, the schools fostered patriotism—American, not tribal. Commissioner Morgan made this goal explicit in an 1889 directive spelling out requirements for displaying and honoring the American flag, singing patriotic songs, and observing national holidays. Teachers, instructed Morgan, "should endeavor to awaken reverence for the nation's power, gratitude for its beneficence, pride in its history, and a laudable ambition to contribute to its prosperity." While pursuing these aims with their pupils, teachers also "should carefully avoid any unnecessary reference to the fact that they are Indians."[21]

The reformers made impressive gains during the 1880s in getting the government into the education business. Acknowledging the identity of education and Christianity, Indian schools had traditionally been the spe-

Henry M. Teller. Senator from Colorado and Interior Secretary under President Arthur (1882–85), Teller allied himself with land boomers and others who would exploit the Indian. He opposed severalty but gave strong support to education. *Denver Public Library Western History Department.*

cial preserve of the missionaries. In 1880, however, Congress appropriated $150,000 for Indian education, and by 1887 the figure had risen to more than a million dollars. High federal officials joined the reformers in urging Congress to yield still more. Even Henry M. Teller, who as a senator fought so stubbornly against severalty, as Interior Secretary vigorously promoted education. Indeed, the money came faster than the officials could use it to create a system of government schools. Instead they turned to the missionary groups, where they found eagerly open hands. Thus about half the appropriations went for "contract schools" in which the missionaries, with partial federal funding, carried out the government's (and their own) educational goals.

The contract school experiment precipitated a nasty feud between Protestants and Catholics. Historically more energetic in missionary and edu-

Henry B. Whipple. One of the most durable and respected of the reformers, Whipple began to influence policy as early as 1859. As Episcopal Bishop of Minnesota, he knew Indians firsthand, and for more than forty years he championed their cause with an effective blend of reason and hyperbole. *Library of Congress.*

cational work among Indians, its Bureau of Catholic Indian Missions adept at manipulating the Washington political levers, the Catholic church soon outdistanced all rivals in the amount of government money garnered for contract schools. Horrified by the spectacle of federal funds promoting Romanism among the Indians, Protestants fought back by uniting behind a move to replace all contract schools with government schools. For Protestants, this was the lesser of two evils: they disliked losing their own contracts, but they could be assured that government schools, like the public schools, would exclude Catholic dogma while fostering Protestant verities.

The fight reached a peak, both of combativeness and public vituperation, during the tenure of Thomas J. Morgan as head of the Indian Bureau, from 1889 to 1893. Already, as a Baptist educator, Morgan had castigated parochial schools as a "challenge to everything we Americans cherish today." Now, as Commissioner of Indian Affairs, he worked hard to substitute government schools for contract schools of whatever denomination. Stigmatizing Morgan as "a full-blooded religious bigot . . . an arrogant, dictatorial, domineering fanatic," Father Joseph A. Stephan, head of the Bureau of Catholic Indian Missions, led the Catholic counterattack. Morgan did not win quick victory, but he set in motion a process that by 1900 had phased out all the contract schools.[22]

Not only did Catholics and Protestants brawl over education. The three kinds of schools that made up the system set passionate critics against equally passionate defenders. Day schools sprouted across the reservations in the vicinity of the Indian camps. Because near home, they could draw large numbers of pupils. But also because near home, they relinquished the children each evening to a family environment scarcely conducive to rapid acculturation. By contrast, the reservation boarding schools, usually a fixture of the agency, could hold the children comparatively distant from home influences, though not from scenes and values of the reservation communuity. Actually, a good case could be made for both kinds—for day schools to impart the rudiments of reading, writing, and arithmetic to beginners, and for boarding schools to provide the advanced work of industrial training for boys and domestic training for girls.

Much the more severe controversy erupted over reservation schools versus off-reservation schools, and in the thick of the dispute raged the vigorous chief of the first and greatest of the off-reservation schools, Carlisle. Captain Richard Henry Pratt had served as jailer to the Plains Indians imprisoned in Florida after the Red River War and had discovered his life's calling. With some of these Indians and the unused military barracks at Carlisle, Pennsylvania, he had enlisted government backing to found the Carlisle Indian School in 1879. Here, hundreds or even thousands of miles from the countervailing influences of tipi and wickiup, he could truly experiment with the civilizing process. Dogmatic, stubborn, inflexible, outspoken, combative, and above all determined, Pratt championed his theories for a quarter of a century. He warred against the Indian Bureau and its entrenched bureaucracy, which he would have abolished, along with the reservations, had he been able. He warred against ethnologists and anthropologists, the U.S. Bureau of Ethnology, and all others who glorified or even studied Indian culture. He warred against all critics of his ideas, especially critics of his school, and he fought against those of like mind who simply believed that he wanted to go too fast.

Pratt advocated sudden, total immersion, as he told a religious convention in 1883: "In Indian civilization I am a Baptist because I believe in immersing the Indians in our civilization and when we get them under holding them there until they are thoroughly soaked."[23] The soaking process had to take place a long way from the reservation. Carlisle provided the model. He would establish enough Carlisles to accommodate all the Indian children of the United States, enroll them by force if necessary, and from these prep schools in civilization feed them into the public school system and thus into American life. As Pratt told Lyman Abbott, the solution to the Indian problem lay in putting all the Indians on special trains which would crisscross the nation dropping off seven Indians in each county.[24] Pratt could display some impressive specimens of his work, and he did so regularly at world's fairs and other exhibitions. And Carlisle did in truth serve as a model for other off-reservation schools, in Indian Territory, Kansas, Nebraska, and Oregon, but never on the scale Pratt judged essential.

Despite all the furor over means, the reformers shared the basic faith in and commitment to education as a crucial bridge between savagery and civilization. After 1880, in contrast to earlier years, the possibility and thus the necessity of Indian education never occasioned serious debate, only how much to spend and what to spend it for. Education represented the second great triumph of the reformers.

The third major quest of the reformers was to give the Indians a system of law to replace the sanctions of their traditional society. The proposition seemed simple on its face, but it plunged reformers into a legal quagmire and embroiled them in endless controversies. Traditionally the United States had regarded Indians as members of the "domestic dependent nations" of John Marshall's formulation and thus, consistent with the treaty relationship, subject to tribal governance. Now they lived on reservations, their tribal institutions collapsing under government assault, the agent supreme in all his individual caprice, and no system in place to ensure uniform treatment in matters of injury or dispute—between Indians, between Indians and whites, or between Indians and their government overseers. No longer citzens of "domestic dependent nations," and not yet citizens of the United States, Indians existed in a nightmarish realm of legal chaos.

Administrative stratagems filled part of the void. As a means of preserving order without calling on the army, the Indian Bureau established Indian police forces on most of the reservations. Though wholly a tool of the agent and thus subject to misuse, the police generally proved highly effective. More dubious of purpose were the Courts of Indian Offenses. Indian judges presided, and, although they performed good service in mediating disputes, their principal task was to enforce a list of "Indian offenses" compiled by the Indian Bureau and aimed not at the usual criminal offenses or civil disputes but at feasts and dances, the practices of medicine men, and a large body of customs judged "demoralizing and barbarous." Such expedients could not be regarded as substitutes for a code of laws and a system of jurisprudence.[25]

The issue burst dramatically in 1883. On the Sioux reservation of Dakota, intricate currents of tribal politics blew up a blood feud between Crow Dog and the longtime Brule chief Spotted Tail. In an act of cold-blooded murder uncomplicated by any hint of open combat or self-defense, Crow Dog gunned down Spotted Tail. The territorial courts moved in at once and Crow Dog wound up in the dock convicted of murder and sentenced to die. But in December 1883, in a landmark decision, the U.S. Supreme Court ordered him freed. The United States, the justices ruled in *Ex Parte Crow Dog*, had no jurisdiction over crimes committed by one Indian against another. In 1885 the Congress met this crisis by extending U.S. jurisdiction over Indians for seven major crimes, but this, like Indian police and judges, still left great legal needs uncovered.

In reformist debates, the issue of law became entangled with the issue of citizenship. Only a year after *Ex Parte Crow Dog*, the Supreme Court, in *Elk v. Wilkins*, had also ruled definitively on the question of citizenship: Indians would not be citizens until made so by Congress. Many activists urged this step, not only as a means of clarifying the Indian's legal status, but also as a means also of automatically taking care of the need for law: Indian citizens would stand in the same relationship to law as white citizens. Others, fearing demoralizing haste or constitutional objections, preferred to harness citizenship to land in severalty and thus let the orderly process of allotment take care of law as it took care of citizenship. Senator Dawes led these forces, and in the General Allotment Act of 1887 his view prevailed. But a substantial block of the reform community still believed fervently that law should be promptly thrown over the Indians. Professor James Bradley Thayer of Harvard Law School spoke for these people. Dawes, convinced that the slower pace of allotment provided essential protection to the Indian, opposed Thayer and managed to scuttle all attempts in the Congress to enact his program.[26]

Unlike severalty and education, the reformers' record on law and citizenship turned out to be mixed. This happened because the reformers themselves were badly divided on tactics, and also because Congress partly

Reformers looked to education as a major tool in transforming the Indians into copies of white Christian farmers. Richard Henry Pratt's Carlisle in Pennsylvania was the flagship of the off-reservation boarding schools. Pratt (above) remained in the army, on detached duty, throughout his entire quarter century as school superintendent; this portrait was made about 1898.

addressed the need in the Major Crimes Act of 1885 and in the Dawes Severalty Act of 1887. As issues, law and citizenship thus sputtered along into the future, now and then agitated but never wholly resolved, until, as Dawes had advocated, they faded into larger issues.

In contrast to law and citizenship, purification of the Indian Bureau found no crack in the reformers' unity. All believed in it fervently, and all labored together to bring it about. But like law and citizenship, the record showed less success than failure.

As a surge of clean wind, the Hayes administration swept into the Interior Department in 1877. Friends of the Indian hailed a new day as an able, honest, crusading Secretary took over from the scandal-wracked Columbus Delano. With characteristic energy and gusto, Carl Schurz embarked on a thorough housecleaning. Not even a faint stain of corruption would touch his department, especially the Indian Bureau. But the bright promise faded. Schurz at once clashed with Indian friends by op-

(*Opposite*) Sioux girls arrive at Carlisle as part of the first class, in October 1879. The first graduating class (above), 1889, impressed reformers, but the Carlisle diploma had no more relevance to the realities of the reservation than the hair styles, starched collars, and bustles of the graduation portrait. *Yale University Library.*

223

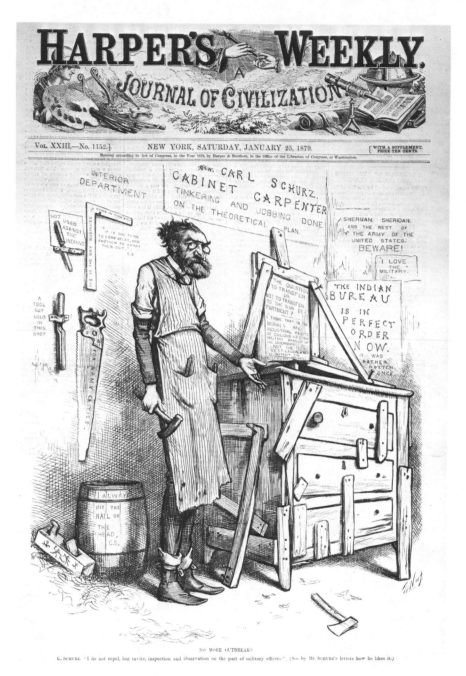

Carl Schurz, President Hayes' energetic Secretary of the Interior (1877–81), set forth to reform Indian policy and clean up the Indian Bureau, only to discover his Indian commissioner deep in fraud. The cartoon in an 1879 issue of *Harper's Weekly* chides Schurz during a wordy and vitriolic battle with General Sheridan that reflected no credit on either combatant. *Library of Congress* and *State Historical Society of Wisconsin*.

Carl Schurz, a German emigré, served as President Hayes's reformist Secretary of the Interior. *National Archives.*

posing their views in the Ponca controversy, and in the end, as he grappled with substantive matters, the dirt settled back in unnoticed. His Commissioner of Indian Affairs, Ezra A. Hayt, got caught in fraudulent transactions on the San Carlos Reservation in Arizona, and an outraged Schurz summarily fired him.[27] Thereafter, in spite of a succession of presidents, secretaries, and commissioners who said all the right words and appeared to be trying hard to cleanse the machinery, it was business as usual in the Indian Bureau and its field service.

On the reservations employees came and went with the rise and fall of the political fortunes of their mentors. The spoils system reigned supreme, squeezing out all considerations of merit. Many were unfit for their jobs, many corrupt, many both. Herbert Welsh told of a state governor who laughingly admitted that for party hacks fit for nothing else, he could usually find jobs in the Indian Service.[28] An Indian inspector reported finding an "abandoned woman" running an Indian school, a lunatic in charge of another.[29] Until good competent people could be placed in the reservation posts, reformers knew, the civilization programs could not work their magic, and the reservations could not be abolished.

The communicants at Lake Mohonk looked to civil service reform as the all-encompassing panacea. A national civil service movement was then gaining momentum, and a statutory basis existed in the Pendleton Civil

Service Act of 1883. The Indian reformers pressured presidents to extend the provisions of the Pendleton Act to all positions in the Indian Bureau. The Indian Rights Association took the lead. Its publications cited flagrant abuses and gathered political support; its Washington lobbyist worked assiduously.

The reformers elicited much fine rhetoric but little more. A committee of Lake Mohonk conferees, for example, called on President-elect Grover Cleveland early in 1885 and obtained what they interpreted as favorable responses to their pleas not to turn out competent employees of the previous administration. And that autumn at Lake Mohonk, Cleveland's Superintendent of Indian Schools, John H. Oberly, urged his audience to "thank the Lord that the Democratic Party has come into power, and is determined to make merit and competency, instead of partisan considerations, paramount tests."[30] Yet within a year, virtually every Republican agent had yielded to a Democrat, and lesser reservation functionaries had almost all been replaced too. President Harrison's appointees uttered similar fine words, only to inaugurate a plan called "Home Rule," under which Republican senators and congressmen dictated appointments in their home districts.

In truth, whatever their personal convictions, political leaders were prisoners of the spoils system, and only slowly, against stubbornly entrenched habit, could reformers make headway. At last, however, they made a first modest breakthrough. It came as a reward for persistence, but especially as a response to the terrible tragedy at Wounded Knee in 1890. But for a woefully incompetent agent, the Ghost Dance excitement might have been contained and Wounded Knee avoided. The reformers made the most of the opportunity, and on April 13, 1891, President Harrison extended the civil service rules to cover medical and educational posts in the Indian Bureau. It was an encouraging beginning, one that moved the reformers to press forward toward the more substantial gains that came later.

Not amid the cushioned comforts of Lake Mohonk, but on the reservations, where spoilsmen ran the programs, were the theories of the reformers put to the test. Lake Mohonk provided the perfect setting for spinning the theories, for it so perfectly mirrored the life and values of the reformers themselves, and therefore the life and values considered ideal for the Indians. But the polished lobby of Mohonk House differed from the hard environment and society of the reservation as night differed from day, and what seemed so ideal and attainable at Mohonk proved considerably less so on the reservation. There, to their pain and sorrow, several generations of Indians were fated to grapple with the legacy of Mohonk.

8

The Reservation, 1880–1890

Sioux Falls, South Dakota, sported a festive air as the United States District Court opened on April 23, 1891. The streets teemed with townspeople, farmers, rough-hewn frontiersmen, and reporters from eastern newspapers come to cover the trial of a bewildered Sioux youth of twenty-two named Plenty Horses. He stood charged with the murder of an army officer during the recent Ghost Dance troubles on the Pine Ridge Reservation. His acquittal on the grounds that he acted as a combatant during a state of war made legal history, and his trial, incidentally, drew a stark contrast between the theories evolved at Lake Mohonk and their actual workings on the reservation. But the trial also set the stage for a scene somberly symbolic of what had happened to the Indians of the American West in the short span of a decade.

On the edge of town an imaginative entrepreneur had built a corral and succeeded in assembling a herd of seventeen buffalo. The eastern visitors and, for that matter, the local residents themselves came to gawk at the shaggy, lumbering animals. Most had never seen one in the flesh. Among the viewers was a delegation of Sioux brought from Pine Ridge Agency to testify in the trial. The sight of the buffalo gave such joy to the Indians that they cavorted about like excited children. Broken Arm and He Dog even climbed into the pen and tried to hug the animals, only to be thrown roughly aside by a surly shake of the head. They then, as a reporter described it, "scampered about, although at the risk of their lives, and in general made so free with the animals that the latter looked around as though dazed at the proceedings."[1]

Scarcely twenty-five years earlier, perhaps thirteen million buffalo darkened the Great Plains. They provided the Plains Indians with food and almost every other material want and contributed vitally to the shape of

Plenty Horses. A Carlisle graduate, the Sioux youth shot and killed an army officer during the Ghost Dance troubles of 1890—to "make a place for myself among
my people," he testified. Tried for murder, he was set free when the court found
that he had acted as a belligerent during a state of war. He is shown here at Fort
Meade, South Dakota, in the spring of 1891. *Library of Congress*.

The slaughter of the buffalo doomed the Plains Indians' way of life and forced them to settle on reservations. Indians and whites alike were responsible, but the main culprits were the hide-hunters who killed the buffalo for their hides alone and left their carcasses by the millions to rot on the prairie. From Richard I. Dodge, *The Plains of the Great West* .

their political and social institutions and spiritual beliefs. They made possible the nomadic way of life that had endured for more than a century. In 1867–68 the Union Pacific Railroad divided the buffalo into two great herds, northern and southern. In 1871 an eastern tannery hit upon buffalo hides as a source of commercial leather. By the hundreds "hide hunters" spread over the Plains, slaughtering the buffalo at the rate of three million a year. By 1878 the southern herd had been obliterated. By 1883 a scientific expedition could find only two hundred buffalo in all the West.[2]

For the Plains Indians, the disappearance of the buffalo was a shattering cultural catastrophe, and it had another portentous consequence: it left no alternative to the reservation. Now a breakout from the reserva-

At first the reservation Indians lived in their traditional dwellings but later, responding to official pressures to adopt white ways, moved into dark, unhealthful cabins. Left is Sitting Bull's camp on the Standing Rock Reservation in 1883 or 1884. Right is a typical Sioux cabin on the Pine Ridge Reservation. *Denver Public Library Western History Department.*

tion no longer held the hope of old that food could be found and pursuing bluecoats eluded or fought off. For the first time the reservation actually offered a testing ground for the government's civilization program. In other parts of the West, too, outside the buffalo ranges, Indians confronted a similar reality. Game and other resources that supported a roving life of freedom—not least of these resources open land itself—shrank as swiftly as the country filled up with white settlers.

"All our people now were settling down in square gray houses, scattered here and there across this hungry land," recalled the holy man Black Elk of the Teton Sioux Reservation in the 1880s, "and around them the Wasichus had drawn a line to keep them in. . . . The people were in despair. . . . Hunger was among us often now, for much of what the Great Father in Washington sent us must have been stolen by Wasichus

231

who were crazy to get money. There were many lies, but we could not eat them. The forked tongue made many promises."[3]

Life was every bit as bleak as Black Elk remembered, and it grew bleaker as nostalgia burnished yet more brightly the memory of the old free life that had been lost. It could never be recaptured, for now the line that so disturbed Black Elk truly locked the people in, forcing them to cope with rather than run from the efforts of government agents to destroy all vestiges of the old life. On most of the reservations the story was basically the same, varied only by personality, plot, and tempo. Black Elk's people, the Sioux, offer graphic personification of a process repeated among Indians all over the West.[4]

The Great Sioux Reservation, legacy of the Fort Laramie Treaty of 1868, sprawled over the southwestern quarter of Dakota Territory. Even after the cession of the Black Hills in 1877, it encompassed some 43,000 square miles of arid plains stretching westward from the Missouri River. The tribes of Teton Sioux held the land in common, but for administrative purposes they reported to six separate agencies. On the Missouri River, Hunkpapa, Blackfoot, Sans Arc, Miniconjou, and Two Kettle Sioux drew rations at Standing Rock and Cheyenne River agencies. To the south and west, Oglalas enrolled at Pine Ridge and Brules at Rosebud. These agencies had been established in 1878 as successors to Red Cloud and Spotted Tail agencies, which were abandoned at last because they lay outside the reservation, in Nebraska. Smaller and less important, Lower Brule and Crow Creek completed the six. Some sixteen thousand Tetons resided on the Great Sioux Reservation during the 1880s. Few, even among the half who had stayed on the reservation during the great wars of 1876–81, had been sufficiently contaminated by white associations to affect their clear cultural identity as the powerful, free-spirited people that for more than a century had dominated the northern Plains.

Some determined to keep this identity at all costs. Predictably, one was Sitting Bull. Following a three-year confinement at Fort Randall, he came to Standing Rock Agency in 1883 as stubbornly resistant as ever to all the ways of the white man. In James McLaughlin he encountered an agent as stubborn and possibly as able as he. The powerful support of the Catholic church insulated McLaughlin from the spoils system, and a half-Sioux wife gave him a window on his Indians that was denied most agents. With time out to tour Europe as an attraction of Buffalo Bill's Wild West Show, Sitting Bull feuded incessantly with McLaughlin, contesting his every initiative for civilization and struggling with him for domination of the Standing Rock Sioux. "Crafty, avaricious, mendacious, and ambitious,"

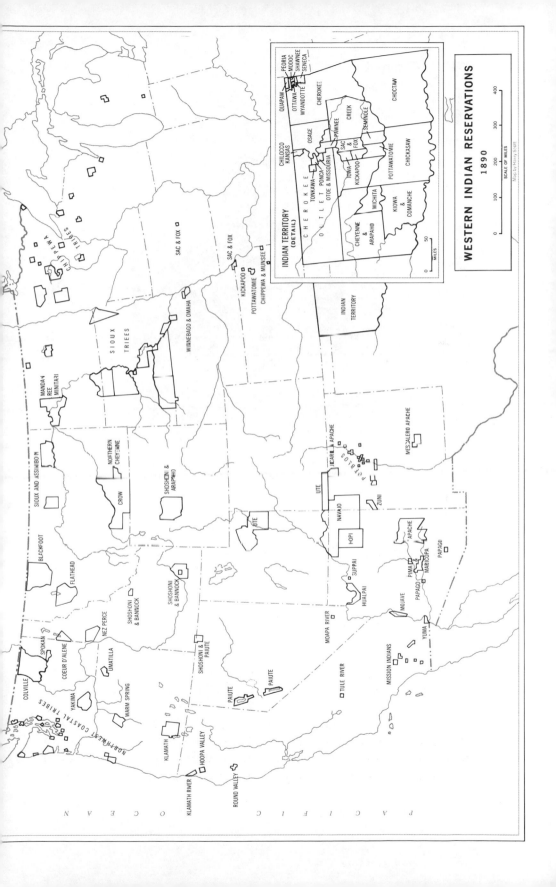

WESTERN INDIAN RESERVATIONS

1890

Map by Harry Scott

SCALE OF MILES

0   100   200   300   400

INDIAN TERRITORY
(DETAIL)

0   50   100

MILES

QUAPAW	PEORIA
	MODOC
OTTAWA	SHAWNEE
WYANDOTTE	SENECA

CHILOCCO
KANSAS

CHEROKEE

OSAGE

CHEROKEE

TONKAWA

PONCA

OTOE & MISSOURI

SAC & FOX

PAWNEE

CREEK

SEMINOLE

CHOCTAW

IOWA & KICKAPOO

POTTAWATOMIE

CHICKASAW

TONKAWA

WICHITA

KIOWA & COMANCHE

CHEYENNE & ARAPAHO

INDIAN TERRITORY

CHIPPEWA TRIBES

SAC & FOX

KICKAPOO

POTTAWATOMIE

CHIPPEWA & MUNSEE

SAC & FOX

WINNEBAGO & OMAHA

MANDAN
REE
MINITARI

SIOUX TRIBES

SIOUX AND ASSINIBOIN

NORTHERN CHEYENNE

SHOSHONI & ARAPAHO

CROW

MESCALERO APACHE

JICARILLA APACHE

PUEBLOS

UTE

NAVAJO

ZUNI

UTE

HOPI

BLACKFOOT

FLATHEAD

SHOSHONI & BANNOCK

SHOSHONI & BANNOCK

SUPPAI

HUALPAI

APACHE

PAPAGO

NEZ PERCE

SPOKAN

COEUR D'ALENE

UMATILLA

WARM SPRING

SHOSHONI & PAIUTE

MOAPA RIVER

MOJAVE

PIMA

MARICOPA

PAPAGO

COLVILLE

YAKIMA

PAIUTE

PAIUTE

TULE RIVER

YUMA

MISSION INDIANS

NORTHWEST COASTAL TRIBES

KLAMATH

KLAMATH RIVER

HOOPA VALLEY

ROUND VALLEY

P A C I F I C   O C E A N

Oglala chiefs at Pine Ridge Agency. Left is Little Wound, right American Horse and Red Cloud (with feathered bonnet). *Smithsonian Institution National Anthropological Archives* and *Library of Congress*.

the agent characterized his adversary in words that probably summed up with fair accuracy Sitting Bull's own estimate of McLaughlin.[5] Like Standing Rock, each agency had its reactionaries—"nonprogressives," the whites called them. At Cheyenne River, the leaders were Hump and Big Foot; at Rosebud, Crow Dog and Two Strike; at Pine Ridge, Little Wound and Big Road.

At the opposite pole from the "nonprogressives" stood the "progressives"—those sincerely convinced that the only salavation lay in cooperation with the whites or cynically motivated to go along in hope of the benefits that flowed from the agent's favor. At Pine Ridge the leaders were American Horse and Young-Man-Afraid-of-His-Horse. Both had been notable warriors in the old days and had built up the stature to wield considerable power on the reservation. Both usually supported the agent

in the civilization program and in the political battles for the allegiance of the Oglalas. Young-Man-Afraid's motivations tended toward personal ambition. American Horse, a man of great dignity and oratorical distinction, had visited the Great Father and traveled with Buffalo Bill; what he had seen convinced him that the white people's way held out the only promise of Indian survival. At Standing Rock, McLaughlin enjoyed even more helpful progressives in John Grass, Gall, and Crow King. The last two, once warrior-lieutenants of Sitting Bull who had played leading roles in wiping out Long Hair Custer, now gave crucial aid to McLaughlin in the battle with their old chief.

Then, at each agency, there were those who tried to walk both sides of the road. Often called nonprogressive, rarely progressive, they resisted when they could get away with it, gave in when they could not. Red Cloud and Spotted Tail excelled in this role, the former at Pine Ridge, the latter at Rosebud. Crow Dog's murder of Spotted Tail in 1883 left a power vacuum at Rosebud, for no other chief could rise to Spotted Tail's commanding eminence, and a host of contending lesser chiefs kept the Brules in a state of political anarchy for years. At Pine Ridge Red Cloud conducted a six-year conflict with an agent as honest and fearless as McLaughlin, though considerably more mercurial—a balding, spectacularly mustached former army surgeon with the distinctive name of Valentine T. McGillycuddy. Indeed, the clash of wills between these two men gained Pine Ridge a niche in the Sioux lexicon as the "Place Where Everything is Disputed;" several times it came close to plunging the agency into violence, but each time Red Cloud, unlike Sitting Bull, drew back from the brink. He had learned well the arts of conflict and compromise: he knew when to pursue conflict in the interest of gaining the support of his people, and he knew when to compromise in order to mollify government officials.[6]

No matter what the reaction of individuals or factions, the government programs relentlessly chewed up the old ways, but without substituting the new life so glowingly pictured at Lake Mohonk. The tribal identity, the tribal character, began to change, abruptly and swiftly, as soon as the Sioux faced the reality of reservation confinement. Almost overnight, a whole way of life had vanished, and thus whole clusters of habits and customs, activities, attitudes, values, and institutions lost relevance and meaning and likewise began to vanish.

Once warfare had consumed much of the men's time and thought and energy. With fidelity to prescribed ritual, they had fashioned and decorated weapons, planned and carried out raids on enemy tribes and invad-

Valentine T McGillycuddy. The energetic and combative agent presided over the Pine Ridge Sioux in the early reservation years, warring both with his superiors and the chiefs, notably Red Cloud (right), who resisted his rule. *South Dakota State Historical Society.*

ing whites, celebrated success, and mourned failure. War societies united men in common purpose, triumph, tragedy, and loyalty. Warfare opened the way to prestige, honor, wealth, and high rank. Now warfare no longer provided a foundation for this elaborate cultural edifice, and it crumbled.

Once the hunt had given order and organization to the yearly life cycle of band and tribe. The tribal circle, the police societies (Akicitas) that regulated its movement and configuration and saw that the hunt proceeded according to approved custom, the deeply embedded beliefs that formed a spiritual connection between Sioux and buffalo, and the constant preoccupation of women with the preparation of meat and hides and the crafting of clothing, tipis, utensils, and artwork—all ended as the buffalo and the life it supported vanished.

Pathetically, the Sioux tried to preserve a faint taste of the hunt. Like

238

Issue day. About every two weeks the Indians came in from their scattered settlements to draw government rations. Left, Oglalas hold council against backdrop of tipis in which they camped during issue days at Pine Ridge Agency, 1890. Right, Brule women line up for beef handout at Rosebud Agency. *National Archives* and *Library of Congress*.

the buffalo of old, steers issued as rations were gunned down by breech-clouted horsemen, after which the women moved in to butcher the carcasses. But a visiting government commission saw this as "a disgrace to our civilization" that could only "perpetuate in a savage breast all the cruel and wicked propensities of his nature," and the Indian Bureau moved to stamp out the practice.[7]

To take the place of the buffalo and the hunt, the agents constantly demanded that the Sioux turn to farming. For the time being, there would be the beef, coffee, sugar, and other rations promised in the treaties. But these would not last forever, and the Indians must learn to till the soil. These Indians had not tilled the soil since drifting out onto the Plains generations before. Labor of this sort demeaned Sioux manhood. As Red Cloud informed McGillycuddy, "the Great Spirit did not make us to work.

He made us to hunt and fish." And, he added, not illogically, "the white man owes us a living for the lands he has taken from us."[8] Besides, it required little foresight to see that growing crops would put an end to free rations. And so the Sioux resisted. But as the years passed, more and more moved out from the agencies and scattered over the land, built rude cabins, broke a patch of sod, and planted just enough seed to keep the agent from hounding them.

Even these halfhearted efforts earned no reward. Year after year the would-be farmers watched the corn and other crops burn up and blow away, or vanish under great clouds of grasshoppers, or disintegrate under pulverizing hail. Outside the reservation, whites just venturing onto the northern Plains experienced the same disheartening failure. That experience should have said something to the Indian policy theorists about the land and climate of Dakota, but the agents never ceased pestering the Sioux to plant and tend crops just like the white farmers back in Illinois and Pennsylvania.

Not that agents like McLaughlin and McGillycuddy failed to recognize the drawbacks to conventional argiculture west of the Missouri River. They simply could not overcome the image of the Indian farmer concocted at Lank Mohonk and unswervingly pursued by their superiors in Washington. What the agents could do, however, was to help in finding other means of self-support.

One means of great promise was stockraising. In 1879 the Indian Bureau distributed three thousand head of cattle among the Sioux agencies. The Indians took good care of them and liked this pastime far better than plowing and weeding the sandy Dakota soil. But, obsessed with farming, the government never sent enough breeding stock to give the experiment a true test. Then the terrible winter of 1886–87 wiped out most of the herds on the northern Plains, those tended by whites as well as by Indians, and this disaster incidentally decreed an end to the open range. The promise of cattle raising faded.

Another activity that the Sioux liked was freighting. For considerably less cash than the regular contractors demanded, they hauled their own annuities and other goods and supplies from railroad to agency. But this source of income could scarcely support a people as numerous as the Sioux, and besides, the white freighters, who usually had sturdy political connections, greeted the innovation less than enthusiastically.

The Sioux political system did not collapse as quickly as the economic, but it endured severe stresses that contributed greatly to the cultural breakdown. Some political institutions simply disappeared because the context in which they had existed, the tribal circle, had disappeared. Others persisted but came under vigorous government attack—none more so than the chieftainship.

The war on the chiefs bewildered the Sioux. On the one hand, the agents tore down the chiefs. On the other hand, they did things that built them up. McGillycuddy, for example, "deposed" Red Cloud and declared every man his own chief. Instead of chiefs drawing rations and redistributing them among their people, now every man might draw rations for his family. Yet when McGillycuddy needed Indian cooperation or acquiescence in some especially unpopular measure, the Oglalas observed that he dealt through Red Cloud. In fact, the government provided Red Cloud with a shiny black carriage, built him a frame house more imposing than the agent's own, and periodically brought him to Washington for a state visit replete with all the ceremony accorded a foreign potentate. As if this were not confusing enough, the government still could not resist manufacturing chiefs. As agents ignored or tried to undermine the established chiefs, they also turned for support to chiefs of lesser stature but of progressive bent, or, failing that, they simply elevated deserving progressives. There were so many chiefs, real and counterfeit, strong and weak, that one never knew where authority actually resided—if indeed anywhere.

Theoretically, supreme authority resided in the agent, and with strong agents like McLaughlin and McGillycuddy this was largely true. But agents came and went, and more were weak than strong. During the tenure of weak agents, the established chiefs usually asserted themselves, only to be suppressed when a strong agent inherited the post. Agents enjoyed a number of advantages in the contest for supremacy. For example, rations could be withheld to enforce conformity in a wide range of official demands, such as requiring that children be placed in school or that crops be planted. Another advantage lay in the Indian police force. Police service involved enough attributes of the old life to be popular and to inculcate in the policeman a sense of duty and loyalty to the agent. In the hands of a forceful agent, the police proved highly effective. Finally, the slow but steady dispersal of the people in family groups across the reservation weakened the chieftainship simply because a chief's hold depended in part on the proximity of families in band groups. By the close of the 1880s the chieftainship still existed, but it had been badly weakened and subjected to such mishandling by whites and Indians alike that a chaos of authority plagued the Sioux.

In the reservation environment the spiritual life the Sioux also eroded.

Indian police kept the peace on the reservations and enforced the agent's orders. The policemen were generally loyal to the government and effective in carrying out their responsibilities. This is the contingent at Rosebud Agency in Dakota. *Colorado Historical Society.*

Here, too, the passing of the old ways undermined established beliefs and practices. The vision quest, for example, once marked a boy's passage to manhood and determined intensely personal and intensely sacred meanings and habits that guided his course through life. Their relevance, however, depended in large part on war and the hunt, and these no longer occupied the Sioux.

The more visable expressions of the Indian spiritual world drew direct government fire when the Indian Bureau issued its "List of Indian Offenses" in 1883. Now a medicine man could be hauled before the Court of Indian Offenses for providing his people with spiritual counsel or for practicing the rituals and incantations of his calling. One by one the old-time shamans died without passing their lore to apprentices.

But the hardest blow came with the ban on the Sun Dance. Once the centerpiece of the social and religious fabric of the Sioux, the Sun Dance provided an annual forum for spiritual communication and comfort. No other institution afforded so pervading a sense of religious security. No other event so strengthened the values and institutions of society. Of all the voids that settled into Sioux life in the early reservation years, this emotional void was the worst.

Missionaries hastened to fill the void. Except at Standing Rock, with its Catholic agent, Episcopalians led the field, followed closely by Congregationalists and Presbyterians. They contradicted one another in their teachings and forever ridiculed the old Indian ways, but they made progress. They were kind, they conducted rituals that the Sioux liked, and their churches were about the only place where Indians actually experienced the Christian precept that all people, even Indians, stood equal in the eyes of God. But the main explanation for the spread of Christianity lay in the nature of the Indian spiritual belief, which did not bar the new from living comfortable next to the old—so long as the Christian holy men did not demand too insistently that the old be cast aside. The Indian spiritual life centered on a quest for personal power. The white man quite visibly possessed power. Therefore, his God might also be petitioned for power along with all the traditional Sioux deities.

Explaining his own religious experience, one of Pine Ridge's staunchest progressives, George Sword, also explained what had happened to many of his people under the influence of missionary teachings:

> When I believed the Oglala Wakan Tanka was right I served
> him with all my powers. . . . In war with the white people I found
> their Wakan Tanka the Superior. I then took the name of Sword

Pine Ridge Agency, Dakota, about 1885. A typical agency, Pine Ridge consisted of offices (3), agent's house (8), quarters for police and employees (6,7,9), council room and physician's office (2), commissary (5), storehouse (4), stable and annuity center (12), ice and meat house (11), shops (15), boarding school (1). The frame house the government built for Red Cloud is in the distance, slightly left of the flagpole (14). *National Archives.*

and have served Wakan Tanka according to the white people's manner with all my power. I became the chief of the United States Indian police and held the office until there was no trouble between the Oglala and the white people. I joined the church and am a deacon in it and shall be until I die. I have done all I was able to do to persuade my people to live according to the teachings of the Christian ministers.

I still have my Wasicun [ceremonial pouch containing personal sacred objects] and I am afraid to offend it, because the spirit of an Oglala may go to the spirit land of the Lakota.[9]

Like Christianity, education elicited ambivalent reactions from the Sioux. On the one hand, they sensed its importance in helping them to cope with the white people in the new world forced upon them. On the other hand, they feared what it would do to the hearts and minds, indeed the Sioux identity, of their children. On both counts, of course, they were right.

The Oglalas and Brules had hardly settled at their new agencies in 1879 when Captain Richard H. Pratt descended on them to recruit pupils for his new school at Carlisle, Pennsylvania. He left with sixty boys and twenty-four girls—and left behind parents anguished over the parting and fearful for their children's fate in a far-off place peopled only by whites. Spotted Tail visited Carlisle a few months later and had his worst fears confirmed: his own children, locks shorn, Indian garb discarded in favor of tightly buttoned military dress, engaged in chores no Indian had ever done before. After an angry scene with Pratt, he stormed out with his children and thereafter set his influence against Carlisle. Even so, Sioux continued to enroll and receive a rudimentary classroom and industrial education. But then they came home to find themselves almost aliens among their own people and with no place to apply their newly acquired skills and learning. One such Carlisle graduate was Plenty Horses, the youth arraigned for murder but acquitted in the federal court at Sioux Falls in 1891. To the jurors he explained his motive:

> I am an Indian. Five years I attended Carlisle and was edu-
> cated in the ways of the white man. . . . I was lonely. I shot the
> lieutenant so I might make a place for myself among my people.
> Now I am one of them. I shall be hung and the Indians will bury
> me as a warrior. They will be proud of me. I am satisfied.[10]

Day schools and boarding scools proved less repugnant than Carlisle and its sister institutions because the children stayed closer to home. Even so, parents found many of the rules and routines deeply offensive, and they resisted. Agents frequently had to resort to suspension of rations to fill the classrooms. At Standing Rock in 1884, for example, McLaughlin assigned quotas to the various bands and stopped issues until they were met. "But I afterward learned," he later confessed, "that there was not an *orphan child* over five years of age left in the camps after this 'con-scription.' "[11] And so, like the churches, the schools had their effect whether the Sioux resisted or not. By the close of the 1880s, the adults were confused and resentful, and the children, exposed to both white and Indian environments, were torn by conflicting values.

As the reservation program shredded the old values and institutions, the reservation itself attracted pressures that kept the Sioux constantly apprehensive of losing still more of their land. Pressed by the reformers, the government never let the Sioux forget that farming and land allotment went hand in hand and that sooner or later they must take up individual homesteads. Even after the Black Hills cession of 1877, the Great Sioux Reservation contained about nine million acres more than needed for the allotment program. Dakota land boomers eyed this "surplus" hungrily; it would provide homesteads for thousands of immigrants, and, once it was removed from the reservation, it would open railroad and other communication routes between eastern Dakota and the burgeoning mining districts of the Black Hills. Mohonk's faithful raised no dissenting voice to such disposition of surplus land, and indeed they agreed wholeheartedly, so long as such moves were carried out in accordance with treaty stipulations and with scrupulous regard for the Indian's welfare. Although land boomer and reformer never acted in concert, their similarity in viewpoint joined them in a practical political combination that doomed a vast acreage of Indian lands that the owners hardly viewed as surplus.

The first assault occurred in 1883. Dakota's delegate in Congress, Richard F. Pettigrew, had slipped a rider onto unrelated legislation calling for a commission to find out whether the Sioux would exchange their one large reservation for six small ones and would also, in the process, cede their unneeded land. Secretary of the Interior Henry M. Teller, a sympathetic westerner, named Newton Edmunds to head the commission. Former Dakota governor and chief negotiator of the fraudulent treaties of 1865 with the upper Missouri Sioux (see p. 96), Edmunds knew how to deal with Indians. Instead of simply sounding out the Sioux, as instructed by the legislation, he set forth to sell the proposition. At each agency he talked up a storm, misrepresented the proposal, exerted blatant pressure, and triggered a stampede of confused Indians that gained him the signatures of 384 chiefs and headmen. Triumphantly, Edmunds announced acceptance of the agreement. But his tactics had stirred up the reformers and they moved to block the cession—easily enough done since the Treaty of 1868 required the signatures of three-fourths of all adult males. Congress sent the agreement back to the reservation, but this time the Indians firmly rejected it. The experience left the Sioux shaken, resentful, and deeply fearful of any more talk about land.

There would be more talk, however, as the Dawes General Allotment Act of 1887 made amply clear. Backed by this law, the Dakota promoters moved swiftly to revive the Edmunds project. The Sioux Act of 1888 applied the principles of the Dawes Act to the Great Sioux Reservation. But it reversed the intended procedure: Negotiate the cession of the surplus lands first, and then allot the remaining reservation lands to the Indians. In return for "joint undivided occupancy," the Sioux would gain clear title to six separate reservations coinciding with the existing agencies, cede the nine million acres not needed for allotments, receive payment in specified sums as settlers took up homesteads in the opened district, and deal with their own allotment program at whatever pace they wanted. It was a complicated piece of legislation, replete with sweeteners thrown in to make it more palatable, but it aimed chiefly at moving half the Great Sioux Reservation out of Sioux ownership.

At each agency the Sioux braced to withstand the new land commission, headed by the familiar figure of Captain Richard H. Pratt, the stern officer with the big nose who took their children away to distant Carlisle. Like Edmunds, Pratt and his associates talked a great deal, painted the proposal in glowing terms, and indulged in scarcely veiled intimidation. But the Sioux had learned a lesson from the Edmunds Commission. They decided not to argue, simply to say no. So loudly and firmly did they say no at Standing Rock, the first agency on the commission's itinerary, that Pratt clearly foresaw the failure of his mission. A subsequent meeting at Lower Brule of delegates from all the agencies resoundingly confirmed the failure. Angrily, Pratt urged that the agreement be placed into effect even without the signatures required by the Treaty of 1868.[12]

But already the Indians themselves had broken ranks. Characteristically, the Sioux spokesmen had been unable simply to say no. They could not resist complaining about certain provisions of the law, which they saw as clever traps for unwary Indians. Once they began to debate, they inevitably implied that a more liberal measure might be acceptable. Also, and fatally for the plan of resistance, the delegates at Lower Brule suggested that a trip to Washington and talks with the Great Father and the Secretary of the Interior might yield a compromise. The chiefs got their trip, and although it did not end with a compromise, it gave new heart to proponents of the agreement, led to another Sioux Act, and confronted the Indians with still another land commission in the summer of 1889.

The chairman of this commission knew little about Indians, but one of the members assuredly did. Major General George Crook understood Sioux psychology and tribal politics. He had fought and negotiated with these very Indians little more than a decade earlier. Many of them knew him personally and perhaps even accorded him a trust denied most whites. Champions of the new Sioux Act looked to Crook to sell the proposition

The Crook Commission at Standing Rock, 1889. In often stormy sessions featuring divide-and-conquer tractics, the commission persuaded the Sioux to part with nine million acres of the Great Sioux Reservation. The experience badly shook the Indians and, with other setbacks, made them receptive to the teachings of the Ghost Dance religion. General Crook is seated third from left. *National Archives*.

to the Indians. He did not disappoint them. At each agency he feasted the Sioux and even allowed the old dances so offensive to the Indian Bureau. With infinite patience he explained over and over the provisions of the proposed agreement. He also spoke with stern paternalism. "It strikes me," he told them, "that you are in the position of a person who had his effects in the bed of a dry stream when there was a flood coming down, and instead of finding fault with the Creator for sending it down, you should try and save what you can."[13]

Finally, and most critically, Crook made heavy use of the old technique, so often effective in dealing with Indians, of divide and conquer. At Standing Rock, for example, there was no hope of winning over Sitting Bull, but Crook and McLaughlin got John Grass in the agent's office for a night of persuasion that threw his formidable weight behind the measure. At

Pine Ridge the same treatment brought American Horse around. On June 21 Crook noted in his diary, "Had a big council this afternoon in which American Horse, Bear Nose and a couple of others made speeches in favor of the bill for the first time since we first met the Indians here. American Horse's band commenced signing. I had coached Bear Nose."[14]

In fact, the Sioux *were* like people in a dry wash with a flood coming down. Crook clearly saw that Congress would never come up with a more liberal measure than the one now before the Indians, and he succeeded in convincing enough tribal leaders to swing more than the three-fourths majority of adult males necessary to put over the agreement. But he left behind a badly divided and thoroughly demoralized people. Almost unanimously they had opposed the land agreement. Yet overwhelmingly they had voted for it and put their marks on the paper. Bewildered over how it had happened, angry with themselves for letting it happen, fearful that the government had once more played them false, bickering among themselves, they waited to see what would happen next.

In addressing particular concerns of the Indians, the commissioners had made promises that went beyond the precise content of the agreement. Carefully and repeatedly they had explained that these were not unqualified promises, only promises to use their influence with Congress and the President to secure certain concessions—a subtle distinction that, not surprisingly, eluded most of the Sioux. One promise, however, did not have to be qualified. Over and over the Indian spokesmen had voiced a deep-seated fear that the government, once having taken their land, would cut down on their rations. Over and over the commissioners promised that this could not happen: the treaties fixed the rations; the land agreement had nothing to do with the treaties; and both would run side by side until the end of the period specified in the treaties. The Sioux remained skeptical, and not without good reason.

Two weeks after the departure of the commission, orders arrived from Washington reducing the annual beef issue at Rosebud by two million pounds, at Pine Ridge by one million, and at the other agencies by proportional amounts. Crook had not lied. In an economizing mood, Congress had simply cut the Sioux appropriation, leaving the Indian Bureau no choice but to cut rations—another technicality unappreciated by the victims. Then all the other promises seemed to get lost too. Again, the commissioners had acted in good faith: they had indeed used their influence. But again the proper order of execution was reversed. Secretary of the Interior John W. Noble advised President Harrison that Congress could surely be expected to make good the promises of the Crook Commission

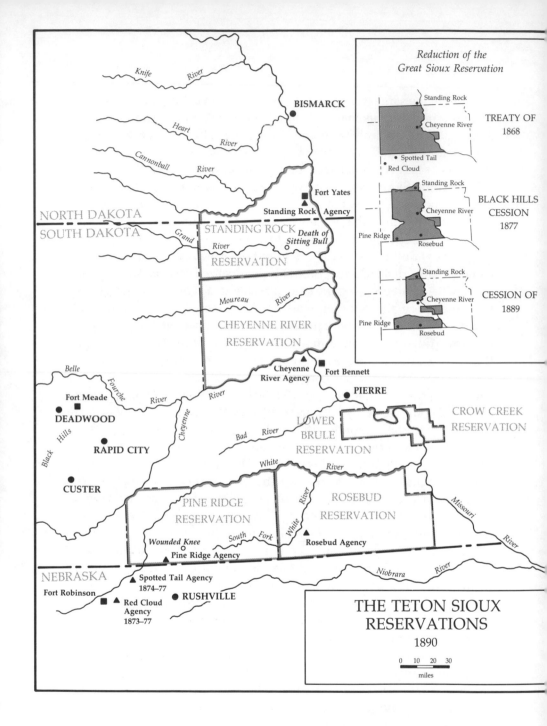

THE TETON SIOUX RESERVATIONS
1890

0   10   20   30
miles

Reduction of the Great Sioux Reservation

TREATY OF 1868

BLACK HILLS CESSION 1877

CESSION OF 1889

and that implementation of the agreement need not be held up until that happened. On February 10, 1890, therefore, the President stunned the Sioux by announcing their acceptance of the land agreement and throwing open the ceded territory to settlement. "They made us many promises," observed an old Sioux with a long memory, "more than I can remember, but they never kept but one; they promised to take our land and they took it."[15]

And so the Teton Sioux ended the decade of the 1880s depressed, despairing, and drained of hope for improvement. The old values, the old verities, the old ways, and the old institutions fell irrevocably away. Nothing solid or satisfying took their place. That the people could not help giving up the old, that they could not help sampling or even embracing some of the new, only deepened the malaise. The long and exhausting battle over land, ending in defeat accompanied by a dramatic show of government bad faith—or so it appeared to the Indians—made matters even worse. The winter of 1889–90 brought hunger and perhaps even some starvation, which was in part a consequence of the ration cut. Epidemics of measles, influenza, and whooping cough swept the reservation with fatal effect. Summer drought in 1890 blasted into total ruin such crops as had been planted. Never had the fortunes of the Sioux reached lower ebb. Never had their sense of who they were been more blurred.

Other Indian tribes endured similar though usually less demoralizing stresses during the 1880s. The reservation program tore down the traditional culture without substituting the new at which it aimed. The Dawes Act set in motion a concerted drive for allotment in severalty and the cession of surplus lands. All over the West, Indians closed the decade beset by more or less cultural disintegration and by feelings of helplessness and hopelessness. Symptomatic of their condition was the fervor with which most greeted the stirring message that came out of the west in 1890, bringing with it the promise of a way out of the morass into which the white people had forced them.

A prophet had appeared among the Paiutes of Nevada. He preached a new religion. It was a religion that offered hope for the Indian race—hope not dependent upon promises of the white men. He held forth a vision of paradise in which all Indians would at last be free of the white burden and reside for eternity in a blissful land, a land without white people, a land inhabited by all the generations of Indians that had gone before, a land bounteous in game and all the other riches of the natural world, a land free of sickness and want, a land where all peoples dwelt in peace with one another. It was a religion that combined many of the old spiritual beliefs with the new teachings of the Christian missionaries. The injunction to live in peace, for example, drew on Christian dogma. Indeed, the prophet came to be known as the Messiah, and when pilgrims from reservations all over the West gathered at his brush lodge he showed them scars on his hands where centuries before the whites had nailed him to a cross. But his promise was of an exclusively Indian world, and it could be simply attained by practicing the tenets of his faith and dancing a prescribed "Ghost Dance."

The Indians of the American West thus responded to their plight in the only way left, a way that called on the spiritual rather than the worldly. Throughout history, peoples similarly afflicted have sought similar solutions. A wise and articulate government ethnologist who studied the Ghost Dance shortly after it broke over the West discerned in it this universal instinct of peoples in crisis. "When the race lies crushed and groaning under an alien yoke," he wrote, "how natural is the dream of a redeemer, an Arthur, who shall return from exile or awake from some long sleep to drive out the usurper and win back for his people what they have lost. The hope becomes a faith and the faith becomes the creed of priests and prophets, until the hero is a god and the dream a religion, looking to some great miracle of nature for its culmination and accomplishment."[16] Such was the promise that the Ghost Dance religion held forth to the Indians of the American West in 1890.

9

The Passing of the Frontier, 1890

No Indian agency exhibited a more conspicuous personification of the evils of the spoils system than Pine Ridge. Under the Harrison administration's "Home Rule," Pine Ridge was recognized as "Pettigrew's Place." Richard F. Pettigrew, senator from the new state of South Dakota, pledged the post to Daniel F. Royer, physician, pharmacist, and local politician of Alpena, South Dakota. Middle-aged, with thinning hair, stringy mustache, and cherubic face, Royer had fallen on bad times and now needed a chance to recoup his finances. Although he wanted to be registrar of the Huron land office, Pettigrew could offer only an Indian agency. But another candidate with good Republican credentials and equal need appeared in the person of Bishop J. Gleason. Not until the middle of 1890 did Pettigrew work out a solution: Royer would get the agency and would at once appoint Gleason his chief clerk. With understandable though not necessarily inaccurate bias, the man fired as chief clerk recalled of Royer and Gleason: They were "broken down small politicians . . . overwhelmingly in debt. They came to the reservation as political adventurers in search of fortunes."[1]

Royer installed himself at Pine Ridge Agency on October 1, 1890, just in time to confront the Ghost Dance. The Sioux pilgrims to Nevada had returned with word of the new Messiah during the previous March, but not until after a summer of cascading afflictions did the Sioux turn seriously to the hope he held forth. Cannily, old Red Cloud steered his usual ambiguous course. If the story were true, he said, "it would spread all over the world." If false, "it would melt like the snow under the hot sun."[2] Little Wound agreed, but he spoke for most of the chiefs in urging the people not to take a chance. "You better learn this dance," he warned, "so if the Messiah does come he will not pass us by."[3]

And they did learn the dance. All over Pine Ridge Reservation, and on the others as well, the people abandoned their cabins and pitched their tipis in the cottonwood groves. Hypnotically, in slow shuffling cadence, they danced around sacred prayer trees. As the intensity and excitement mounted, some fell to the ground, to die and go to heaven and there talk with the Indian Messiah and see the beautiful new world foretold. They came back to describe their experiences and to urge others to dance with a passion that would reveal to them, too, a vision of the promised land.

Unhappily for Royer and the other Sioux agents, the apostles who preached the new religion among the Sioux, chief among them Short Bull and Kicking Bear, added a feature that formed no part of Wovoka's message. The prophet taught nonviolence, even in thought. The millennium would occur through divine instrumentality; Indians need only follow the rituals and precepts of the new religion. But among the Sioux the travail and resentment of recent events allowed the priests to twist Wovoka's pacifistic doctrine. Now they suggested that the time of deliverance might be advanced by direct action, and that the people should not fear such a drastic course because the special "Ghost Shirt" worn by the dancers would turn the white man's bullets. With this assurance, the Sioux, in contrast to the faithful on other reservations throughout the West, grew increasingly turbulent and defiant.

Whether a steadier agent could have contained the trouble at Pine Ridge can never be known. Suggestively, McLaughlin succeeded at Standing Rock, and McGillycuddy had weathered crises as bad. But Royer, one of the worst specimens ever produced by the spoils system, was weak, excitable, and easily panicked, so much so that the Sioux named him "Young-Man-Afraid-of-Indians." He quickly made himself a target of contempt and ridicule, and he proved utterly wanting in any ability to stem the drift to anarchy. Repeatedly he ordered the dancers to stop dancing and return to their cabins, but they simply laughed at him. Repeatedly he bombarded his superiors with frantic appeals for soldiers. At last, in late November 1890, he could no longer be denied, for the Pine Ridge Sioux and a sizable infusion from Rosebud had got so far out of hand as to threaten the lives of agency personnel and spread fear of massacre among settlers outside the reservation.[4]

The appearance of troops at Pine Ridge and Rosebud united the Sioux Ghost Dancers in the armed defense of their religion. While the "friendlies" gathered at Pine Ridge Agency, the "hostiles" fled with Short Bull and Kicking Bear to the remote northwestern corner of the reservation. Some three thousand strong, they took positions on an elevated tableland that could not be stormed without great loss of life. Appropriately, it was called the "Stronghold."

The army had no wish to assault the Stronghold, and in fact it badly wanted to end the whole affair without violence. General Crook had died suddenly of a heart attack, and a new commander had recently taken over the military division in which South Dakota fell—none other than Crook's old nemesis, Major General Nelson A. Miles. Breathing fire but intent on diplomacy, Miles concentrated most of the army's combat units, more than five thousand soldiers, in western South Dakota. Backed by overwhelming force, he set about trying to coax the suspicious, nervous fugitives out of the Stronghold. Two developments dashed his hopes and decreed that, like a jarring postscript to the long history of warfare that Miles himself had seemingly closed out in Skeleton Canyon in 1886, one final clash of arms would poison relations between Indian and white.

The first occurred on the Standing Rock Reservation on December 15. For some weeks Agent McLaughlin had plotted to remove a potential spark from the powder keg by seizing Sitting Bull and putting him behind bars in some distant place until the Ghost Dance blew over. Learning that Sitting Bull planned to leave his home and join the Brule and Oglala dancers in the Stronghold, McLaughlin moved swiftly. He dispatched a contingent of forty-three Indian policemen, supported at a distance by cavalry from Fort Yates, to make a dawn arrest at Sitting Bull's cabin on Grand River, some thirty miles south of the agency. The police accomplished their mission, but a fatal delay intervened in saddling the old chief's horse—a handsome gray circus animal presented to him by Buffalo Bill Cody. Angry, shouting Indians swarmed around the cabin, vowing that the *ceska maza*, the "metal breasts," should not take their chief. A gun went off, and a brief, furious fight erupted. Amid the smoke and noise, the old circus horse, doubtless prompted by memories of the Wild West Show, sat on its haunches and began to perform tricks. When the cavalry reached the scene and the smoke lifted, Sitting Bull and seven of his followers lay dead around the cabin, while inside were four dead and three wounded policemen, two of whom died later.

The second misfortune arose out of another intended arrest, one founded on a mistaken assumption. Big Foot and his Miniconjou band lived on the south side of the Cheyenne River about ten miles below its forks. They belonged to the Cheyenne River Reservation, but the land agreement of 1889 had left them outside its boundaries. A leading nonprogressive, Big Foot had warmly embraced the Ghost Dance and thus had got his name on the list of troublemakers who should be arrested. Actually, his ardor for the new religion had cooled considerably, and his reputation as a peacemaker had elicited an invitation from Red Cloud and other "friendlies" at Pine Ridge to come down and help end the troubles there. When Big Foot and his people started south, their ranks swelled by Hunkpapa refugees from the melee at Sitting Bull's cabin, General Miles and everyone else assumed they were headed for the Stronghold to cast their lot with the dancers.

Goaded by a furious Miles, military units combed the frozen plains looking for Big Foot. They failed chiefly because Big Foot was not aiming for the Stronghold but for Pine Ridge. At last, on December 28, a squadron of the Seventh Cavalry found the fugitives. Big Foot, prostrated in a wagon with pneumonia, agreed with the officer in charge to accompany the soldiers to their camp. It lay in the valley of Wounded Knee Creek about twenty miles east of Pine Ridge Agency. That night the rest of the Seventh Cavalry rode out to Wounded Knee, and Colonel James W. Forsyth took command. Daybreak of December 29, gray with threatening storm, revealed Big Foot's tipis, sheltering some 350 people, closely surrounded by five hundred cavalrymen and commanded from a nearby hilltop by four small-caliber Hotchkiss cannon. It was not a reassuring sight.

No one on either side that morning had any thought of a fight. Certainly not the Indians, as the army later charged; they were outnumbered, surrounded, poorly armed, and had their women and children present. Certainly not the soldiers; they clearly saw their advantages, and so unconcerned was Colonel Forsyth that he failed to dispose his units so that their fire would not endanger one another. But Forsyth had orders to disarm Big Foot's people, and taking an Indian's gun from him always unleashed emotions that could override logic. That, not an outbreak of treacherous Indians or a massacre plotted by brutal soldiers, is what happened at Wounded Knee.

As the search progressed, powerful tensions rose on both sides. A medicine man pranced about inciting the men to fight; their Ghost Shirts would protect them, he said. Nervous troopers fingered their carbine triggers. One seized a deaf man and grasped his rifle. It went off. The chanting priest threw a handful of dirt into the air. A knot of Indians dropped their blankets and leveled Winchester repeaters at a rank of soldiers. Both sides fired at once, and the fight that neither side intended or expected burst upon them.

In a murderous melee at close range, soldiers and Indians shot, stabbed, and clubbed one another. Weakly, Big Foot rose from his pallet to watch.

A volley killed him and most of the headmen lined up behind him. Abruptly the two sides separated, and from the hill the artillery went into action. Exploding shells flattened the Sioux tipis and filled the air with deadly shrapnel. In less than an hour most of the fighting had ended, leaving the battlefield a horror of carnage. Nearly two-thirds of Big Foot's band had been cut down, at least 150 dead and 50 wounded, and perhaps more who were never reported. The army lost 25 dead and 39 wounded.[5]

Wounded Knee ruined General Miles's peace initiative, which had so far succeeded that the "hostiles" had abandoned the Stronghold and were on their way to Pine Ridge Agency when word of the tragedy reached them. Even the "friendlies" bolted, taking Red Cloud with them, and they joined with the dancers north of the agency. On the day after Wounded Knee, warriors ambushed the Seventh Cavalry at Drexel Mission and tasted a measure of revenge before black cavalrymen rescued their white comrades.

But now this great camp of some four thousand Sioux of both progressive and nonprogressive bent suffered confusion and hesitation. Miles knew how to exploit the divisions in the Indian leadership. He sent in conciliatory messages urging surrender while also expertly bringing his huge army into an ever tightening ring around the village. Thus combining force and diplomacy in just the right proportions, Miles turned the deadly incident of December 29 into a complete surrender on January 15, 1891.

Wounded Knee was the last major armed encounter between Indians and whites in North America. A few scattered clashes occurred later, but Wounded Knee was the last of great consequence. Even so, neither Wounded Knee nor the Ghost Dance "outbreak" that formed its backdrop deserves to be viewed as an episode in the Indian Wars of the United States. More fittingly, warfare ended in 1886 at Skeleton Canyon, Arizona, with the collapse of the last armed resistance to the reservation system. Instead of armed challenge to the reservation, the Ghost Dance was a desperate bid for divine salvation where all else had failed. Among the Sioux it assumed a militant form, but still it need not have ended in violence save for an incompetent Indian agent and a tragic accident born of mutual distrust, misunderstanding, and fear.

Rather, both in fact and in symbol, Wounded Knee assumes a larger significance, for it marks the passing of the Indian frontier. A little more than two years after Wounded Knee, the young historian Frederick Jackson Turner appeared before a convention of the American Historical As-

258

Among the Sioux the Ghost Dance troubles led to armed confrontation between Indians and soldiers and to the tragic slaughter at Wounded Knee. Left, Big Foot's Miniconjou Ghost Dancers mingle peaceably with soldiers near the forks of Cheyenne River in the autumn of 1890. Right, the field of Wounded Knee two days after the fight, with the medicine man Yellow Bird in foreground. *Library of Congress* and *Smithsonian Institution National Anthropological Archives.*

sociation in Chicago. Pointing out that the census of 1890 had failed for the first time to trace a frontier of white settlement in the West, he expounded his provocative interpretation of "The Significance of the Frontier in American History." For generations to come the Turner thesis would profoundly influence American historical thought and spark heated controversy among historians. For more than four hundred years, Indian conflicts had flashed across the successive frontiers that Turner postulated. Coincidentally, the last serious conflict occurred in the very year, 1890, that he chose as the end of America's frontier era.

Turner never mentioned this coincidence. Indeed, his conceptions gave little emphasis to the Indians. With so many of his countrymen of the nineteenth century, he regarded Indians less as people than as fixtures of a wilderness that civilized man must conquer and transform. Like the

Pine Ridge after the surrender, January 1891. The great tipi village recalled scenes of the old free life whose end Wounded Knee so tragically dramatized. *Library of Congress.*

forests and mountains and plains and the wild beasts they contained, Indians formed a barrier to the march of Anglo-Saxon civilization. All, not just the Indian, must be overcome for civilization to prevail. His preoccupation was with the pioneers, and how their experience with the wilderness shaped and distinguished the American character.[6]

Especially in its ethnocentric neglect of the Indians, Turner's monolithic Anglo-Saxon frontier advancing irresistibly across the continent has been challenged as too simplistic. Even so, although Turner never stressed it, the last gasp of the Indians at Wounded Knee gave support to his choice of 1890 as the close of the frontier period. In the more sophisticated views of the frontier evolved since Turner's time, however, Wounded Knee may still be seen as validating the significance of 1890 and as containing meaning not only for Turner's Anglo-Saxon civilization but for the Indian's civilization as well.

More plausibly than as a single line that disappeared when whites conquered the wilderness, the Indian frontier may be viewed as zones of ethnic interaction that faded when whites established political domination over the Indians. In this formulation as well as in Turner's, the Ghost Dance and Wounded Knee signal the end of the frontier period. For the Sioux, despite a decade of reservation experience, the loss of their freedom and traditional way of life seemed unthinkable until the bullets of the Seventh Cavalry penetrated their Ghost Shirts and shattered the dream held out by the Indian Messiah. After Wounded Knee, the Sioux resignedly submitted to the reservation system and thus implicitly surrendered the last vestiges of sovereignty to the invader. In varying degree, although no other Wounded Knees dramatized the surrender, the same thing happened on reservations all over the West. Indians embraced the Ghost Dance and the last hope of salvation it offered. When the miracles failed to occur, the reality of their political subordination could no longer be denied or ignored. Thus on December 29, 1890, the Indian frontier of the American West vanished in the smoke of Hotchkiss shells bursting over the valley of Wounded Knee Creek.

Yet history, mirroring life, is rarely that tidy. Although for most western tribes the events of 1890 added up to overwhelming evidence of the Great Father's complete and unchallengeable dominion over their destinies, three exceptions spoil the neatness of the generalization. In Indian Territory the Five Civilized Tribes clung precariously to sovereignty, in Alaska native sovereignty had yet to be seriously threatened, and in the Southwest special circumstances pointed the Pueblos in directions different from almost all other groups.

The Five Civilized Tribes had made a rapid recovery from the devastation and demoralization of the Civil War. Throwing off the Reconstruction yoke in 1870, rapidly healing the bitter factionalism spawned by the war, all of the Five Tribes had attained, by 1880, a comfortable prosperity that set them apart from all other Indians of the West.

As foreshadowed by the Fort Smith council of 1865 (p. 117), however, their sovereignty came under heavy attack after the Civil War. The federal objective was to merge the five Indian nations into one, which would then be organized as a U.S. territory. The tribes did not need Cherokee Chief John Ross's alarmed warnings to see this as the death knell of the autonomy guaranteed in the removal treaties. Threatened by legislation

Dressed as the reformers wanted them dressed, Sioux delegation to the Great Father poses with an impeccably groomed Commissioner of Indian Affairs, Thomas J. Morgan (4), in the spring of 1891. The group includes some of the most famous Teton chiefs, among them John Grass (2), Two Strike (3), American Horse (5), High Hawk (6), Young-Man-Afraid-of-His-Horse (8), Hollow Horn Bear (9), Little Wound (14), Big Road (23), Hump (24), He Dog (27), No Heart (31), and Sword (35). Noted mixed-blood scouts of past wars, now serving as interpreters, include Louis Richard (20), Baptiste Pourier (39), and Louis Shangreau (41). *Library of Congress.*

262

pending in the Congress, however, they got together in 1870 and drafted the Oklmulgee Constitution. This enlightened document would have accomplished the government's aim, but it contained a measure more Indian independence than the Congress cared for, and anyway it failed of ratification by the tribes themselves. The controversy over the Okmulgee Constitution unified the Five Tribes in opposition to further pressures, but the pressures continued all the same. Other forces combined to make them even more threatening.[7]

The most serious and troublesome force was the influx of non-Indians, black and white alike, to Indian Territory after the Civil War. By 1890 more than seventy percent of the population of the five nations consisted of these immigrants. As U.S. citizens, they were not subject to tribal law, and only the barest shadow of U.S. law protected them from violence and crime. Postwar Indian Territory thus became a nightmare both of law and of outlawry. Controlling a small army of deputy marshals, the U.S. District Court at Fort Smith, Arkansas, with the legendary "hanging judge" Isaac Parker presiding, gradually reduced crime in this judicial no-man's land. But civil disputes between U.S. citizens and between tribal and U.S. citizens remained unregulated. Also, U.S. citizens had no public school system for the education of their children and enjoyed none of the other services traditionally furnished by state and local government.

In truth, the "domestic dependent nation" concept simply no longer worked in the Indian nations, and the chief victims, the non-Indians, advocated the elimination of tribal governments and the incorporation of Indian Territory into the U.S. political system. The railroads that had won rights-of-way across the five nations in the Reconstruction treaties had a large stake in the issue too. Whites provided most of their way business, and political reorganization would mean vastly more whites and vastly more way business. In Washington their powerful lobbyists took up the cause. Reformers joined the chorus. Blind to how close the people of the Five Tribes came to fitting their image of the ideal Indian, they saw only a tribal ownership of land that prevented allotment in severalty. The Dawes Act of 1887 exempted the Five Tribes, but it served warning that time was running out. About the only supporters the Five Tribes could look to were Texas cattlemen who leased Indian grasslands and had no wish to see their monopoly ended.

Other pressures came from the former western lands surrendered at the close of the Civil War to accommodate Plains and immigrant tribes. These pressures took two forms, one a noisy campaign of land "boomers"

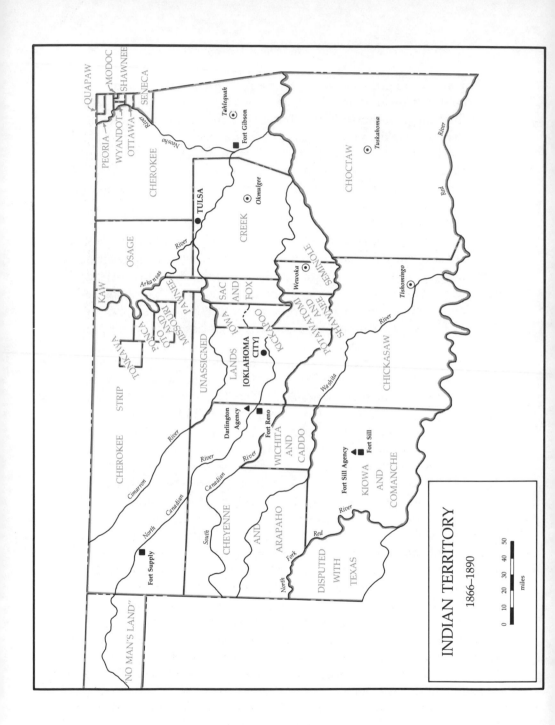

QUAPAW
MODOC
SHAWNEE
SENECA
PEORIA
WYANDOTTE
OTTAWA

Neosho River

Tahlequah ⊙

Fort Gibson ■

CHEROKEE

OSAGE

TULSA ●

CREEK

Okmulgee ⊙

CHOCTAW

Tuskahoma ⊙

Red River

KAW

Arkansas River

PAWNEE

PONCA
OTO AND MISSOURI
TONKAWA

SAC AND FOX

IOWA

KICKAPOO

Wewoka ⊙

SEMINOLE

POTAWATOMI AND SHAWNEE

Tishomingo ⊙

CHEROKEE STRIP

UNASSIGNED LANDS

[OKLAHOMA CITY] ●

CHICKASAW

River

Washita

Darlington Agency ▲
Fort Reno ■

WICHITA AND CADDO

Fort Sill Agency ▲
Fort Sill ■

Cimarron River

North Canadian

South Canadian River

River

CHEYENNE

AND

ARAPAHO

KIOWA AND COMANCHE

Red River

Fort Supply ■

North Fork

DISPUTED WITH TEXAS

NO MAN'S LAND

INDIAN TERRITORY
1866–1890

0   10   20   30   40   50
miles

The fate of Indian lands. The Dawes Severalty Act of 1887 laid the groundwork for the cession of "surplus" Indian lands, which were then opened to white settlement (left). Here (right) is the great rush to the Cherokee Strip of Indian Territory in 1893. *Oklahoma Historical Society.*

advocating the opening to homesteaders of land not yet assigned to any Indians, and the other the systematic program inaugurated by the Dawes Act to open land on the reservations themselves that was not needed for allotment. In 1889, responding to a public clamor generated by the boomers, Congress threw open the unassigned district and thus set off the first of the great land rushes. Established as Oklahoma Territory a year later, the new political creation then provided a convenient base on which to erect, county by county, the products of subsequent rushes. Most of these accretions came as a result of the labors of the Jerome Commission, sort of a southern counterpart of the Crook Commission to the Sioux. Between 1889 and 1894 the Jerome Commission negotiated the cession of more than fifteen million acres of "surplus" Indian lands. A large chunk came from the Cheyenne-Arapaho Reservation, but much the largest,

six million acres, was the Cherokee Strip. At first the Cherokees refused
to sell because the Strip earned large grazing revenues from Texas cattlemen, but in 1890 a presidential proclamation declared the grazing leases
illegal and ordered the area vacated of all cattle. The Cherokees then sold
for $8.6 million. With the final additions from the Kiowa-Comanche Res-
ervation in 1901, Oklahoma Territory consisted of virtually all the present state west of the five nations.

Now the assault on the five nations focused less on the old idea of an
Indian state than on their union with Oklahoma Territory in a single state.
Beginning in 1894, still another commission went to work on the Five
Tribes. Headed by no less an eminence than former Senator Henry L.
Dawes, the body set forth to persuade the Indians to break up their tribal
holdings and to allot them in severalty. One after another the tribes ada-
mantly refused. Then in 1895 Congress empowered the Dawes Commission to survey and allot lands without tribal consent. Faced with this
prospect, one after another the tribes gave in and concluded agreements
with the commission. They faced another reality too: the erosion of their
tribal governments. The most severe blow came in 1898, when Congress
abolished tribal courts and placed everyone—Indian, white, black, and
mixed-blood—under U.S. law enforceable in the U.S. courts that had been
established in Indian Territory beginning in 1889. In the agreements with
the Dawes Commission, therefore, the tribes agreed to phase out their
national governments altogether by 1906. A year later, in 1907, Oklahoma
entered the Union as a state. For the Five Civilized Tribes the Indian frontier passed out of existence.

Less by far than the Five Civilized Tribes can Alaska's Indian frontier
be forced into the temporal and conceptual framework of the continental
frontier of the American West. Indeed, the Alaskan frontier cannot even
be accurately labeled Indian, but rather Native—with a capital N to de-
note Eskimo, Aleut, and Indian and to distinguish them from white *natives*.
Eskimos peopled the coastal areas fronting the Bering Sea and the Arctic
Ocean, Aleuts the Aleutian Islands, Athabascan Indians the interior, and
Tlingit and Haida Indians the Alexander Archipelago and the bordering
mainland.

Alaska's colonial period, beginning in the middle of the eighteenth century and featuring Russian and British fur-gathering frontiers advancing
toward each other from west and east, saw the beginnings of frontier
zones that brought Native and European into political, economic, and
cultural interaction. The most intense relations, immensely destructive
to the Natives, occurred in areas colonized by the Russians—principally

Sitka, Kodiak, Cook Inlet, and the lower Yukon—but significant contacts also developed with British traders in the middle and upper Yukon Basin.

Although the process continued after the United States purchased Alaska in 1867, it differed fundamentally both in tempo and substance from what was transpiring at the same time in the American West. For one thing, no Indian warfare occurred in Alaska. A brief spate of violence springing from liquor marred military-Native harmony in 1869, but otherwise only a few scattered incidents, more properly viewed as disorders than as hostilities, shed any blood. Indeed, the army reduced its presence in Alaska to a mere token in 1870 and withdrew altogether in 1877. Largely as a consequence of the absence of hostilities, therefore, Washington felt no impulse to throw the mantle of federal Indian policy over Alaska. No treaty extinguished Native title to land, no reservation restricted Native freedom and independence, and no agent sought to impose civilization programs.

Scholarship has not addressed the question of why Indian warfare did not disrupt Alaskan frontiers. One explanation may lie in cultural factors, such as the essential pacifism of Alaskan Natives, even in the face of severe provocation, and the receptivity of many Natives to the ways of the newcomers. Another explanation may be Alaska's immensity in relation to Native and white populations. One-fifth the size of the continental United States, containing 365 million acres, it harbored but 50,000 to 75,000 Indians in the late nineteenth century. The census of 1880 counted less than five hundred non-Natives in all Alaska, and they lived mostly in Sitka. The number had grown to nearly seven thousand by 1890, but still they remained all but invisible in the enormity of the land.

Although Alaska therefore featured less competition between races for land and natural resources, this cannot entirely explain the differing experiences here and in the American West. In local situations, whites intruded into Native homelands and in some instances even dispossessed Native groups, especially during the turn-of-the-century gold rushes to the Klondike, Nome, and Fairbanks. Russians severely depleted the sea mammals on which Eskimos depended, while Americans later excluded Indians from traditional fishing places on the interior rivers. In both the colonial and American periods, moreover, significant cultural and economic interaction occurred, with the Natives embracing new forms that brought about major changes both in material culture and in social, political, and economic institutions and values. Christian missionaries, in particular, had great influence on Native spiritual beliefs and practices.

Still the Natives did not resist. Nor did questions of land title pose serious problems. The treaty of cession with Russia acknowledged Native title. So did the Organic Act of 1884, which ended the era of military rule and provided for a rudimentary civil government that existed until the advent of territorial status in 1912. The Organic Act reserved land issues for later congressional action, but, between Native and white, land issues did not become acute enough to prompt congressional action until well into the twentieth century.

And so a history as yet imperfectly probed and chronicled gave the Natives of Alaska a breathing space denied their brethren on other frontiers. It was a critical breathing space, for, by the time the issues grew pressing, public attitudes had changed so far as to admit Natives to a meaningful participation in the political process. One result was a comprehensive and just resolution of land title in the Alaska Native Claims Settlement Act of 1971. Another was the emergence of strong institutions of Native political autonomy. Thus one searches in vain for a plainly identifiable time or symbol to represent the loss of Native sovereignty. In terms of conventional frontier concepts, Alaska reveals no clear end to the frontier period.[8]

In the Southwest, by 1890 the Pueblos found themselves in a predicament that made considerations of sovereignty the least of their concerns. In fact, they remained loosely self-governing through political institutions blending traditional forms with those imposed by Spain and Mexico. The Pueblos' severest problems, however, sprang from their ambiguous status under U.S. law. Since their Spanish land grants had been confirmed, territorial officials held that their lands did not constitute reservations and could be sold or otherwise disposed of as the owners saw fit. When the Supreme Court upheld this interpretation in 1876, it placed the Pueblos, for all practical purposes, beyond U.S. Indian law and outside the U.S. Indian system. Deprived of even the theoretical protection of federal authority, Pueblo lands beckoned squatters in ever increasing numbers. Powerless to cope, the true owners could only watch helplessly as their holdings dwindled. By the time the Supreme Court got around to reversing itself in 1913, the Pueblo land situation had become an almost hopeless muddle that would take twenty-five years to straighten out.[9]

Despite the exceptions, American Indian frontiers can be seen as essentially closed by 1890. For the Indians, however, the legacy of the frontier period endured through the first three decades of the twentieth century and, in many respects, even beyond.

Most devastating were the relentless workings of the Dawes General

Allotment Act. The Dawes Act and its subsequent modifications achieved but one of the goals of the reformers, and that spectacularly, for it swiftly moved Indian land into white ownership. Between 1887 and 1934 the purchase of reservation lands not needed for allotment, coupled with the sale of allotments by their owners after the trust period, reduced Indian holdings by sixty percent, from 138 million acres to 55 million. In its other objectives the Dawes Act failed as spectacularly as it succeeded in the first. It did not protect Indians in the ownership of an economically viable homestead: by sale, lease, or other forms of alienation, and by infinite subdivision through inheritance, allotments disintegrated into unproductive parcels or escaped Indian ownership altogether. It did not transform the Indian into a self-sufficient yeoman farmer: fragmentation and alienation of holdings, lack of government aid, unsuitability of lands for agriculture, and cultural conservatism united to discourage Indian effort and actually produce a decline in Indian farming between 1900 and 1930. It did not promote civilization and assimilation: the scientific assumptions that underlay that objective were erroneous. And it did not reduce Indian dependency on federal assistance: quite the reverse, for by fostering poverty it increased dependency. The Dawes Act, then, turned out to be a disaster for the Indians, relieved only by its demise in the Wheeler-Howard Act of 1934, with its promise of an Indian "New Deal."[10]

Although the Dawes Act at least confirmed the Indians in the ownership of their shrunken reservations, it is difficult to discern any other benefit to them. Yet the Dawes Act cannot be understood in the simplistic terms of white lust for Indian land, however generously it fed that undeniable lust. While recognizing its catastrophic consequences, one must also acknowledge the altruistic motives of its framers and promoters. As an article of faith—of Protestant evangelical faith—the reformers genuinely believed that land must not be suffered to lie unused in the approved Anglo-Saxon fashion—a conviction that incidentally supported the notions of land boomers who wasted no altruism on Indians. Thus Indians must learn to use the land in the approved fashion, and all they did not need must be turned over to whites to use in the same way. Beyond satisfying the imperative to make the land blossom, reformers also sincerely foresaw a host of civilizing influences accruing from individual ownership of land and the values, attitudes, and way of life thus forced on the individual owner. Though scarcely a recompense to the victims, the evidence of high-minded motivation is simply too overwhelming to be buried in a later generation's guilt over the hardship and injustice inflicted on the Indians.

The same is true of the civilization program. Its authors honestly saw nothing worth saving in Indian culture. They honestly thought the Indian would greatly benefit economically, politically, socially, and culturally by incorporation into the life of white America. Although they recognized obstacles, they honestly believed that with proper legislation and administration the obstacles could be overcome and the Indian would be hastened from savagery to a condition of civilized grace in which only his color would mark him as different. Several generations of advances in anthropology, sociology, history, and other social sciences now reveal all these assumptions to be false. Such a body of knowledge and insight did not exist in the 1880s. Of scientific authorities, only Lewis Henry Morgan sounded a note of caution, and even he did not question the basic premises but only the time needed to reach the goal. Today the goal and the process have been rejected and the consequences lamented. At the same time, the essentially humanitarian intent of the authors has to be credited.

In truth, the thought and action of the reformers simply expressed their culture. Just as the Indians responded to the vision of the reformers in ways entirely consistent with their culture, so the reformers themselves behaved no more or less consistently with their own culture. Although radically different, white culture also controlled its possessors. From the beginning of the Republic, U.S. Indian policy has sharply reflected the prevailing religious and intellectual mood of the age, and at no time until well into the twentieth century was there any room for different ways of life.[11] The reformers were indeed ethnocentric. In certitude, rectitude, righteousness, and faith in the superiority of their culture over all others, they were perhaps every bit as ethnocentric as the Indian whose transformation they sought. But as belied by their passionate dedication to the welfare of the Indian, racist they assuredly were not.

How then should white Americans have approached those frontiers in which they came into contact with Indians? In the 1870s some Canadians, extolling the superiority of their own policies and programs, looked with unconcealed condescension on American bungling,[12] and occasionally U.S. officials urged that the Canadian example be heeded. With accurate foresight, however, Interior Secretary Carl Schurz pointed out that the Canadians, too, would have their day of reckoning. "When in the British possessions agricultural and mining enterprise spreads with the same energy and eagerness as in the United States," he wrote in 1881, "when railroads penetrate their Indian country, when all that is valuable in it becomes thus accessible and tempting to the greed of white men, when game becomes scarce and ceases to furnish sufficient sustenance to the Indians, the Canadian authorities in their management of Indian affairs will find themselves confronted with the same difficulties."[13] They did indeed. That the Indian-Metis uprising of 1885 was the only major war of the Canadian West is explained less by enlightened Canadian policies than by the vastness of the land in relation to the Indian and white population.

In ends as well as means, and even in the land greed of settlers and the unfitness and occasional corruption of officials, Canadian policy and Canadian experience did not differ all that much from American. Treaties extinguished Indian title to land and set aside reservations dedicated both to removing the Indians from the paths of expansion and to transforming them into "civilized" and assimilated Canadians. Like Americans, Canadian theorists and administrators approached their task within the framework of their own culture, which of course closely resembled that of white Americans. In one major respect, the United States might have profited by a closer look at Canadian experience. The North-West Mounted Police enjoyed an authority and prestige with the Indians based on justice and fairness. Unlike the U.S. Army, it was a civil constabulary that could deal with individuals as well as tribes. It did not have to go to war with a whole people in order to enforce order. Yet even the vaunted Mounties could not stem the outbreak of 1885, which had to be suppressed by regular troops dispatched from the East.[14]

If Canada offers no basically better model, how then might the United States have managed the process differently so as to have produced an outcome consistent with today's concepts of justice, humanity, and pluralism? Although hindsight permits such speculation, in order to have validity any speculative alternatives must reflect the state of the social sciences in the nineteenth century and the values, attitudes, and assumptions—the culture—of white Americans of the nineteenth century. Given who these people were, what they knew, and what they believed, it is difficult to see how they might have behaved differently enough to have brought about a resultthat would be acceptable today.

What seems today more useful than postulating how previous generations should have behaved is to turn a clear and objective eye on why they behaved as they did. In such scrutiny the word *civilization* has to be neutralized—divested of its nineteenth-century meaning of the peak of human progress—and equated with the word *culture*. In the absence of any standards of worth that are not expressions of ethnocentrism, assumptions of the comparative worth of civilizations must be avoided as irrelevant. Thus, within the frontier zones of the American West, white and Indian civilizations met in a variety of relationships, fertilized each other, and left both permanently and significantly changed. Within this framework, not only is a more truthful view of history attainable, but moral judgments reflecting modern standards and values may be pronounced without indicting earlier generations for acting consistently with their time and place.

Such a framework also opens vistas of America's frontier process more sophisticated than Frederick Jackson's Turner's one-dimensional interpretation. In the Anglo-Saxon frontiersman's conquest of the wilderness, the Indian included, Turner saw a profound explanation of America's uniqueness. Perhaps an even more profound explanation lies in the cultural cross-fertilization that occurred first in the frontier zones and, more recently, in an America that welcomes and encourages the cultural, spiritual, political, and economic revival of the Indians and increasingly recognizes the rich contributions they have made and continue to make to American life. Although Indians still harbor deep and compelling grievances, modern America rejects the aim of nineteenth-century Indian policy and applauds their progress in combating its legacy. Modern America is uniquely, as Turner failed to perceive, a blend of its immigrant and native heritages.[15]

Notes

Preface

1. Joseph Epes Brown, "The Roots of Renewal," in Walter Holden Capps, ed., *Seeing with a Native Eye: Essays on Native American Religion* (New York, 1976), p. 34.

2. Calvin Martin, "The Metaphysics of Writing Indian-White History," *Ethnohistory*, XXVI (Winter 1981), p. 158.

3. Particularly useful in surveying the literature and postulating concepts are Leonard Thompson and Howard Lamar, "Comparative Frontier History," and Robert F. Berkhofer, Jr., "The North American Frontier as Process and Context," in Lamar and Thompson, eds., *The Frontier in History: North America and Southern Africa Compared* (New Haven, Conn., 1981), pp. 3-13, 43-75. Provocative too is Jack D. Forbes, "Frontiers in American History and the Role of the Frontier Historian," *Ethnohistorian*, XIV (Spring 1968), pp. 203-35.

Chapter 1: The Indian West at Midcentury

1. "Report of Lieut. J. W. Abert, of His Examination of New Mexico, in the Years 1846-'47," *Senate Executive Documents*, 30th Cong., lst sess., no. 23 (1848), p. 10. Stan Hoig, *The Peace Chiefs of the Cheyennes* (Norman, Okla., 1980), chap. 3.

2. Estimating Indian population is fraught with peril. Figures here are derived mainly from John R. Swanton, *The Indian Tribes of North America*, Bureau of American Ethnology Bulletin no. 45 (Washington, D.C., 1952).

3. This capsule look at the Nez Perces is drawn principally from Alvin M. Josephy, Jr., *The Nez Perce Indians and the Opening of the Northwest* (New Haven, Conn., 1965).

4. In addition to Josephy, see Sue Whalen, "The Nez Perces' Relationship to Their Land," *The Indian Historian*, n.s., IV (Fall 1971), pp. 30-33.

5. Josephy, *Nez Perce Indians and the Opening of the Northwest*, Frontispiece. See also Whalen, "Nez Perces' Relationship to Their Land."

6. Lucullus V. McWhorter, *Yellow Wolf: His Own Story* (Caldwell, Idaho, 1948), p. 296.

7. Quoted in Josephy, *Nez Perce Indians and the Opening of the Northwest*, p. 488.

8. For discussion of this point see Francis Jennings, *The Invasion of America: Indians, Colonialism, and the Cant of Conquest* (Chapel Hill, N.C., 1975), pp. 158–59.

9. Two sources well illustrate this often overlooked point: Richard White, "The Winning of the West: The Expansion of the Western Sioux in the Eighteenth and Nineteenth Centuries," *Journal of American History*, LXV (September 1978), pp. 319–43; and John C. Ewers, "Intertribal Warfare as the Precursor of Indian-White Warfare on the Northern Great Plains," *Western Historical Quarterly*, VI (October 1975), pp. 397–410.

10. Edward P. Dozier, "Rio Grande Pueblos," in Edward H. Spicer, ed., *Perspectives in American Indian Culture Change* (Chicago, 1961), chap. 3.

11. Sherburne F. Cook, *The Conflict between the California Indian and White Civilization* (Berkeley and Los Angeles, 1976), pts. 1 and 2. Edward D. Castillo, "The Impact of Euro-American Exploration and Settlement [on California Indians]," in Robert F. Heizer, ed., *California* (William C. Sturtevant, ed., *Handbook of North American Indians*, VIII, Washington, D.C., 1978), pp. 88–107.

12. Wilbur R. Jacobs, "The Indian and the Frontier in American History," *Western Historical Quarterly*, IV (January 1973), pp. 44–48. For a survey of the literature on this important subject, see Henry F. Dobyns, *Native American Historical Demography: A Critical Bibliography* (Bloomington, Ind., 1976).

13. Morton H. Fried, *The Notion of Tribe* (Menlo Park, Calif., 1975). Alfred L. Kroeber, "Nature of the Land-Holding Group," *Ethnohistory*, II (Fall 1955), pp. 304–15. Elman R. Service, "War and Our Contemporary Ancestors," in Morton H. Fried, Marvin Harris, and Robert Murphy, eds., *War: The Anthropology of Armed Conflict and Aggression* (Garden City, N.Y., 1968), pp. 160–67.

14. These premises form a theme that runs throughout Jennings, *Invasion of America*, but see also Service, "War and Our Contemporary Ancestors."

15. William Brandon, "American Indians and American History," *The American West*, II (Spring 1965), p. 24.

16. Two outstanding studies of the interaction thus fostered are Lewis O. Saum, *The Fur Trader and the Indian* (Seattle, 1965), and Arthur J. Ray, *Indians in the Fur Trade: Their Role as Hunters, Trappers, and Middlemen in the Lands Southwest of Hudson Bay, 1660–1870* (Toronto, 1974).

17. Bernard W. Sheehan, *Seeds of Extinction: Jeffersonian Philanthropy and the American Indian* (Chapel Hill, N.C., 1973), p. 232.

18. Craig MacAndrew and Robert B. Edgerton, *Drunken Comportment: A Social Explanation* (Chicago, 1969), chaps. 6 and 7. See also Nancy Oestreich Lurie, "The World's Oldest On-Going Protest Demonstration: North American Indian Drinking Patterns," *Pacific Historical Review*, XL (August 1971), pp. 311–32.

19. Quoted in Walter O'Meara, *Daughters of the Country: The Women of the Fur Traders and Mountain Men* (New York, 1968), p. 182. The nature and significance of this feature of trade is well set forth in John C. Ewers, "Mothers of the Mixed Bloods: The Marginal Woman in the History of the Upper Missouri," in K. Ross Toole et al., eds., *Probing the American West: Papers from the Santa Fe Conference* (Santa Fe, 1962), pp. 62–70; and Harry H. Anderson, "Fur Traders as Fathers:

The Origins of the Mixed-Blood Community among the Rosebud Sioux," *South Dakota History,* III (Summer 1973), pp. 233–70.

20. P. Richard Metcalf has pointed out that the missionary and other white influences did not so much create factionalism as reinforce existing factionalism; see Metcalf, "Who Shall Rule at Home? Native American Politics and Indian-White Relations," *Journal of American History,* LXI (December 1974), pp. 651–65. Excellent insights into the nature of the interaction of missionaries and Indians are in Robert F. Berkhofer, Jr., *Salvation and the Savage: An Analysis of Protestant Missions and American Indian Response, 1787–1862* (Lexington, Ky., 1965). The story of missionaries in the Pacific Northwest is exceptionally well told in Josephy, *Nez Perce Indians and the Opening of the Northwest,* and Robert Ignatius Burns, S.J., *The Jesuits and the Indian Wars of the Northwest* (New Haven, Conn., 1966).

21. Quoted in Saum, *The Fur Trader and the Indian,* p. 75. Two articles by John C. Ewers are especially good in portraying Indian views of whites: "Indian Views of the White Men Prior to 1850: An Interpretation," in Daniel Tyler, ed., *Red Men and Hat Wearers: Viewpoints in Indian History* (Fort Collins, Colo., 1976), pp. 7–24; and "When Red and White Men Met," *Western Historical Quarterly,* II (April 1971), pp. 132–50. See also Preston Holder, "The Fur Trade as Seen from the Indian Point of View," in John Francis McDermott, ed., *The Frontier Reexamined* (Urbana, Ill., 1967), pp. 129–40.

22. Ewers, "Indian Views of White Men," p. 11.

23. Ibid., p. 20.

24. Ewers, "When Red and White Men Met," pp. 139–40.

25. Richard Slotkin, *Regeneration through Violence: The Mythology of the American Frontier, 1600–1860* (Middletown, Conn., 1973), p. 26.

26. The following paragraphs are drawn from John C. Ewers, *The Blackfeet: Raiders of the Northwestern Plains* (Norman, Okla., 1958); Oscar Lewis, *The Effects of White Contact upon Blackfoot Culture, with Special Reference to the Role of the Fur Trade,* Monographs of the American Ethnological Society, no. 6 (New York, 1942); Polly Pope, "Trade in the Plains: Affluence and Its Effects," *Kroeber Anthropological Society Papers,* XXIV (Spring 1966), pp. 53–61; and Clark Wissler, *Indians of the United States: Four Centuries of Their History and Culture* (New York, 1940), chap. 9.

27. Alexander Henry, quoted in Ewers, *Blackfeet,* p. 35.

28. Quoted in ibid., p. 41.

Chapter 2: Foundations of a New Indian Policy, 1846–1860

1. Ralph E. Twitchell, *The History of the Military Occupation of the Territory of New Mexico from 1846 to 1851* (Denver, 1909), pp. 49–52.

2. The following paragraphs are drawn chiefly from the following: Robert F. Berkhofer, Jr., *The White Man's Indian: Images of the American Indian from Columbus to the Present* (New York, 1978); Roy Harvey Pearce, *The Savages of America: A Study of the Indian and the Idea of Civilization* (Baltimore, 1953); Roy Harvey Pearce, "The Metaphysics of Indian-Hating," *Ethnohistory,* IV (Winter 1957), pp. 27–40; Richard Slotkin, *Regeneration through Violence: The Mythology of the American Frontier,*

1600–1860 (Middletown, Conn., 1973); Bernard W. Sheehan, *Seeds of Extinction: Jeffersonian Philanthropy and the American Indian* (Chapel Hill, N.C., 1973); Francis Jennings, *The Invasion of America: Indians, Colonialism, and the Cant of Conquest* (Chapel Hill, N.C., 1975); and Francis Paul Prucha, "The Image of the Indian in Pre-Civil War America," *Indiana Historical Society Lectures, 1970–71* (Indianapolis, 1971), pp. 2–19 (also printed in Prucha, *Indian Policy in the United States: Historical Essays* [Lincoln, Nebr., 1981], pp. 49–62).

3. This point is nicely expressed in Jennings, *Invasion of America*, p. 32.

4. Quoted in Berkhofer, *White Man's Indian*, p. 47.

5. Wilbur R. Jacobs, "The Indian and the Frontier in American History—A Need for Revision," *Western Historical Quarterly*, IV (January 1973), pp. 43–56.

6. Slotkin, *Regeneration through Violence*, pp. 366–67.

7. Recent historians of racism contend that nineteenth-century thought linked race with traits not subject to change and that this view conditioned public attitudes toward the Indian. This thesis is effectively disputed in Francis Paul Prucha, "Scientific Racism and Indian Policy," in Prucha, *Indian Policy in the United States*, pp. 180–97.

8. Cf. Slotkin, *Regeneration through Violence*, p. 45. A sensitive examination of Indian religion is Hartley Burr Alexander, *The World's Rim: Great Mysteries of the North American Indians* (Lincoln, Nebr., 1953)

9. Quoted in Berkhofer, *White Man's Indian*, p. 138.

10. Ronald N. Satz, *American Indian Policy in the Jacksonian Era* (Lincoln, Nebr., 1975), p. 1.

11. Quoted in Berkhofer, *White Man's Indian*, p. 138.

12. Removal has inspired a vast literature, of which the following are notable: Satz, *American Indian Policy in the Jacksonian Era* (from which the above statistics are taken, see p. 97); Reginald Horsman, *The Origins of Indian Removal, 1815–1824* (East Lansing, Mich., 1970); Francis Paul Prucha, "Andrew Jackson's Indian Policy: A Reassessment," *Journal of American History*, LVI (December 1969), pp. 527–39; Prucha, "Indian Removal and the Great American Desert," *Indiana Magazine of History*, LIX (December 1963), pp. 299–322; Michael Paul Rogin, *Fathers and Children: Andrew Jackson and the Subjugation of the American Indian* (New York, 1975). Prucha's two articles are reprinted in Prucha, *Indian Policy in the United States*, pp. 138–52, 92–116.

13. The Census of 1860 disclosed the following non-Indian population: Kansas 107,206; Nebraska 28,841; Dakota 4,837; Texas 604,215; New Mexico 93,516; Nevada 6,857; Utah 40,273; Colorado 34,277; Washington 11,594 ; Oregon 52,465; and California 379,994.

14. Three studies are basic to understanding Indian policy in the decade following the Mexican War: Robert A. Trennert, Jr., *Alternative to Extinction: Federal Indian Policy and the Beginnings of the Reservation System, 1846–51* (Philadelphia, 1975); James C. Malin, *Indian Policy and Westward Expansion* (Lawrence, Kans., 1921); and Alban W. Hoopes, *Indian Affairs and their Administration, with Special Reference to the Far West, 1849–60* (Philadelphia, 1932).

15. The 1855 expansion raised the ceiling on army strength to eighteen thousand, but the lag of actual behind authorized strength, the diversion of personnel to detached service, and the assignment of about one-third of the army to eastern

stations thinned the ranks available for frontier service. For the army in this period see Robert M. Utley, *Frontiersmen in Blue: The United States Army and the Indian, 1848–1865* (New York, 1967).

16. John Griener in "Condition of the Indian Tribes," *Senate Reports*, 39th Cong., 2d sess., no. 156 (1867), p. 328. He meant it literally; he sang at political rallies. The standard history of the Indian Bureau is Laurence F. Schmeckebier, *The Office of Indian Affairs: Its History, Activities, and Organization* (Baltimore, 1927).

17. Quoted in Frederick J. Dockstader, *Great North American Indians: Profiles in Life and Leadership* (New York, 1977), p. 150. For a good discussion of the treaty system see Wilcomb E. Washburn, *The Indian in America* (New York, 1975), pp. 97–103. All ratified treaties are printed in Charles J. Kappler, comp., *Indian Affairs: Laws and Treaties*, 5 vols. (Washington, D.C., 1904–41), II. Many treaties were negotiated but not ratified. The text of those that have survived may usually be found in the Indian Bureau records in the National Archives.

18. The subject is well treated in Robert A. Trennert, *Indian Traders on the Middle Border: The House of Ewing, 1827–1854* (Lincoln, Nebr., 1981). See also Francis Paul Prucha, "American Indian Policy in the 1840s: Visions of Reform," in John G. Clark, ed., *The Frontier Challenge: Responses to the Trans-Mississippi West* (Lawrence, Kans., 1971), pp. 81–110 (reprinted in Prucha, *Indian Policy in the United States*, pp. 153–79).

19. The origins and evolution of the reservation policy are set forth in Trennert, *Alternative to Extinction*. See also Trennert's biographical sketch of Medill in Robert N. Kvasnicka and Herman J. Viola, eds., *The Commissioners of Indian Affairs, 1824–1977* (Lincoln, Nebr., 1979), pp. 29–40. Mix' role is apparent in the successive biographies of this volume.

20. Quoted in Donald J. Berthrong, "Changing Concepts: The Indians Learn about the 'Long Knives' and Settlers," in Daniel Tyler, ed., *Red Men and Hat Wearers: Viewpoints in Indian History* (Fort Collins, Colo., 1976), p. 48.

21. This account is drawn mainly from Frank McNitt, *Navajo Wars: Military Campaigns, Slave Raids, and Reprisals* (Albuquerque, 1972), chap. 14; and McNitt, ed., *Navaho Expedition: Journal of a Military Reconnaissance from Santa Fe, New Mexico, to the Navaho Country Made in 1849 by Lieutenant James H. Simpson* (Norman, Okla. 1964), which deals with the subject in a detailed epilogue, pp. 193–201.

22. W. H. H. Davis, *El Gringo, or, New Mexico and Her People* (1856; reprint, Santa Fe, 1938), p. 233.

23. Malcolm Edwards, ed., *The California Diary of General E. D. Townsend* (Los Angeles, 1970), p. 55. Entry of June 2, 1852. Townsend was a captain and division adjutant general.

24. W. A. Croffut, ed., *Fifty Years in Camp and Field: The Diary of Major General Ethan Allen Hitchcock* (New York, 1909), p. 395. Captain Townsend, cited in the previous note, recorded the same incident in his journal, July 31, 1851; see p. 68.

25. *Annual Report of the Secretary of the Interior, 1851*, pp. 484–88. For the California reservations, see Hoopes, *Indian Affairs*, Chap. 3; William H. Ellison, "The Federal Indian Policy in California, 1846–1860," *Mississippi Valley Historical Review*, IX (June 1922), pp. 37–67; and Richard E. Crouter and Andrew F. Rolle, "Edward Fitzgerald Beale and the Indian Peace Commissioners in California, 1851–1854," *Historical Society of Southern California Quarterly*, XLII (June 1960), pp. 107–32.

26. Harry Kelsey, "The California Indian Treaty Myth," *Southern California Quarterly*, LV (Fall 1973), pp. 225–38, traces the tortured origins of the treaties and shows that the question of title was among the reasons for rejection.

27. *California Diary of General E. D. Townsend*, p. 146. Entry of October 27, 1855.

28. Sherburne F. Cook, *The Population of the California Indians, 1769–1970* (Berkeley and Los Angeles, 1976), pp. 42–43, 44, 59, 69, 70, 199–202. See also Cook, *The Conflict between the California Indians and White Civilization* (Berkeley and Los Angeles, 1976), pt. 1; Edward D. Castillo, "The Impact of Euro-American Exploration and Settlement [on California Indians]," in Robert F. Heizer, ed., *California* (William C. Sturtevant, ed., *Handbook of North American Indians*, VIII, Washington, D.C., 1978), pp. 107–12; and Robert F. Heizer, ed., *The Destruction of the California Indians* (Santa Barbara, 1974).

29. Hoopes, *Indian Affairs*, pp. 79–86, covers this topic. See also C. F. Coan, "The First Stage of the Federal Indian Policy in the Pacific Northwest, 1849–1852," *Oregon Historical Quarterly*, XXII (March 1921), pp. 46–89; and idem., "The Adoption of the Reservation Policy in the Pacific Northwest, 1853–1855," ibid., XXIII (March 1922), pp. 1–38.

30. Hoopes, *Indian Affairs*, summarizes the principal events in the Pacific Northwest. Especially good accounts of the Stevens treaties are in Alvin M. Josephy, Jr., *The Nez Perce Indians and the Opening of the Northwest* (New Haven, Conn., 1965); and Robert Ignatius Burns, S.J., *The Jesuits and the Indian Wars of the Northwest* (New Haven, Conn., 1966). For military aspects see Utley, *Frontiersmen in Blue*, chap. 9.

31. For developments in Texas see Trennert, *Alternative to Extinction*, chap. 4; George D. Harmon, "The United States Indian Policy in Texas, 1846–1860," *Mississippi Valley Historical Review*, XVII (December 1930), pp. 377–403; and Lena Clara Koch, "The Federal Indian Policy in Texas, 1845–1860," *Southwestern Historical Quarterly*, XXVIII (January 1925), pp. 223–34; (April 1925), pp. 259–86; XXIX (July 1925), pp. 19–35; (October 1925), pp. 98–127.

32. The story of the Texas reservations is recounted in a series of articles by Kenneth F. Neighbours: "Robert S. Neighbors and the Founding of the Texas Indian Reservations," *West Texas Historical Association Year Book*, XXXI (1955), pp. 65–74; "Chapters from the History of the Texas Indian Reservations," ibid., XXXIII (1957), pp. 3–16; and "The Assassination of Robert S. Neighbors," ibid., XXXIV (1958), pp. 38–49.

33. For these three administrations, see Annie H. Abel, ed., *The Correspondence of James S. Calhoun* (Washington, D.C., 1915); Abel, ed., "Indian Affairs in New Mexico under the Administration of William Carr Lane, from the Journal of John Ward," *New Mexico Historical Review*, XVI (April 1941), pp. 206–32; (July 1941), pp. 328–58; Ralph E. Twitchell, *Historical Sketch of Governor William Carr Lane* (Santa Fe, 1917); and David Meriwether, *My Life in the Mountains and on the Plains*, ed. Robert A. Griffin (Norman, Okla., 1965). No good synthesis exists of Indian policy in the 1850s in New Mexico (which then included Arizona). See, in addition to McNitt, *Navajo Wars*; Ralph H. Ogle, *Federal Control of the Western Apaches, 1848–1886* (Albuquerque, 1970); and Frank D. Reeve, "The Government and the Navaho, 1846–1858," *New Mexico Historical Review*, XIV (January 1939), pp. 82–114.

34. Marc Simmons, "History of the Pueblos since 1821," in Alfonso Ortiz, ed.,

Southwest (William C. Sturtevant, ed., *Handbook of North American Indians*, IX, Washington, D.C., 1979), pp. 206–23.

35. Trennert, *Alternative to Extinction*, chap. 6. Among the tribes native to this area were Pawnee, Ponca, Oto, Missouri, and Omaha. Transplants from the East included Potawatomi, Ottawa, Chippewa, Winnebago, Sac and Fox, Kickapoo, Delaware, Shawnee, Peoria, Wea, Miami, Kaskaskia, and Piankashaw. The treaties are in Kappler, *Indian Affairs*, II, pp. 608–46.

36. H. Craig Miner and William E. Unrau, *The End of Indian Kansas: A Study of Cultural Revolution, 1854–1871* (Lawrence, Kans., 1978).

37. There is no satisfactory history of the Five Tribes as a group, although Grant Foreman, *The Five Civilized Tribes* (Norman, Okla., 1934) is often cited, and the main themes emerge in several chapters of Angie Debo, *A History of the Indians of the United States* (Norman, Okla., 1970). Rather, one must turn to individual tribal histories: Grace Steele Woodward, *The Cherokees* (Norman, Okla., 1963); Angie Debo, *The Road to Disappearance: A History of the Creek Indians* (Norman, Okla., 1941); Debo, *The Rise and Fall of the Choctaw Republic*, 2d ed. (Norman, Okla., 1967); Arrell M. Gibson, *The Chickasaws* (Norman, Okla., 1971); and Edwin C. McReynolds, *The Seminoles* (Norman, Okla., 1957). Excellent tribal sketches appear in Muriel H. Wright, *A Guide to the Indian Tribes of Oklahoma* (Norman, Okla., 1951).

38. This Mexican problem was stubbornly troublesome for decades. Involved were Indians from the Great Plains, Texas, New Mexico, and Arizona. See especially J. Fred Rippy, "The Indians of the Southwest in the Diplomacy of the United States and Mexico, 1848–1853," *Hispanic-American Historical Review*, II (August 1919), pp. 363–96; and Joseph F. Park, "The Apaches in Mexican-American Relations, 1846–1861: A Footnote to the Gadsden Treaty," *Arizona and the West*, III (Summer 1961), pp. 129–46.

39. LeRoy R. Hafen and W. J. Ghent, *Broken Hand: The Life Story of Thomas Fitzpatrick, Chief of the Mountain Men* (Denver, 1931).

40. Quoted in Trennert, *Alternative to Extinction*, p. 190, which gives a good account of Plains events in chaps. 6 and 7. See also Harry H. Anderson, "The Controversial Sioux Amendment to the Fort Laramie Treaty of 1851," *Nebraska History*, XXXVII (September 1956), pp. 201–20.

41. *Annual Report of the Commissioner of Indian Affairs, 1853*, p. 370.

Chapter 3: When the White People Fought Each Other, 1861–1865

1. Eve Ball, *In the Days of Victorio: Recollections of a Warm Springs Apache* (Tucson, 1970), p. 47.

2. Robert M. Utley, "The Bascom Affair: A Reconstruction," *Arizona and the West*, II (Spring 1961), pp. 59–68. Benjamin Sacs, ed., "New Evidence on the Bascom Affair," ibid., IV (Autumn 1962), pp. 261–78. These two sources should be used together, for the second makes important revisions in the first.

3. John C. Cremony, *Life among the Apaches* (San Francisco, 1868), p. 164.

4. Robert M. Utley, *Frontiersmen in Blue: The United States Army and the Indian, 1848–1865* (New York, 1967), pp. 251–52, recounts this episode and cites pertinent evidence.

5. Quoted in Angie Debo, *A History of the Indians of the United States* (Norman, Okla., 1970), p. 137. In addition to sources cited in chap. 2, n. 36, see two studies by Annie H. Abel long considered standard: *The American Indian as Slaveholder and Secessionist: An Omitted Chapter in the Diplomatic History of the Southern Confederacy* (Cleveland, 1915) and *The American Indian as a Participant in the Civil War* (Cleveland, 1919). See also, for military aspects, LeRoy H. Fisher, ed., *The Civil War Era in Indian Territory* (Los Angeles, 1974).

6. William W. Folwell, *A History of Minnesota*, 4 vols. (St. Paul, 1924), II, p. 232. The literature of the Minnesota outbreak is extensive. See especially C. M. Oehler, *The Great Sioux Uprising* (New York, 1959) and Kenneth Carley, *The Sioux Uprising of 1862* (St. Paul, 1961). Extensive documentation is in *Minnesota in the Civil and Indian Wars*, 2 vols. (St. Paul, 1899).

7. These people made up the "Indian Ring," that elusive phantom that looms so large in the literature of the Indian frontier. No formal, organized ring existed, but when some or all these parties worked toward the same end, the Indian lost just as surely. The Indian Ring as it developed in Kansas is expertly dissected in H. Craig Miner and William E. Unrau, *The End of Indian Kansas: A Study of Cultural Revolution, 1854–1871* (Lawrence, Kans., 1978).

8. Quoted in David A. Nichols, *Lincoln and the Indians: Civil War Policy and Politics* (Columbia, Mo., 1978), p. 132. My account is based on chaps. 4–6. For a good study of this same period, though with somewhat different focus, see Edmund J. Danzinger, Jr., *Indians and Bureaucrats: Administering the Reservation Policy during the Civil War* (Urbana, Ill., 1974).

9. Nichols, *Lincoln and the Indians*, p. 87.

10. Frank McNitt, *Navajo Wars: Military Campaigns, Slave Raids, and Reprisals* (Albuquerque, 1972), pp. 390–98. Marc Simmons, *The Little Lion of the Southwest: A Life of Manuel Antonio Chaves* (Chicago, 1973), pp. 159–63.

11. "Condition of the Indian Tribes," *Senate Reports*, 39th Cong., 2d sess., no. 156 (1867), p. 117. This source contains most of the official correspondence relating to the Navajo Wars and the Bosque Redondo experience. See also Utley, *Frontiersmen in Blue*, pp. 237–48; Gerald Thompson, *The Army and the Navajo: The Bosque Redondo Reservation Experiment, 1863–1868* (Tucson, 1976); Clifford E. Trafzer, *The Kit Carson Campaign: The Last Great Navajo War* (Norman, Okla., 1982); Lynn R. Bailey, *The Long Walk: A History of the Navajo Wars, 1846–68* (Los Angeles, 1964) and his *Bosque Redondo: An American Concentration Camp* (Pasadena, Calif., 1970); and Charles Amsden, "The Navajo Exile at Bosque Redondo," *New Mexico Historical Review*, VIII (January 1933), pp. 31–50. A richly detailed chronicle of the Long Walk is Frank McNitt, "The Long March, 1863–1867," in Albert H. Schroeder, ed., *The Changing Ways of Southwestern Indians* (Glorieta, N.M., 1973), pp. 145–69.

12. Stan Hoig, *The Peace Chiefs of the Cheyennes* (Norman, Okla., 1980), chap. 8.

13. The literature of Sand Creek and its antecedents, both original and secondary, is voluminous. The standard monographic treatment is Stan Hoig, *The Sand Creek Massacre* (Norman, Okla., 1961). Excellent recent scholarship is contained in the Sand Creek centennial issue of the *Colorado Magazine*, XLI (Fall 1964): Raymond G. Carey, "The Puzzle of Sand Creek," pp. 279–98; William E. Unrau, "A Prelude to War," pp. 299–314 (a good treatment of the Fort Wise Treaty); and Janet Lecompte, "Sand Creek," pp. 314–35. Also notable are two works by Harry Kelsey:

"Background to Sand Creek," ibid., XLV (Fall 1968), pp. 279–300; and *Frontier Capitalist: The Life of John Evans* (Denver, 1969), chap. 10. Donald J. Berthrong, *The Southern Cheyennes* (Norman, Okla., 1963), contains provocative interpretations. I found useful and reliable Lonnie J. White, "From Bloodless to Bloody: The Third Colorado Cavalry and the Sand Creek Massacre," in White, ed., *Hostiles and Horse Soldiers: Indian Battles and Campaigns in the West* (Boulder, Colo., 1972), chap. 1.

14. The Indian account of this fight is in George Bird Grinnell, *The Fighting Cheyennes*, 2d ed. (Norman, Okla., 1956), pp. 144–47. For Lean Bear see Hoig, *Peace Chiefs of the Cheyennes*, chap. 6.

15. Utley, *Frontiersmen in Blue*, chap. 15.

16. Richard N. Ellis, *General Pope and U.S. Indian Policy* (Albuquerque, 1970), pp. 98–103, 111–12. Howard R. Lamar, *Dakota Territory, 1861–1889: A Study of Frontier Politics* (New Haven, Conn., 1956), chap. 2. For the text see Charles J. Kappler, comp., *Indian Affairs: Laws and Treaties*, 5 vols. (Washington, D.C., 1904–41), II, pp. 883–87, 896–908.

17. William E. Unrau, "Indian Agency vs. the Army: Some Background Notes on the Kiowa-Comanche Treaty of 1865," *Kansas Historical Quarterly*, XXX (Summer 1964), pp. 129–52. For the text see Kappler, *Indian Affairs*, II, pp. 887–95.

Chapter 4: War and Peace: Indian Relations in Transition, 1865–1869

1. Red Cloud and the history of relations between his people and the whites are outstandingly chronicled in James C. Olson, *Red Cloud and the Sioux Problem* (Lincoln, Nebr., 1965); and George E. Hyde, *Red Cloud's Folk: A History of the Oglala Sioux Indians* (Norman, Okla., 1937).

2. The best account of this council is in Olson, *Red Cloud and the Sioux Problem*, chap. 3.

3. *Congressional Globe*, 40th Cong., 1st sess. (July 17, 1867), p. 681.

4. Quoted in Robert G. Athearn, *William Tecumseh Sherman and the Settlement of the West* (Norman, Okla., 1956), p. 219.

5. The travels of the committee are followed in Lonnie J. White, ed., *Chronicle of a Congressional Journey: The Doolittle Committee in the Southwest, 1865* (Boulder, Colo., 1975); and Doolittle to Mrs. L. F. S. Foster, March 7, 1881, printed in *New Mexico Historical Review*, XXVI (April 1951), pp. 149–58.

6. For succinct treatments of the civil-military issue, see Donald J. D'Elia, "The Argument over Civilian or Military Control, 1865–1880," *Historian*, XXIV (February 1962), pp. 207–25; and Loring Benson Priest, *Uncle Sam's Stepchildren: The Reformation of United States Indian Policy, 1865–1887* (New Brunswick, N.J., 1942; Lincoln, Nebr., 1975), pp. 17–27. For Pope's role see Richard N. Ellis, *General Pope and U.S. Indian Policy* (Albuquerque, 1970), chaps. 5–6; Ellis, ed., "General Pope's Report on the West, 1866," *Kansas Historical Quarterly*, XXXV (Winter 1969), pp. 345–67; and Ellis, ed., "Bent, Carson, and the Indians, 1865," *Colorado Magazine*, XLVI (Winter 1969), pp. 55–68.

7. The Fetterman Massacre has inspired a voluminous literature. I have writ-

ten of it and cited the principal sources in Robert M. Utley, *Frontier Regulars: The United States Army and the Indian, 1866–1891* (New York, 1973), chap. 7. But see especially Dee Brown, *Fort Phil Kearny: An American Saga* (New York, 1962); J. W. Vaughn, *Indian Fights: New Facts on Seven Encounters* (Norman, Okla., 1966), chap. 2; and Robert A. Murray, *Military Posts in the Powder River Country of Wyoming, 1865–1894* (Lincoln, Nebr., 1968), pt. 1. For the Indian side of the story, see Hyde, *Red Cloud's Folk*, chap. 9; and George Bird Grinnell, *The Fighting Cheyennes*, 2d ed. (Norman, Okla., 1956), chap. 18.

8. *Senate Executive Documents*, 40th Cong., 1st sess., no. 13 (1867), p. 27.

9. The Doolittle report, "Condition of the Indian Tribes," was published separately by the Government Printing Office and also as *Senate Reports*, 39th Cong., 2d sess., no. 156 (1867). See also, for analysis, Harry Kelsey, "The Doolittle Report of 1867: Its Preparation and Shortcomings," *Arizona and the West*, XVII (Summer 1975), pp. 107–20; and Donald Chaput, "Generals, Indian Agents, Politicians: The Doolittle Survey of 1865," *Western Historical Quarterly*, III (July 1972), pp. 269–82.

10. *House Executive Documents*, 39th Cong., 2d sess., no. 71 (1866), pp. 12–13. Ibid., no. 88 (1866). Lewis V. Bogy to Secretary Browning, February 11, 1867, Secretary of the Interior, Letters Received, Indian Division, Record Group 98, National Archives, Washington, D.C.

11. James G. Randall, ed., *The Diary of Orville Hickman Browning*, 2 vols. (Springfield, Ill., 1933), II, pp. 126, 128, 137–38, 140. *Senate Executive Documents*, 40th Cong., 1st sess., no. 13 (1867), pp. 55–56.

12. *Congressional Globe*, 39th Cong., 2d sess. (1867), pp. 843–44, 878–82, 891–99, 1623–24, 1988.

13. Randall, *Diary of Orville Hickman Browning*, II, p. 147. I have dealt with the Hancock campaign in Utley, *Frontier Regulars*, chap. 8.

14. *Annual Report of the Secretary of War, 1866*, pp. 18–23; *Annual Report of the Secretary of War, 1867*, pp. 65–68. *Senate Executive Documents*, 40th Cong., 1st sess., no. 13 (1867), pp. 17–18. Athearn, *William Tecumseh Sherman and the Settlement of the West*, pp. 95–97, chap. 7.

15. The law creating the Taylor Peace Commission is 15 Stat. 17–18, also printed in Francis Paul Prucha, ed., *Documents of United States Indian Policy* (Lincoln, Nebr., 1975), pp. 105–06. Good biographical sketches of Bogy and Taylor, by William E. Unrau, are in Robert M. Kvasnicka and Herman J. Viola, eds., *The Commissioners of Indian Affair, 1824–1977* (Lincoln, Nebr., 1979), pp. 109–22. Taylor's program and the recommendations of the Sully commissioners (they wrote separate reports over a three-month period) are in *Senate Executive Documents*, 40th Cong., 1st sess., no. 13 (1867), pp. 1–6, 57–64, 115–16, 123–24.

16. Olson, *Red Cloud and the Sioux Problem*, pp. 63–68. Hyde, *Red Cloud's Folk*, pp. 156–61. Utley, *Frontier Regulars*, pp. 122–25.

17. For these events see Donald J. Berthrong, *The Southern Cheyennes* (Norman, Okla., 1963), Chaps. 11–12; Grinnell, *Fighting Cheyennes*, Chap. 19; and George E. Hyde, *Life of George Bent Written from His Letters*, ed. Savoie Lottinville (Norman, Okla., 1967), chaps. 9–10.

18. The best account of Kiowa and Comanche relations with the whites is in two works by Wilbur S. Nye: *Carbine and Lance: The Story of Old Fort Sill* (Norman,

Okla., 1937); and *Plains Indian Raiders: The Final Phases of Warfare from the Arkansas to the Red River* (Norman, Okla., 1968). The Texas perspective is set forth in two studies by Rupert N. Richardson: *The Comanche Barrier to South Plains Settlement* (Glendale, Calif., 1933); and *The Frontier of Northwest Texas, 1846 to 1876* (Glendale, Calif., 1963). Tribal histories are Mildred P. Mayhall, *The Kiowas* (Norman, Okla., 1962); and Ernest Wallace and E. Adamson Hoebel, *The Comanches: Lords of the South Plains* (Norman, Okla., 1952). For this period in particular, see Forrest D. Monahan, "Kiowa-Federal Relations in Kansas, 1865–68," *Chronicles of Oklahoma*, XLIX (Winter 1971–72), pp. 477–91.

19. Monahan, "Kiowa-Federal Relations," p. 49, doubts that Satanta conducted this raid, ascribing it instead to Cheyennes. Nye, *Plains Indian Raiders*, p. 80, gives the above version based on official correspondence in the Fort Dodge Letter Book.

20. As recorded in shorthand by reporter Henry M. Stanley, who would one day find Dr. Livingstone in the African jungle. See Stanley, "A British Journalist Reports the Medicine Lodge Peace Councils of 1867," *Kansas Historical Quarterly*, XXXIII (Autumn 1967), pp. 285–86. Stanley's dispatches to the *Missouri Democrat* contain much of the dialogue. Berthrong, *Southern Cheyennes*, presents a thorough and accurate account of the proceedings, based on official documents in the National Archives. See also Douglas C. Jones, *The Treaty of Medicine Lodge: The Story of the Great Treaty Council as told by Eyewitnesses* (Norman, Okla., 1966). For the treaty text see Charles J. Kappler, comp., *Indian Affairs: Laws and Treaties*, 5 vols. (Washington, D.C. 1904–41), II, pp. 977–89.

21. Stanley again, this time as recorded in Stan Hoig, *The Western Odyssey of John Simpson Smith, Frontiersman, Trapper, Trader, Interpreter* (Glendale, Calif., 1974), p. 189.

22. *Annual Report of the Commissioner of Indian Affairs, 1865*, pp. 312–53, contains the proceedings of the Fort Smith meeting. The treaties are in Kappler, *Indian Affairs*, II, pp. 910–15, 918–37, 942–50. See also Grace Steele Woodward, *The Cherokees* (Norman, Okla., 1963), chap. 14. The postwar history of the Five Tribes is the subject of the third volume of Annie Abel's trilogy, *The American Indian under Reconstruction* (Cleveland, 1925).

23. The text of the report is printed in Prucha, *Documents of United States Indian Policy*, pp. 106–10. See also Francis Paul Prucha, *American Indian Policy in Crisis: Christian Reformers and the Indian, 1865–1900* (Norman, Okla., 1976), pp. 20–23.

24. Quoted in Athearn, *William Tecumseh Sherman and the Settlement of the West*, pp. 210–11.

25. Olson, *Red Cloud and the Sioux Problem*, pp. 74–75.

26. John L. Kessell, "General Sherman and the Navajo Treaty of 1868: A Basic and Expedient Misunderstanding," *Western Historical Quarterly*, XII (July 1981), pp. 251–72. For Bosque Redondo see Gerald Thompson, *The Army and the Navajo: The Bosque Redondo Reservation Experiment, 1863–1868* (Tucson, 1976); and Lynn R. Bailey, *Bosque Redondo: An American Concentration Camp* (Pasadena, Calif., 1970). The text is in Kappler, *Indian Affairs*, II, pp. 1015–20.

27. Robert Winston Mardock, *The Reformers and the American Indian* (Columbia, Mo., 1971), pp. 34–35. Athearn, *William Tecumseh Sherman and the Settlement of the West*, pp. 209–10.

28. *Senate Executive Documents*, 40th Cong., 3d sess., no. 13 (1869), pp. 18–20.

Annual Report of the Secretary of War, 1868, pp. 10–16. Berthrong, *Southern Cheyennes,* pp. 305–06.

29. The resolutions are in Prucha, *Documents of United States Indian Policy,* pp. 116–17. See also Athearn, *William Tecumseh Sherman and the Settlement of the West,* pp. 226–28.

30. *The New York Times,* October 16, 1868.

31. There is confusion over whether Man-Afraid signed at this time or had signed the previous spring. I follow Olson, whose case for November seems strongest. See Olson, *Red Cloud and the Sioux Problem,* pp. 75 n. 79, 79 n. 99. For the text of the Fort Laramie Treaty, see Kappler, *Indian Affairs,* II, pp. 998–1007; and Prucha, *Documents of United States Indian Policy,* pp. 110–14.

32. For this celebrated engagement, which established the reputation of George Armstrong Custer as an Indian fighter, see Stan Hoig, *The Battle of the Washita: The Sheridan-Custer Indian Campaign of 1867–69* (New York, 1976).

Chapter 5: Grant's Peace Policy, 1869–1876

1. William S. McFeely, *Grant: A Biography* (New York, 1981), pp. 286–87.

2. Thomas C. Battey's introduction to Lawrie Tatum, *Our Red Brothers and the Peace Policy of President Ulysses S. Grant* (Philadelphia, 1899), pp. 17–18. See also Joseph E. Illick, "'Some of our Best Indians are Friends. . . .': Quaker Attitudes and Actions Regarding the Western Indians during the Grant Administration," *Western Historical Quarterly,* II (July 1971), pp. 283–94.

3. Boston *Daily Advertiser,* February 25, 1869, quoted in Robert Winston Mardock, *The Reformers and the American Indian* (Columbia, Mo., 1971), p. 50.

4. This account of the Peace Policy owes a large debt to Henry G. Waltmann, "Circumstantial Reformer: President Grant and the Indian Problem," *Arizona and the West,* XIII (Winter 1971), pp. 323–42. Cf. McFeely, *Grant,* chap. 9, which portrays the Peace Policy as more the product of Grant's initiative and also links it more firmly to Grant's youthful experience on the Pacific Coast. There is a vast literature on the Peace Policy, from which I have used in particular Francis Paul Prucha, *American Indian Policy in Crisis: Christian Reformers and the Indians, 1865–1900* (Norman, Okla., 1976), chaps. 2–4; Mardock, *Reformers and the American Indian,* chaps. 4–5; Henry E. Fritz, *The Movement for Indian Assimilation, 1860–1890* (Philadelphia, 1963), chaps. 3–7; and Loring Benson Priest, *Uncle Sam's Stepchildren: The Reformation of United States Indian Policy, 1865–1887* (New Brunswick, N.J., 1942; Lincoln, Nebr., 1975), pts. 1–3.

5. An excellent biography is William H. Armstrong, *Warrior in Two Camps: Ely S. Parker, Union General and Seneca Chief* (Syracuse, N.Y., 1978). See also biographical sketch by Henry G. Waltmann in Robert M. Kvasnicka and Herman J. Viola, eds., *The Commissioners of Indian Affairs, 1824–1977* (Lincoln, Nebr., 1979), pp. 123–33.

6. The act authorizing the board and its instructions from the President are printed in Francis Paul Prucha, ed. *Documents of United States Indian Policy* (Lincoln, Nebr., 1975), pp. 126–29. The first appointees were William Welsh, John V. Farwell,

George H. Stuart, Robert Campbell, William E. Dodge, E. S. Toby, Felix R. Brunot, Nathan Bishop, and Henry S. Lane.

7. Paul A. Hutton, "Phil Sheridan's Pyrrhic Victory: The Piegan Massacre, Army Politics, and the Transfer Debate," *Montana, the Magazine of Western History,* XXXII (Spring 1982), pp. 32–43.

8. *Memoirs of General William T. Sherman,* 2 vols. (New York, 1891), II, p. 436.

9. Quoted in Prucha, *American Indian Policy in Crisis,* p. 52. The sequence here presented by which church nomination became embedded in the Peace Policy is most clearly set forth in Waltmann, "Circumstantial Reformer," pp. 332–34.

10. Prucha, *Documents of United States Indian Policy,* p. 136.

11. Prucha, *American Indian Policy in Crisis,* p. 30.

12. Quoted in Dan L. Thrapp, *Victorio and the Mimbres Apaches* (Norman, Okla., 1974), p. 100. This is the most detailed and reliable account of the peace offensive against the Apaches and has been extensively used in what follows. See also Thrapp, *The Conquest of Apacheria* (Norman, Okla., 1967), chaps. 6–12; and Ralph H. Ogle, *Federal Control of the Western Apaches, 1848–1886* (Albuquerque, 1970), chaps. 3–6.

13. In addition to Thrapp, *Victorio,* chap. 10, see Drew's letters in *First Annual Report of the Board of Indian Commissioners, 1869,* pp. 64–70.

14. James R. Hastings, "The Tragedy at Camp Grant in 1871," *Arizona and the West,* I (Summer 1959), pp. 146–60.

15. Colyer's success in obtaining military rations is documented in *Second Annual Report of the Board of Indian Commissioners, 1870,* pp. 9–10, 102–04. His report of his Arizona mission is in *Annual Report of the Commissioner of Indian Affairs, 1871,* pp. 41–95.

16. For Howard's reminiscences see Oliver O. Howard, *My Life and Experiences among our Hostile Indians* (Hartford, Conn., 1907), chaps. 12–14. His report is in *Annual Report of the Commissioner of Indian Affairs, 1872,* pp. 175–78.

17. Tatum, *Our Red Brothers,* pp. 29–30. Tatum's excellent book is a standard source for these events. See also W. S. Nye, *Carbine and Lance: The Story of Old Fort Sill* (Norman, Okla, 1937), chap. 6; Nye, *Plains Indian Raiders: The Final Phases of Warfare from the Arkansas to the Red River* (Norman, Okla., 1968), chaps. 16–17; and William T. Hagan, *United States-Comanche Relations: The Reservation Years* (New Haven, Conn., 1976), chap. 4. I have dealt with these events from the military point of view in Robert M. Utley, *Frontier Regulars: The United States Army and the Indian, 1866–1891* (New York, 1973), pp. 207–12.

18. Tatum, *Our Red Brothers,* pp. 116–18.

19. In addition to Tatum, Nye, and Utley, cited above, see Sherman's account in *House Reports,* 43d Cong., 1st sess., no. 395 (1874), pp. 270–75. An excellent account is J'Nell Pate, "Indians on Trial in a White Man's Court," *Great Plains Journal,* XIV (Fall, 1974), pp. 56–71. See also C. C. Rister, "The Significance of the Jacksboro Indian Affair of 1871," *Southwestern Historical Quarterly,* XXIX (January 1926), pp. 181–200.

20. *Annual Report of the Commissioner of Indian Affairs, 1872,* p. 228.

21. These events are authoritatively detailed in James C. Olson, *Red Cloud and the Sioux Problem* (Lincoln, Nebr., 1965), chaps. 6–10.

22. Prucha, *American Indian Policy in Crisis,* pp. 33–46, is a good account of the

origin and progress of the board. The published annual reports of the board are also informative and contain descriptions of the annual meetings.

23. Priest, *Uncle Sam's Stepchildren*, chap. 8, contains an analysis.

24. Quoted in Prucha, *American Indian Policy in Crisis*, p. 58. Priest, *Uncle Sam's Stepchildren*, chap. 3, cites examples of discord. Fritz, *Movement for Indian Assimilation*, chap. 4, analyzes the Catholic reaction.

Chapter 6: Wars of the Peace Policy, 1869–1886

1. Azor H. Nickerson, "Major General George Crook and the Indians [c. 1890]," typescript in W. S. Schuyler Papers, Huntington Library, San Marino, Calif.

2. Schuyler's daily journal of this scouting mission is in the Schuyler Papers at the Huntington Library. Dan L. Thrapp chronicles it in detail in *Al Sieber, Chief of Scouts* (Norman, Okla., 1964), pp. 128–37.

3. Recounted by a participant, An-pay-kau-te, son of Satank, in Wilbur S. Nye, *Bad Medicine and Good: Tales of the Kiowas* (Norman, Okla., 1962), chap. 29.

4. Sheridan's annual report in *Annual Report of the Secretary of War, 1869*, p. 38.

5. Schuyler to his father, Camp Verde, Ariz., July 6, 1873, in Schuyler Papers, Huntington Library.

6. Cheyenne *Daily Leader*, March 9, 1870, quoted in Henry E. Fritz, *The Movement for Indian Assimilation, 1860–1890* (Philadelphia, 1963), p. 115.

7. *House Reports*, 43d Cong., 1st sess., no. 384 (1874), p. 276.

8. Robert M. Utley, *Frontier Regulars: The United States Army and the Indian, 1866–1891* (New York, 1973), chap. 3. See also Utley, *The Contribution of the Frontier to the American Military Tradition*, Harmon Memorial Lectures in Military History no. 19, U.S. Air Force Academy (Colorado Springs, Colo., 1977).

9. General Alfred Sully to Commissioner of Indian Affairs, June 22, 1867, in *Senate Executive Documents*, 40th Cong., 1st sess., no. 13 (1867), p. 124. At the close of the Civil War the army passed out so many brevet, or honorary, ranks for Civil War services that the distinction became almost meaningless.

10. Quoted in Robert G. Athearn, *William Tecumseh Sherman and the Settlement of the West* (Norman, Okla., 1956), p. 197.

11. For the Modoc War, see Keith A. Murray, *The Modocs and Their War* (Norman, Okla., 1959); Richard Dillon, *Burnt-Out Fires: California's Modoc Indian War* (New York, 1973); and Erwin N. Thompson, *The Modoc War: Its History and Topography* (Sacramento, Calif., 1971).

12. For the effect of the Modoc War on public opinion and policy, see Robert Winston Mardock, *The Reformers and the American Indian* (Columbia, Mo., 1971), pp. 117–28; and Francis Paul Prucha, *American Indian Policy in Crisis: Christian Reformers and the Indian, 1865–1900* (Norman, Okla., 1976).

13. Standard histories of the Red River War are James L. Haley, *The Buffalo War: The History of the Red River Indian Uprising of 1874* (New York, 1976); William F. Leckie, *The Military Conquest of the Southern Plains* (Norman, Okla., 1963); Donald J. Berthrong, *The Southern Cheyennes* (Norman, Okla., 1963); W. S. Nye, *Carbine*

and Lance: The Story of Old Fort Sill (Norman, Okla., 1937); and William T. Hagan, *United States-Comanche Relations: The Reservation Years* (New Haven, Conn., 1976), chap. 5. See also Joe F. Taylor, ed., *The Indian Campaign on the Staked Plains, 1874–75: Military Correspondence from War Department, Adjutant General's Office, File 2815 - 1874* (Canyon, Tex., 1962).

14. Thomas B. Marquis, *A Warrior Who Fought Custer* (Minneapolis, 1931), p. 383 (reprinted as *Wooden Leg, A Warrior who Fought Custer* [Lincoln, Nebr., 1962]). The standard biography of Sitting Bull is Stanley Vestal, *Sitting Bull, Champion of the Sioux*, 2d ed. (Norman, Okla., 1957), but it must be used with great caution.

15. Quoted in Mark H. Brown, *The Plainsmen of the Yellowstone: A History of the Yellowstone Basin* (New York, 1961), p. 229.

16. The literature of the Sioux War of 1876 is voluminous. For the Indian side see George E. Hyde, *Red Cloud's Folk: A History of the Oglala Sioux Indians* (Norman, Okla., 1937); and Hyde, *Spotted Tail's Folk: A History of the Brule Sioux* (Norman, Okla., 1961); George B. Grinnell, *The Fighting Cheyennes*, 2d ed. (Norman, Okla., 1956); and Marquis, *A Warrior Who Fought Custer*. For the military side, see Utley, *Frontier Regulars*, chaps. 14–15; John S. Gray, *Centennial Campaign: The Sioux War of 1876* (Fort Collins, Colo., 1976); and Edgar I. Stewart, *Custer's Luck* (Norman, Okla., 1955). For the reservation background see especially James C. Olson, *Red Cloud and the Sioux Problem* (Lincoln, Nebr., 1965).

17. A good view of the Sioux refugees in Canada is George F. G. Stanley, "Displaced Red Men: The Sioux in Canada," in A. L. Getty and Donald B. Smith, eds., *One Century Later: Western Canadian Reserve Indians Since Treaty 7* (Vancouver, B.C., 1978), pp. 55–81.

18. Of the extensive literature of the Nez Perce War, three books are especially useful: Alvin M. Josephy, Jr., *The Nez Perce Indians and the Opening of the Northwest* (New Haven, Conn., 1965); Merrill D. Beal, *"I Will Fight No More Forever:" Chief Joseph and the Nez Perce War* (Seattle, 1963); and Mark H. Brown, *The Flight of the Nez Perce: A History of the Nez Perce War* (New York, 1967). See also Utley, *Frontier Regulars*, chap. 16.

19. For the Bannock War, see George F. Brimlow, *The Bannock Indian War of 1878* (Caldwell, Idaho, 1938); and R. Ross Arnold, *The Indian Wars of Idaho* (Caldwell, Idaho, 1932). The Sheepeater conflict is treated in W. C. Brown, *The Sheepeater Campaign* (Caldwell, Idaho, 1926). For the Utes, see Robert Emmitt, *The Last War Trail: The Utes and the Settlement of Colorado* (Norman, Okla., 1955); Wilson Rockwell, *The Utes, A Forgotten People* (Denver, 1956); and Marshall Sprague, *Massacre: The Tragedy at White River* (Boston and Toronto, 1957). For all, see Utley, *Frontier Regulars*, chap. 17.

20. Jason Betzinez with W. S. Nye, *I Fought with Geronimo* (Harrisburg, Pa., 1959), p. 58. Standard histories of the Victorio and Geronimo wars by Dan L. Thrapp are: *The Conquest of Apacheria* (Norman, Okla., 1967); *Al Sieber, Chief of Scouts; Victorio and the Mimbres Apaches* (Norman, Okla., 1974); and *General Crook and the Sierra Madre Adventure* (Norman, Okla., 1972). Others include: Alexander B. Adams, *Geronimo: A Biography* (New York, 1971); Ralph H. Ogle, *Federal Control of the Western Apaches, 1848–1886* (Albuquerque, 1970); Donald E. Worcester, *The Apaches: Eagles of the Southwest* (Norman, Okla., 1979); James L. Haley, *Apaches:*

A History and Culture Portrait (Garden City, N.Y., 1981); Eve Ball, *In the Days of Victorio: Recollections of a Warm Springs Apache* (Tucson, 1970); Eve Ball, *Indeh: An Apache Odyssey* (Provo, Utah, 1980); and Utley, *Frontier Regulars*, chaps. 18–19.

21. Ball, *In the Days of Victorio*, p. 28.

Chapter 7: The Vision of the Reformers, 1865–1890

1. Frederick E. Partington, *The Story of Mohonk*, 4th ed. (Annandale, Va. 1962). Lyman Abbott, *Silhouettes of My Contemporaries* (Garden City, N.Y., 1921), pp. 18–31.

2. Or at least so remembered conference chairman Clinton B. Fisk, in *Proceedings of the Seventh Annual Meeting of the Lake Mohonk Conference of Friends of the Indian, 1889*, p. 6. Smiley recounts the origins of the conferences in *Proceedings of the Twelfth Annual Meeting of the Lake Mohonk Conference of Friends of the Indian, 1894*, p. 38.

3. *Proceedings of the Seventh Annual Meeting of the Lake Mohonk Conference of Friends of the Indian, 1889*, p. 16. See also Francis Paul Prucha's biographical sketch of Morgan in Robert M. Kvasnicka and Herman J. Viola, eds., *The Commissioners of Indian Affairs, 1824–1977* (Lincoln, Nebr., 1979), pp. 193–203.

4. The progress of the reform movement in the 1870s is traced in Robert Winston Mardock, *The Reformers and the American Indian* (Columbia, Mo., 1971), chaps. 8 and 9. See, in addition, Alfred B. Meacham, *Wigwam and War-Path; or The Royal Chief in Chains* (Boston, 1875); Thomas A. Bland, *Life of Alfred B. Meacham* (Washington, D.C., 1883); and Ruth Odell, *Helen Hunt Jackson* (New York, 1939).

5. See, for example, Smith's policy statement of October 30, 1876, reproduced in Francis Paul Prucha, ed., *Documents of United States Indian Policy* (Lincoln, Nebr., 1975), pp. 147–48.

6. All three of these episodes and their relationship to Indian policy are treated in Francis Paul Prucha, *American Indian Policy in Crisis: Christian Reformers and the Indian, 1865–1900* (Norman, Okla., 1977), chaps. 4 and 5; and Mardock, *The Reformers and the American Indian*, chaps. 9 and 10. A prime agitator in the Ponca affair wrote a contemporary view of it: Thomas H. Tibbles, *Buckskin and Blanket Days* (1905; Garden City, N.Y., 1957). For Chief Joseph see Alvin M. Josephy, Jr., *The Nez Perce Indians and the Opening of the Northwest* (New Haven, Conn., 1965), pp. 634–644, but especially Joseph's own appeal to public opinion: Chief Joseph, "An Indian's View of Indian Affairs," *North American Review*, CXXVIII (April 1879), pp. 431–33. The Cheyenne tragedy is treated in George Bird Grinnell, *The Fighting Cheyennes*, 2d ed. (Norman, Okla., 1956), chaps. 19 and 20.

7. Prucha, *American Indian Policy in Crisis*, Chap. 3. Richard N. Ellis, "The Humanitarian Generals," *Western Historical Quarterly*, III (April 1972), pp. 169–78. James T. King, "George Crook: Indian Fighter and Humanitarian," *Arizona and the West*, IX (Winter 1967), pp. 333–48.

8. *Tenth Annual Report of the Indian Rights Association, 1892* (Philadelphia, 1893), pp. 3–4. Herbert Welsh, *A Brief Statement of the Objects, Achievements and Needs of the Indian Rights Association* (Philadelphia, 1887). Both Prucha, *American Indian Policy*

in Crisis, pp. 138–43, and Mardock, *The Reformers and the American Indian,* pp. 200–01 and passim, deal with the emergence of the Indian Rights Association.

9. The quotation is from a Senate speech, quoted in Prucha, *American Indian Policy in Crisis,* p. 136.

10. *Proceedings of the Eighth Annual Meeting of the Lake Mohonk Conference of the Friends of the Indian, 1890,* p. 70.

11. The linkage of Americanism and evangelical Protestantism to U.S. Indian policy is most clearly established in Prucha, *American Indian Policy in Crisis,* pp. 152–53, 158–61. This chapter owes a significant debt to this and other pioneering works by Prucha.

12. *The Nation,* XXVII (November 28, 1878), pp. 332–33. See also Prucha, *American Indian Policy in Crisis,* pp. 156–57; and Mardock, *The Reformers and the American Indian,* p. 47.

13. The vision, the agenda, and the mind-set of the reformers emerge clearly from their own words as set forth in Francis Paul Prucha, ed., *Americanizing the American Indian: Writings by the 'Friends of the Indian,' 1880–1900* (Cambridge, Mass., 1973).

14. *Proceedings of the Fourteenth Annual Meeting of the Lake Mohonk Conference of the Friends of the Indian, 1896,* p. 11.

15. *Annual Report of the Board of Indian Commissioners, 1879,* pp. 11–12.

16. Quoted in Prucha, *American Indian Policy in Crisis,* pp. 246–247. Prucha's account, chap. 8, is clear, balanced, and thorough, but see also D. S. Otis, *The Dawes Act and the Allotment of Indian Lands,* ed. Francis Paul Prucha (Norman, Okla., 1973); and Loring Benson Priest, *Uncle Sam's Stepchildren: The Reformation of United States Indian Policy,* 2d ed. (Lincoln, Nebr., 1975), pt. 5. A sampler of contemporary writings on severalty is in Prucha, *Americanizing the American Indian,* pt. 2. The Dawes General Allotment Act, 24 Stat. 388–91, is reprinted in Prucha, *Documents of United States Indian Policy,* pp. 171–74.

17. Quoted in Prucha, *American Indian Policy in Crisis,* p. 255.

18. *Proceedings of the Fifth Annual Meeting of the Lake Mohonk Conference of Friends of the Indian, 1887,* p. 9.

19. *Proceedings of the Ninth Annual Meeting of the Lake Mohonk Conference of Friends of the Indian, 1891,* p. 104.

20. *Annual Report of the Commissioner of Indian Affairs, 1882,* p. vi.

21. Prucha (ed.), *Documents of United States Indian Policy,* pp. 180–81.

22. Francis Paul Prucha, *The Churches and the Indian Schools, 1888–1912* (Lincoln, Nebr., 1979), chaps. 1–3. The quotations are on pp. 13 and 25. See also Prucha's broader account of Indian education in *American Indian Policy in Crisis,* chaps. 9–10.

23. Richard Henry Pratt, *Battlefield and Classroom: Four Decades with the American Indian, 1867–1904,* ed. Robert M. Utley (New Haven, Conn., 1964), p. 335. For a biography see Elaine Goodale Eastman, *Pratt, the Red Man's Moses* (Norman, Okla., 1935).

24. Lyman Abbott, *Reminiscences* (Boston, 1923), p. 428.

25. William T. Hagan, *Indian Police and Judges: Experiments in Acculturation and Control* (New Haven, Conn., 1966).

26. Prucha, *American Indian Policy in Crisis*, chap. 11. Samples of reformist writings on law and citizenship are in Prucha, *Americanizing the American Indian*. For *Ex Parte Crow Dog, Elk v. Wilkins*, and other court cases, see Prucha, *Documents of United States Indian Policy*, pp. 166–68.

27. *The Nation*, XXX (February 5, 1880), p. 88. See also biographical sketch of Hayt by Roy W. Meyer in Kvasnicka and Viola, *The Commissioners of Indian Affairs*, pp. 155–66.

28. Welsh, "The Meaning of the Dakota Outbreak," *Scribner's Magazine*, IX (1891), p. 449.

29. *Annual Report of the Board of Indian Commissioners, 1889*, p. 139.

30. *Proceedings of the Third Annual Meeting of the Lake Mohonk Conference of the Friends of the Indian, 1885*, pp. 5–6, 60. For an account of efforts at civil service reform, see Prucha, *American Indian Policy in Crisis*, chap. 12.

Chapter 8: The Reservation, 1880–1890

1. New York *World*, April 26, 1891. For the trial of Plenty Horses see Robert M. Utley, "The Ordeal of Plenty Horses," *American Heritage*, XXVI (December 1974), pp. 15–19, 82–86.

2. E. Douglas Branch, *Hunting the Buffalo* (New York, 1929). M. D. Garretson, *The American Bison* (New York, 1938). Mari Sandoz, *The Buffalo Hunters: The Story of the Hide Men* (New York, 1954). Francis Haines, *The Buffalo* (New York, 1970). Tom McHugh, with the assistance of Victoria Hobson, *The Time of the Buffalo* (New York, 1972).

3. John G. Neihardt, *Black Elk Speaks: Being the Life Story of a Holy Man of the Oglala Sioux* (1932; Pocket Book Ed., New York, 1972), pp. 181–82.

4. Satisfactory tribal histories focused on the reservation period are relatively scarce. I have drawn this picture of the Sioux in large part from my own research incorporated in Robert M. Utley, *The Last Days of the Sioux Nation* (New Haven, Conn., 1963), chaps. 3 and 4; but for the Sioux see also (and use cautiously) George E. Hyde, *A Sioux Chronicle* (Norman, Okla., 1956). Excellent studies of other tribes are Donald J. Berthrong, *The Cheyenne and Arapaho Ordeal: Reservation and Agency Life in the Indian Territory, 1875–1907* (Norman, Okla., 1976) and William T. Hagan, *United States-Comanche Relations: The Reservation Years* (New Haven, Conn., 1976).

5. James McLaughlin, *My Friend the Indian* (Boston and New York, 1910), pp. 180–81. McLaughlin chronicles the feud in fascinating if understandably biased detail.

6. For Red Cloud's clash with McGillycuddy, see James C. Olson, *Red Cloud and the Sioux Problem* (Lincoln, Nebr., 1965), chaps. 14–15. The agent's side is presented in Julia B. McGillycuddy, *McGillycuddy, Agent: A Biography of Dr. Valentine T. McGillycuddy* (Palo Alto, Calif., 1941). For Spotted Tail's reservation years, see George E. Hyde, *Spotted Tail's Folk: A History of the Brule Sioux* (Norman, Okla., 1961), chap. 12.

7. *Senate Executive Documents*, 50th Cong., 2d sess., no. 17 (1888), p. 19. *Annual Report of the Commissioner of Indian Affairs, 1890*, p. clxv.

8. McGillycuddy, *McGillycuddy, Agent*, pp. 103–04.

9. Quoted in J. R. Walker, "The Sun Dance and Other Ceremonies of the Oglala Division of the Teton Dakota," *Anthropological Papers of the American Museum of Natural History*, XVI, pt. 2 (1917), p. 159. For a good discussion of the impact of Christianity, see Gordon MacGregor, *Warriors without Weapons: A Study of the Society and Personality Development of the Pine Ridge Sioux* (Chicago, 1946), pp. 90–92.

10. As recalled by the foreman of the jury, none other than former Pine Ridge Agent Valentine T. McGillycuddy. McGillycuddy, *McGillycuddy, Agent*, p. 272.

11. *Annual Report of the Commissioner of Indian Affairs, 1884*, p. 56.

12. The report of the Pratt Commission is in *Senate Executive Documents*, 50th Cong., 2d sess., no. 17 (1888). For the text of the Sioux Act see *Annual Report of the Commissioner of Indian Affairs, 1888*, pp. 294–301.

13. Report of the Sioux Commission in *Senate Executive Documents*, 51st Cong., 1st sess., no. 51 (1889), p. 172. For the text of the Sioux Act of 1889 see *Annual Report of the Commissioner of Indian Affairs, 1889*, pp. 449–58.

14. Martin F. Schmitt, ed., *General George Crook: His Autobiography* (Norman, Okla., 1946), p. 287. See also McLaughlin, *My Friend the Indian*, pp. 284–85.

15. To Reverend William J. Cleveland, in *Ninth Annual Report of the Indian Rights Association, 1891*, p. 29.

16. James Mooney, *The Ghost-Dance Religion and the Sioux Outbreak of 1890*, 14th Annual Report of the Bureau of American Ethnology, 1892–93, pt. 2 (Washington, D.C., 1896), p. 657.

Chapter 9: The Passing of the Frontier

1. The quotation is from the Robert O. Pugh interview in the Eli S. Ricker Papers, Nebraska State Historical Society. See also Francis E. Leupp, *Civil Service Reform Essential to a Successful Indian Administration* (Indian Rights Association, Philadelphia, 1895), pp. 8–9.

2. Marion P. Maus, "The New Indian Messiah," *Harper's Weekly*, XXXIV (December 6, 1890), p. 944.

3. "Dr. V. T. McGillycuddy on the Ghost Dance," in Stanley Vestal, ed., *New Sources of Indian History* (Norman, Okla., 1934), pp. 88–89.

4. As in the previous chapter, I follow basically the story and sources as presented in Robert M. Utley, *The Last Days of the Sioux Nation* (New Haven, Conn., 1963). As this goes to press, an article by a distinguished anthropologist calls into question some of the assumptions and conclusions of *Last Days of the Sioux Nation*. Were I rewriting that work, I would rephrase some passages to account for his concerns, but I find nothing to change in my account as presented here. Readers may wish to compare the two: Raymond J. DeMallie, "The Lakota Ghost Dance: An Ethnohistorical Account," *Pacific Historical Review*, LI (November 1982), pp. 385–406.

5. Wounded Knee has inspired a vast literature, both first-hand and secondary, the best of which is cited in Utley, *Last Days of the Sioux Nation*, chap. 12. Military reports appear in *Annual Report of the Secretary of War, 1891*. Central to any seri-

ous study are four drawers of official records in Special Case 188, Record Group 75, National Archives, containing Indian Bureau and military correspondence and the transcript of testimony of a court of inquiry General Miles convened to investigate Wounded Knee. Also highly significant are interviews, especially Indian interviews, in the Eli S. Ricker papers at the Nebraska State Historical Society. Finally, all studies of the Ghost Dance and Wounded Knee start with James Mooney, *The Ghost-Dance Religion and the Sioux Outbreak of 1890,* 14th Annual Report of the Bureau of American Ethnology, 1892–93, pt. 2 (Washington, D.C., 1896).

6. David A. Nichols, "Civilization over Savage: Frederick Jackson Turner and the Indian," *South Dakota History,* II (Fall 1972), pp. 383–405.

7. Still standard is Annie H. Abel, "Proposals for an Indian State," *Annual Report of the American Historical Association,* I (1907). The sequence leading to creation of the state of Oklahoma set forth here relies heavily on Francis Paul Prucha, *American Indians Policy in Crisis: Christian Reformers and the Indian, 1865–1900* (Norman, Okla., 1976), chap. 13. For this subject as well as for conditions among the Five Tribes after the Civil War, see Angie Debo, *And Still the Waters Run: The Betrayal of the Five Civilized Tribes,* 2d ed. (Princeton, N. J., 1972); Arrell M. Gibson, *Oklahoma: A History of Five Centuries,* 2d ed. (Norman, Okla., 1981), chaps. 11, 14, and 15; Roy Gittinger, *The Formation of the State of Oklahoma, 1803–1906* (Norman, Okla., 1939); and tribal histories cited in chap. 2, n. 36.

8. Cf. Howard Lamar and Leonard Thompson, eds., *The Frontier in History: North America and Southern Africa Compared* (New Haven, Conn., 1981), p. 311. As suggested, no entirely satisfactory studies exist. I have found useful information in Robert D. Arnold et al., *Alaska Native Land Claims* (Anchorage, 1976); and Harold E. Driver, *Indians of North America* 2d ed. (Chicago, 1969), pp. 546–50. I have also benefited greatly from an unpublished manuscript now in preparation by Melody Webb, tentatively titled *Yukon Frontiers: The Westward Movement to the North Country.*

9. Marc Simmons, "History of the Pueblos since 1821," in Alfonso Ortiz, ed., *Southwest* (William C. Sturtevant, ed., *Handbook of North American Indians,* IX, Washington, D.C., 1979), pp. 206–23.

10. Leonard A. Carlson, *Indians, Bureaucrats, and Land: The Dawes Act and the Decline of Indian Farming* (Westport, Conn., 1981). Wilcomb E. Washburn, *The Assault on Indian Tribalism: The General Allotment Law (Dawes Act) of 1887* (Philadelphia, 1975).

11. Prucha, "Federal Indian Policy in United States History," in Prucha, *Indian Policy in the United States,* pp. 20–35.

12. Cf. editorial in *Army and Navy Journal,* XIV (July 14, 1877), p. 784.

13. Carl Schurz, "Present Aspects of the Indian Problem," *North American Review,,* CXXXIII (July 1881), p. 6. Reprinted in Francis Paul Prucha, ed., *Americanizing the American Indian: Writings by the 'Friends of the Indian,' 1880–1900* (Cambridge, Mass., 1973), pp. 13–26.

14. A comparative study of Canadian and American policy and experience is badly needed, but see Desmond Morris, "Cavalry or Police: Keeping the Peace on Two Adjacent Frontiers, 1870–1900," *Journal of Canadian Studies,* XII (Spring 1977), pp. 27–37. In sketching the above I have used John L. Tobias, "Protection,

Civilization, Assimilation: An Outline History of Canada's Indian Policy," *Western Canadian Journal of Anthropology*, VI, 2 (1976), pp. 13–30; Stewart Raby, "Indian Land Surrenders in Southern Saskatchewan," *Canadian Geographer*, XVII (Spring 1973), pp. 36–52; and Hugh A. Dempsey, "One Hundred Years of Treaty Seven," in Ian A. L. Getty and Donald B. Smith, eds., *One Century Later: Western Canadian Reserve Indians Since Treaty 7* (Vancouver, B.C., 1978), pp. 20–30. For the 1885 rebellion see Desmond Morris, *The Last War Drum* (Toronto, 1972). For the literature of Canadian policy see Robert J. Surtees, *Canadian Indian Policy: A Critical Bibliography* (Bloomington, Ind., 1982).

15. This paragraph owes a considerable debt to Francis Jennings, *The Invasion of America: Indians, Colonialism, and the Cant of Conquest* (Chapel Hill, N.C., 1975), chap. 1.

Bibliography

Bibliographies

Students of Indian-white relations are unusually fortunate to have a comprehensive, well-organized, and up-to-date bibliography: Francis Paul Prucha, *A Bibliographical Guide to the History of Indian-White Relations in the United States* (Chicago, 1977); and Prucha, *Indian-White Relations in the United States: A Bibliography of Works Published 1975–1980* (Lincoln, Nebr., 1982). Also of great value is the series of annotated bibliographies prepared under the auspices of the Newberry Library Center for the History of the American Indian (Francis Jennings, general editor, and William R. Swagerty, assistant editor) and published by Indiana University Press. Those particularly relevant to this study are Martha Royce Blaine, *The Pawnees* (1980); Henry F. Dobyns and Robert C. Euler, *Indians of the Southwest* (1980); Dobyns, *Native American Historical Demography* (1976); Raymond D. Fogelson, *The Cherokees* (1978); Michael D. Green, *The Creeks* (1979); Robert S. Grumet, *Native Americans of the Northwest Coast* (1979); Robert F. Heizer, *The Indians of California* (1976); E. Adamson Hoebel, *The Plains Indians* (1977); Herbert T. Hoover, *The Sioux* (1979); Peter Iverson, *The Navajos* (1976); Clara Sue Kidwell and Charles Roberts, *The Choctaws* (1980); Michael E. Melody, *The Apaches* (1977); Peter J. Powell, *The Cheyennes* (1980); Francis Paul Prucha, *United States Indian Policy* (1977); Robert J. Surtees, *Canadian Indian Policy* (1982); and William E. Unrau, *The Emigrant Indians of Kansas* (1979).

General Works

There are many shelves full of general works on the American Indian, all of which are cited in Prucha's bibliographies. Among the more recent that provide good overviews are William Brandon, *The Last Americans: The Indian in American Culture* (New York, 1974); Angie Debo, *A History of the Indians of the United States* (Norman, Okla., 1970); Harold E. Driver, *Indians of North America*, 2d ed. (Chicago, 1969); William T. Hagan, *American Indians*, rev. ed. (Chicago, 1979); Alvin M. Josephy,

Jr., *The Indian Heritage of America* (New York, 1968); D'Arcy McNickle, *They Came Here First: The Epic of the American Indian,* rev. ed. (New York, 1975); Wilcomb E. Washburn, *The Indian in America* (New York, 1975); and Clark Wissler, *Indians of the United States,* rev. ed. (Garden City, N.Y., 1966).

The Frontier

The historiography of the frontier supports an extensive bibliography in its own right, but a few items are especially useful to an understanding of Indian-white history. Jack D. Forbes has written several pertinent articles, of which the best is "Frontiers in American History and the Role of the Frontier Historian," *Ethnohistory,* XV (Spring 1968), pp. 203–35. Frederick Jackson's Turner's curious neglect of Indians is treated in David A. Nichols, "Civilization over Savage: Frederick Jackson Turner and the Indian," *South Dakota History,* II (Fall 1972), pp. 383–405. Perhaps the most perceptive commentary will be found in Howard Lamar and Leonard Thompson, eds., *The Frontier in History: North America and Southern Africa Compared* (New Haven, Conn., 1981), especially Lamar and Thompson's introduction and epilogue, pp. 3–42 and 308–16, and Robert F. Berkhofer, Jr., "The North American Frontier as Process and Context," pp. 43–75.

Tribal Histories

Some of the best and most reliable material is to be found in histories of individual tribes. For the Five Civilized Tribes consult: Grant Foreman, *The Five Civilized Tribes* (Norman, Okla., 1934) and Angie Debo, *And Still the Waters Run,* rev. ed. (Princeton, N.J., 1972). Studies of individual tribes are Angie Debo, *The Rise and Fall of the Choctaw Republic* (Norman, Okla., 1934); Angie Debo, *The Road to Disappearance* [Creeks](Norman, Okla., 1941); Arrell M. Gibson, *The Chickasaws* (Norman, Okla., 1971); Edwin C. McReynolds, *The Seminoles* (Norman, Okla., 1957); and Grace Steele Woodward, *The Cherokees* (Norman, Okla., 1963). Excellent sketches of all these tribes as well as others of Oklahoma are in Muriel H. Wright, *A Guide to the Indian Tribes of Oklahoma* (Norman, Okla., 1951).

The Indians of the Great Plains have attracted an extensive bibliography. General coverage is in Robert H. Lowie, *Indians of the Plains* (New York, 1954) and Clark Wissler, *North American Indians of the Plains,* 3d ed. (New York, 1927). Tribal studies include: Donald J. Berthrong, *The Southern Cheyenne* (Norman, Okla., 1963); Donald J. Berthrong, *The Cheyenne and Arapaho Ordeal: Reservation and Agency Life in the Indian Territory, 1875–1907* (Norman, Okla., 1976); John C. Ewers, *The Blackfeet: Raiders on the Northwestern Plains* (Norman, Okla., 1958); Arrell M. Gibson, *The Kickapoos: Lords of the Middle Border* (Norman, Okla., 1963); George Bird Grinnell, *The Cheyenne Indians: Their History and Ways of Life,* 2 vols. (New Haven, Conn., 1923); George Bird Grinnell, *The Fighting Cheyennes,* 2d ed. (Norman, Okla., 1956); William T. Hagan, *United States-Comanche Relations: The Reservation Years* (New Haven, Conn., 1976); Royal B. Hassrick, *The Sioux: Life and Customs of a Warrior*

Society (Norman, Okla., 1964); George E. Hyde, *Pawnee Indians*, 3d ed. (Norman, Okla., 1974); George E. Hyde, *Red Cloud's Folk: A History of the Oglala Sioux Indians* (Norman, Okla., 1937); George E. Hyde, *Spotted Tail's Folk: A History of the Brule Sioux* (Norman, Okla., 1961); Mildred P. Mayhall, *The Kiowas* (Norman, Okla., 1962); Roy W. Meyer, *History of the Santee Sioux: United States Indian Policy on Trial* (Lincoln, Nebr., 1967); James C. Olson, *Red Cloud and the Sioux Problem* (Lincoln, Nebr., 1965); Peter J. Powell, *Sweet Medicine: The Continuing Role of the Sacred Arrows, the Sun Dance, and the Sacred Buffalo Hat in Northern Cheyenne History*, 2 vols. (Norman, Okla., 1969); Doane Robinson, *The Sioux Indians: A History*, 3d ed. (Minneapolis, 1956); Virginia C. Trenholm, *The Arapahos, Our People* (Norman, Okla., 1970); and Ernest Wallace and E. Adamson Hoebel, *The Comanches: Lords of the South Plains* (Norman, Okla., 1952).

Overviews of southwestern Indians include Bertha P. Dutton, *American Indians of the Southwest* (Albuquerque, 1983); Alfonso Ortiz, ed., *Southwest*, Vol. IX of William C. Sturtevant, ed., *Handbook of North American Indians* (Smithsonian Institution, Washington, D.C., 1979); and Edward H. Spicer, *Cycles of Conquest: The Impact of Spain, Mexico, and the United States on the Indians of the Southwest, 1533–1960* (Tucson, 1962). For the Apaches, see: Keith H. Basso, *The Cibecue Apache* (New York, 1970); Henry F. Dobyns, *The Apache People* (Phoenix, 1971); Henry F. Dobyns, *The Mescalero Apache People* (Phoenix, 1973); James A. Haley, *Apaches: A History and Culture Portrait* (Garden City, N.Y., 1981); Frank C. Lockwood, *The Apache Indians* (New York, 1938); Ralph H. Ogle, *Federal Control of the Western Apaches, 1848–1886* (Albuquerque, 1970); C. L. Sonnichsen, *The Mescalero Apaches* (Norman, Okla., 1958); and Donald E. Worcester, *The Apaches: Eagles of the Southwest* (Norman, Okla., 1979). For the Navajos, see: Henry F. Dobyns and Robert C. Euler, *The Navajo People* (Phoenix, 1972); Clyde Kluckhohn and Dorothea Leighton, *The Navajo*, rev. ed. (Garden City, N.Y., 1962); and Ruth M. Underhill, *The Navajos* (Norman, Okla., 1956). For the Pueblos, see: Edward P. Dozier, *The Pueblo Indians of North America* (New York, 1970); and Alfonso Ortiz, ed., *New Persectives on the Pueblos* (Albuquerque, 1972).

Authoritative studies of the California tribes are: Sherburne F. Cook, *The Conflict between the California Indian and White Civilization* (Berkeley, 1976); Robert F. Heizer, *Languages, Territories, and Names of California Indian Tribes* (Berkeley, 1966); Robert F. Heizer, ed., *California*, Vol. VIII of William C. Sturtevant, ed., *Handbook of North American Indians* (Smithsonian Institution, Washington, D.C., 1978); Robert F. Heizer and M. A. Whipple, eds., *The California Indians: A Source Book*, 2d ed. (Berkeley, 1971); George H. Phillips, *Chiefs and Challengers: Indian Resistance and Cooperation in Southern California* (Berkeley, 1975); and Verne F. Ray, *Primitive Pragmatists: The Modoc Indians of Northern California* (Seattle,1963).

On the tribes of the Rocky Mountains and Great Basin region, see: Robert C. Euler, *The Paiute People* (Phoenix, 1972); John Fahey, *The Flathead Indians* (Norman, Okla., 1974); Alvin M. Josephy, Jr., *The Nez Perce Indians and the Opening of the Northwest* (New Haven, Conn., 1965); Brigham D. Madsden, *The Bannock of Idaho* (Caldwell, Idaho, 1968); Wilson Rockwell, *The Utes: A Forgotten People* (Denver, 1956); and Virginia C. Trenholm and Maurine Carley, *The Shoshonis: Sentinels of the Rockies* (Norman, Okla., 1964).

Histories of the tribes of the Pacific Northwest include: Richard D. Daugherty,

The Yakima People (Phoenix, 1973); Vine Deloria, Jr., *Indians of the Pacific Northwest from the Coming of the White Man to the Present Day* (Garden City, N.Y., 1977); Pliney E. Goddard, *Indians of the Northwest Coast* (New York, 1924); H. R. Hays, *Children of the Raven: The Seven Indian Nations of the Northwest Coast* (New York, 1975); Sven Liljeblad, *The Idaho Indians in Transition, 1805–1960* (Pocatello, Idaho, 1972); Robert H. Ruby and John A. Brown, *The Cayuse Indians: Imperial Tribesmen of Old Oregon* (Norman, Okla., 1972); Theodore Stern, *The Klamath Tribe: A People and Their Reservation* (Seattle, 1965); Deward E. Walker, Jr., *Indians of Idaho* (Moscow, Idaho, 1978); and George Woodcock, *Peoples of the Coast: The Indians of the Pacific Northwest* (Bloomington, Ind., 1977).

Indian and White Worlds

A growing body of literature probes the Indian and white worlds, their views of themselves and of each other, and their interaction. Some of the studies cited here, it should be noted, deal with Indians and whites generally across the entire span of the contact period, while others are limited to the Indians of the eastern United States. All, however, have some degree of applicability to the subject of this volume. In this study the following have proved helpful: Hartley Burr Alexander, *The World's Rim: Great Mysteries of the North American Indians* (Lincoln, Nebr., 1953); Robert F. Berkhofer, Jr., *The White Man's Indian: Images of the American Indian from Columbus to the Present* (New York, 1978); Walter Holden Capps, ed., *Seeing with a Native Eye: Essays on Native American Religion* (New York, 1976); Brian W. Dippie, "This Bold but Wasting Race: Stereotypes and American Indian Policy," *Montana, The Magazine of Western History*, XXIII (January 1973), pp. 2–13; Richard Drinnon, *Facing West: The Metaphysics of Indian-Hating and Empire Building* (Minneapolis, 1980); John C. Ewers, "When Red and White Men Met," *Western Historical Quarterly*, II (April 1971), pp. 132–50; John C. Ewers, "Indian Views of the White Man Prior to 1850: An Interpretation," in Daniel Tyler, ed., *Red Men and Hat Wearers: Viewpoints in Indian History* (Fort Collins, Colo., 1976), pp. 7–24; John C. Ewers, "Intertribal Warfare as the Precursor of Indian-White Warfare on the Northern Great Plains," *Western Historical Quarterly*, VI (October 1975), pp. 397–410; Morton H. Fried, *The Notion of Tribe* (Menlo Park, Calif., 1975); Preston Holder, "The Fur Trade as Seen from the Indian Point of View," in John Francis McDermott, ed., *The Frontier Reexamined* (Urbana, Ill., 1967), pp. 129–40; Francis Jennings, *The Invasion of America: Indians, Colonialism, and the Cant of Conquest* (Chapel Hill, N.C., 1975); P. Richard Metcalf, "Who Should Rule at Home: Native American Politics and Indian-White Relations," *Journal of American History*, LXI (December 1974), pp. 651–66; Roy Harvey Pearce, *The Savages of America: A Study of the Indian and the Idea of Civilization* (Baltimore, 1953); Roy Harvey Pearce, "The Metaphysics of Indian-Hating," *Ethnohistory*, IV (Winter 1957), pp. 27–40; Francis Paul Prucha, "The Image of the Indian in Pre-Civil War America," in *American Indian Policy: Indiana Historical Society Lectures 1970–1971* (Indianapolis, 1971), pp. 2–19 (reprinted in Prucha, *Indian Policy in the United States: Historical Essays* [Lincoln, Nebr., 1981], pp. 49–63); Arthur J. Ray, *Indians in the Fur Trade: Their Role as Hunters, Trappers, and Middlemen in the Lands Southwest of Hudson's Bay, 1660–1870* (Toronto,

1974); Lewis O. Saum, *The Fur Trader and the Indian* (Seattle, 1963); William W. Savage, Jr., ed., *Indian Life: Transforming an American Myth* (Norman, Okla., 1977); Elman R. Service, "War and Our Contemporary Ancestors," in Morton H. Fried et al., eds., *War: The Anthropology of Conflict and Armed Aggression* (Garden City, N.Y., 1968), pp. 160–67; Bernard W. Sheehan, *Seeds of Extinction: Jeffersonian Philanthropy and the American Indian* (Chapel Hill, N.C., 1973); Richard Slotkin, *Regeneration through Violence: The Mythology of the American Frontier, 1600–1860* (Middletown, Conn., 1973); Edward H. Spicer, ed., *Perspectives in American Indian Culture Change* (Chicago, 1961); Daniel Tyler, ed., *Red Men and Hat Wearers: Viewpoints in Indian History* (Fort Collins, Colo., 1976); and Richard White, "The Winning of the West: The Expansion of the Western Sioux in the Eighteenth and Nineteenth Centuries," *Journal of American History,* LXV (September 1978), pp. 319–43.

Recent works on the writing of Indian history also contain much of interest for this subject. Among the more perceptive are Robert F. Berkhofer, Jr., "The Political Context of a New Indian History," *Pacific Historical Review,* XL (August 1971), pp. 357–82; William Brandon, "American Indians and American History," *American West,* II (Spring 1965), pp. 14–25, 91–93; William T. Hagan, "On Writing the History of the American Indian," *Journal of Interdisciplinary History,* II (Summer 1971), pp. 149–54; Wilbur R. Jacobs, "The Indian and the Frontier in American History—A Need for Revision," *Western Historical Quarterly,* IV (January 1973), pp. 43–56; Wilbur R. Jacobs, "Native American History: How It Illuminates Our Past," *American Historical Review,* LXXX (June 1975), pp. 595–609; Calvin Martin, "Ethnohistory: A Better Way to Write Indian History," *Western Historical Quarterly,* IX (January 1978), pp. 41–56; Calvin Martin, "The Metaphysics of Writing Indian-White History," *Ethnohistory,* XXVI (Winter 1981), pp. 153–59; Francis Paul Prucha, "New Approaches to the Study of the Administration of Indian Policy," *Prologue: The Journal of the National Archives,* III (Spring 1971), pp. 15–19; Wilcomb E. Washburn, "A Moral History of Indian-White Relations: Needs and Opportunites for Study," *Ethnohistory,* IV (Winter 1957), pp. 47–61; and Wilcomb E. Washburn, "The Writing of American Indian History: A Status Report," *Pacific Historical Review,* XL (August 1971), pp. 261–81.

United States Indian Policy

The entire span of U.S. Indian policy is richly documented in the published annual reports of the Secretaries of the Interior, Commissioners of Indian Affairs, and Board of Indian Commissioners; the congressional executive document series; and the *Congressional Globe* and its successor, the *Congressional Record.* Enacted laws and ratified treaties are printed in Charles J. Kappler, comp., *Indian Affairs: Laws and Treaties,* 5 vols. (Washington, D.C., 1904–41). Much original material appears in Felix H. Cohen, comp., *Handbook of Federal Indian Law* (Washington, D.C., 1942). Key documents are printed in Francis Paul Prucha, ed., *Documents of United States Indian Policy* (Lincoln, Nebr., 1975). For policy in terms of personalities, see Robert M. Kvasnicka and Herman J. Viola, eds., *The Commissioners of Indian Affairs, 1824–1977* (Lincoln, Nebr., 1979).

Although antedating the period of this volume, Jacksonian Indian policy, especially Indian removal, is essential to an understanding of what came later. The literature is vast, but the following give a good overview: Francis Paul Prucha, *American Indian Policy in the Formative Years: The Indian Trade and Intercourse Acts, 1790–1834* (Cambridge, Mass., 1962); Francis Paul Prucha, "American Indian Policy in the 1840s: Visions of Reform," in John G. Clark, ed., *The Frontier Challenge: Responses to the Trans-Mississippi West* (Lawrence, Kans., 1971), pp. 81–110; Francis Paul Prucha, "Andrew Jackson's Indian Policy: A Reassessment," *Journal of American History*, LVI (December 1969), pp. 527–39; Francis Paul Prucha, "Indian Removal and the Great American Desert," *Indiana Magazine of History*, LIX (December 1963), pp. 299–322. All the foregoing articles are also printed in Prucha, *Indian Policy in the United States: Historical Essays* (Lincoln, Neb., 1981). See also Michael Paul Rogin, *Fathers and Children: Andrew Jackson and the Subjugation of the American Indian* (New York, 1975); Ronald N. Satz, *American Indian Policy in the Jacksonian Era* (Lincoln, Nebr., 1975); and Wilcomb E. Washburn, "Indian Removal Policy: Administrative, Historical and Moral Criteria for Judging Its Success or Failure," *Ethnohistory*, XII (Summer 1965), pp. 274–78.

General works on Indian policy between removal and the Civil War are scarce. See Alban W. Hoopes, *Indian Affairs and Their Administration, with Special Reference to the Far West, 1849–1860* (Philadelphia, 1932); James C. Malin, *Indian Policy and Westward Expansion* (Lawrence, Kans., 1921); and Robert A. Trennert, Jr., *Alternative to Extinction: Federal Indian Policy and the Beginnings of the Reservation System, 1846–51* (Philadelphia, 1975). See also regional studies for this period: C. F. Coan, "The First Stage of the Federal Indian Policy in the Pacific Northwest, 1849–1852," *Oregon Historical Society Quarterly*, XXII (March 1921), pp. 46–89; C. F. Coan, "The Adoption of the Reservation Policy in the Pacific Northwest, 1853–1855," ibid., XXIII (March 1922), pp. 1–38; Richard E. Crouter and Andrew F. Rolle, "Edward Fitzgerald Beale and the Indian Peace Commissioners in California, 1851–1854," *Historical Society of Southern California Quarterly*, XLII (June 1960), pp. 107–32; William H. Ellison, "The Federal Indian Policy in California, 1846–1860," *Mississippi Valley Historical Review*, IX (June 1922), pp. 37–67; George D. Harmon, "The United States Indian Policy in Texas, 1845–1860," ibid., XVII (December 1930), pp. 377–403; Harry Kelsey, "The California Indian Treaty Myth," *Southern California Quarterly*, LV (Fall 1973), pp. 225–38; H. Craig Miner and William E. Unrau, *The End of Indian Kansas: A Study of Cultural Revolution, 1854–1870* (Lawrence, Kans., 1978); Dale L. Morgan, "The Administration of Indian Affairs in Utah, 1851–1858," *Pacific Historical Review*, XVII (November 1948), pp. 383–409; Kenneth F. Neighbours, *Indian Exodus: Texas Indian Affairs, 1835–1859* (N.p., 1973); Joseph F. Park, "The Apaches in Mexican-American Relations, 1846–1861: A Footnote to the Gadsden Treaty," *Arizona and the West*, III (Summer 1961), pp. 129–46; Frank D. Reeve, "The Government and the Navaho, 1846–1858," *New Mexico Historical Review*, XIV (January 1939), pp. 82–114; J. Fred Rippy, "The Indians of the United States in the Diplomacy of the United States and Mexico, 1848–1853," *Hispanic-American Historical Review*, II (August 1919), pp. 363–96; Lillian B. Shields,

"Relations with the Cheyennes and Arapahoes in Colorado to 1861," *Colorado Magazine*, IV (August 1927), pp. 145–54.

Three recent studies treat Indian policy during the Civil War: Edmund J. Danzinger, Jr., *Indians and Bureaucrats: Administering the Reservation Policy during the Civil War* (Urbana, Ill., 1974); Richard N. Ellis, *General Pope and U.S. Indian Policy* (Albuquerque, 1970); and David A. Nichols, *Lincoln and the Indians: Civil War Policy and Politics* (Columbia,Mo., 1978). For the Five Civilized Tribes, Annie H. Abel's trilogy is still standard: *The American Indian as Slaveholder and Secessionist* (Cleveland, 1915); *The American Indian as Participant in the Civil War* (Cleveland, 1919); and *The American Indian under Reconstruction* (Cleveland, 1925). More specialized studies include: James W. Covington, "Federal Relations with the Colorado Utes," *Colorado Magazine*, XVIII (October 1951), pp. 257–65; Edmund J. Danzinger, "The Steck-Carleton Controversy in Civil War New Mexico," *Southwestern Historical Quarterly*, LXXIV (October 1970), pp. 189–203; Richard N. Ellis, "Civilians, the Army, and the Indian Problem on the Northern Plains, 1862–66," *North Dakota History*, XXXVII (Winter 1970),pp. 20–39; Harry Kelsey, "Abraham Lincoln and American Indian Policy," *Lincoln Herald*, LXXVII (Fall 1975), pp. 139–48; and Michael A. Sievers, "The Administration of Indian Affairs on the Upper Missouri, 1858–1865," *North Dakota History*, XXXVIII (Summer 1971), pp. 367–94.

The postwar period to the end of the century has attracted the greatest attention of historians. The best overviews are to be found in four works: Henry E. Fritz, *The Movement for Indian Assimilation, 1860–1890* (Philadelphia, 1963); Robert Winston Mardock, *The Reformers and the American Indian* (Columbia, Mo., 1971); Loring Benson Priest, *Uncle Sam's Stepchildren: The Reformation of United States Indian Policy, 1865–1887* (New Brunswick, N.J., 1942; Lincoln, Nebr., 1975); and Francis Paul Prucha, *American Indian Policy in Crisis: Christian Reformers and the Indian, 1865–1900* (Norman, Okla., 1976). Important original material appears in Francis Paul Prucha, ed., *Americanizing the American Indian: Writings by the 'Friends of the Indian,' 1880–1900* (Cambridge, Mass., 1973).

On the Peace Commission of 1867–68, see: Donald Chaput, "Generals, Indian Agents, Politicans: The Doolittle Survey of 1865," *Western Historical Quarterly*, III (July 1972), pp. 269–82; Douglas C. Jones, *The Treaty of Medicine Lodge: The Story of the Great Treaty Council as Told by Eyewitnesses* (Norman, Okla., 1966); Harry Kelsey, "The Doolittle Report of 1867: Its Preparation and Shortcomings," *Arizona and the West*, XVII (Summer 1975), pp. 107–20; Arthur P. Mattingly, "The Great Plains Peace Commission of 1867," *Journal of the West*, XV (July 1976), pp. 23–37; and *Proceedings of the Great Peace Commission of 1867–1868*, introduction by Vine Deloria, Jr., and Raymond DeMaillie (Washington, D.C., 1975).

Studies of Grant's Peace Policy include the following: Donald J. D'Elia, "The Argument over Civilian or Military Control, 1865–1880," *Historian*, XXIV (February 1962), pp. 207–25; Henry E. Fritz, "The Board of Indian Commissioners and Ethnocentric Reform," in Jane F. Smith and Robert M. Kvasnicka, eds., *Indian-White Relations: A Persistent Paradox* (Washington, D.C., 1976), pp. 57–78; Joseph E. Illick, "'Some of Our Best Indians are Friends. . .': Quaker Attitudes and Actions Regarding the Western Indians during the Grant Administration," *Western Histori-*

cal Quarterly, II (July 1971), pp. 283–94; Peter J. Rahill, *The Catholic Indian Missions and Grant's Peace Policy, 1870–1884* (Washington, D.C., 1953); Elsie Mitchell Rushmore, *The Indian Policy during Grant's Administration* (Jamaica, N.Y., 1914); Lawrie Tatum, *Our Red Brothers and the Peace Policy of Ulysses S. Grant* (Philadelphia, 1899); Henry G. Waltmann, "Circumstantial Reformer: President Grant and the Indian Problem," *Arizona and the West*, XIII (Winter 1971), pp. 323–42; Donald E. Worcester, "The Friends of the Indian and the Peace Policy," in Worcester, ed., *Forked Tongues and Broken Treaties* (Caldwell, Idaho, 1975), pp. 254–91.

On reform and reformers, see, in addition to works of Mardock and Prucha cited above, three articles by Prucha in *Indian Policy in the United States: Historical Essays* (Lincoln, Nebr., 1981): "Scientific Racism and Indian Policy," pp. 180–97; "Indian Policy Reform and American Protestantism, 1880–1900," pp. 229–41; and "The Decline of the Christian Reformers," pp. 242–62. Also valuable is Prucha, ed., *Americanizing the American Indian: Writings by the 'Friends of the Indian,' 1880–1900* (Cambridge, Mass., 1973). The Indian Rights Association and the Lake Mohonk Conference of the Friends of the Indian published annual reports that contain much of value.

For studies of the reservation, consult: Charles Amsden, "The Navaho Exile at Bosque Redondo," *New Mexico Historical Review*, VIII (January 1933), pp. 31–50; Lynn R. Bailey, *Bosque Redondo: An American Concentration Camp* (Pasadena, Calif., 1970); Donald J. Berthrong, *The Cheyenne and Arapaho Ordeal: Reservation and Agency Life in the Indian Territory,1875–1907* (Norman, Okla., 1976); John Bret Harte, "Conflict at San Carlos: The Military-Civilian Struggle for Control, 1882–1885," *Arizona and the West*, XV (Spring 1973), pp. 27–44; Woodworth Clum, *Apache Agent: The Story of John P. Clum* (Boston, 1936); William T. Hagan, *United States-Comanche Relations: The Reservation Years* (New Haven, Conn., 1976); William T. Hagan, *Indian Police and Judges: Experiments in Acculturation and Control* (New Haven, Conn., 1966); William T. Hagan, "Indian Policy after the Civil War: The Reservation Experience," in *American Indian Policy: Indiana Historical Society Lectures, 1970–71* (Indianapolis, 1971), pp. 20–36; William T. Hagan, "The Reservation Policy: Too Little and Too Late," in Jane F. Smith and Robert M. Kvasnicka, eds., *Indian-White Relations: A Persistent Paradox* (Washington, D.C., 1876), pp. 157–69; George E. Hyde, *A Sioux Chronicle* (Norman, Okla., 1956); Julia B. McGillycuddy, *McGillycuddy, Agent: A Biography of Dr. Valentine T. McGillycuddy* (Palo Alto, Calif., 1941); James Mc-Laughlin, *My Friend the Indian* (Boston and New York, 1910); Forrest D. Monahan, Jr., "The Kiowa-Comanche Reservation in the 1890s," *Chronicles of Oklahoma*, XVL (Winter 1967–68), pp. 451–63; James C. Olson, *Red Cloud and the Sioux Problem* (Lincoln, Nebr., 1965); Flora Warren Seymour, *Indian Agents of the Old Frontier* (Norman, Okla., 1935); Everett W. Sterling, "The Indian Reservation System on the North Central Plains," *Montana, the Magazine of Western History*, XIV (April 1964), pp. 92–100; Gerald Thompson, *The Army and the Navajo: The Bosque Redondo Reservation Experiment, 1863–68* (Tucson, 1976); Robert M. Utley, *The Last Days of the Sioux Nation* (New Haven, Conn., 1963); and Clark Wissler, *Indian Cavalcade: Life on the Old-Time Indian Reservations* (New York, 1938).

Land policies are subjects of the following works: Leonard A. Carlson, *Indians, Bureaucrats, and Land: The Dawes Act and the Decline of Indian Farming* (Westport, Conn., 1981); William T. Hagan, "Private Property: The Indian's Door to Civili-

Bibliography 303

zation," *Ethnohistory*, III (Spring 1956), pp. 126–37; Allan G. Harper, "Salvaging the Wreckage of Indian Land Allotment," in Oliver La Farge, ed., *The Changing Indian* (Norman, Okla., 1942), pp. 84–102; J. P. Kinney, *A Continent Lost—a Civilization Won: Indian Land Tenure in America* (Baltimore, 1937); D. S. Otis, *The Dawes Act and the Allotment of Indian Lands*, ed. Francis Paul Prucha (Norman, Okla., 1973); Charles C. Royce, comp., *Indian Land Cessions in the United States*, 18th Annual Report of the Bureau of American Ethnology, 1896–97, pt. 2 (Washington, D.C., 1899); and Wilcomb E. Washburn, *The Assault on Indian Tribalism: The General Allotment Act (Dawes Act) of 1887* (Philadelphia, 1977).

For studies of educational policies, see: Elaine Goodale Eastman, *Pratt, The Red Man's Moses* (Norman, Okla., 1935); Alice C. Fletcher, *Indian Education and Civilization* (Washington, D.C., 1888); Frederick E. Hoxie, "Redefining Indian Education: Thomas J. Morgan's Program in Disarray," *Arizona and the West*, XXIV (Spring 1982), pp. 5–18; Richard H. Pratt, *Battlefield and Classroom: Four Decades with the American Indian, 1867–1904*, ed. Robert M. Utley (New Haven, Conn., 1964); and Francis Paul Prucha, *The Churches and the Indian Schools, 1888–1912* (Lincoln, Nebr., 1979).

The legal aspects of U.S. Indian policies are covered comprehensively in Wilcomb E. Washburn, *Red Man's Land - White Man's Law: A Study of the Past and Present Status of the American Indian* (New York, 1971).

Indian Warfare

Published original materials on Indian warfare and the U.S. Army on the frontier are in the annual reports of the Secretary of War, the congressional executive documents series, and the *Congressional Globe* and *Congressional Record*.

General overviews or broad studies include: Robert G. Athearn, *William Tecumseh Sherman and the Settlement of the West* (Norman, Okla., 1956); Fairfax Downey, *Indian-Fighting Army* (New York, 1941); S. L. A. Marshall, *Crimsoned Prairie: The Wars between the United States and the Plains Indians during the Winning of the West* (New York, 1972); Don Rickey, Jr., *Forty Miles a Day on Beans and Hay: The Enlisted Soldier Fighting the Indian Wars* (Norman, Okla., 1963); Don Russell, "How Many Indians Were Killed? White Man versus Red Man: The Facts and the Legend," *American West*, X (July 1973), pp. 42–47, 61–63; Martin F. Schmitt and Dee Brown, *Fighting Indians of the West* (New York, 1948); Robert M. Utley, *Frontiersmen in Blue: The United States Army and the Indian, 1848–1865* (New York, 1967); Robert M. Utley, *Frontier Regulars: The United States Army and the Indian, 1866–1891* (New York, 1973); Robert M. Utley and Wilcomb E. Washburn, *The American Heritage History of the Indian Wars* (New York, 1977); and Paul I. Wellman, *Death on Horseback: Seventy Years of War for the American West* (Philadelphia, 1947).

Specialized studies of pre-Civil War conflicts are numerous. For wars on the Great Plains consult: Eugene Bandel, *Frontier Life in the Army, 1854–1861*, ed. Ralph P. Bieber (Glendale, Calif., 1932); LeRoy R. and Ann W. Hafen, eds., *Relations with the Indians of the Plains, 1857–1861: A Documentary Account of the Military Campaigns, and Negotiations of Indian Agents . . .* (Glendale, Calif., 1959); W. J.

Hughes, " 'Rip' Ford's Indian Fight on the Canadian," *Panhandle-Plains Historical Review*, XXX (1957), pp. 1–26; Ray H. Mattison, ed., "The Harney Expedition against the Sioux: The Journal of Capt. John B. S. Todd," *Nebraska History*, XLIII (June 1962), pp. 89–130; Robert L. Munkres, "The Plains Indian Threat on the Oregon Trail before 1860," *Annals of Wyoming*, XL (October 1968), pp. 193–221; W. Stitt Robinson, ed., "The Kiowa and Comanche Campaign of 1860 as Recorded in the Personal Diary of Lt. J. E. B. Stuart," *Kansas Historical Quarterly*, XXIII (Winter 1957), pp. 382–400; and Otis E. Young, *The West of Philip St. George Cooke* (Glendale, Calif., 1955). For warfare in Texas, see: M. L. Crimmins, ed., "Colonel Robert E. Lee's Report on Indian Combats in Texas," *Southwestern Historical Quarterly*, XXXIX (July 1935), pp. 21–32; and Michael L. Tate, "Frontier Defense on the Comanche Ranges of Northwest Texas, 1846–1860," *Great Plains Journal*, XIII (January 1974), pp. 67–77. Studies of warfare in the Southwest include: Averam B. Bender, *The March of Empire: Frontier Defense in the Southwest, 1848–1860* (Lawrence, Kans., 1952); Frank McNitt, *Navajo Wars: Military Campaigns, Slave Raids, and Reprisals* (Albuquerque, 1972); and Morris F. Taylor, "Action at Fort Massachusetts: The Indian Campaign of 1855," *Colorado Magazine*, XLII (Fall 1965), pp. 292–310; Morris F. Taylor, "Campaigns against the Jicarilla Apache, 1854," *New Mexico Historical Review*, XLIV (October 1969), pp. 269–91; Morris F. Taylor, "Campaigns against the Jicarilla Apache, 1855," ibid., XLV (April 1970), pp. 119–36. For the Pacific Northwest wars, see: William N. Bischoff, "The Yakima Indian War, 1855–1856: A Problem in Research," *Pacific Northwest Quarterly*, XLI (April 1950), pp. 162–69; Robert Ignatius Burns, *The Jesuits and the Indian Wars of the Northwest* (New Haven, Conn., 1966); Robert C. Clark, "Military History of Oregon, 1849–59," *Oregon Historical Quarterly*, XXXVI (March 1935), pp. 14–59; Lawrence Kip, *Army Life on the Pacific: A Journal of the Expedition against the Northern Indians, the Tribes of the Coeur d'Alenes, Spokans, and Pelouzes, in the Summer of 1858* (New York, 1859); Bernard C. Nalty and Truman R. Strobridge, "The Defense of Seattle, 1856: 'And Down Came the Indians,'" *Pacific Northwest Quarterly*, LV (July 1964), pp. 105–10; and Kent Richards, "Isaac I. Stevens and Federal Military Power in Washington Territory," ibid., LXV (July 1972), pp. 81–86.

Specialized studies of conflicts during the Civil War era are voluminous. The Minnesota uprising and its aftermath are treated in the following: Kenneth Carley, *The Sioux Uprising of 1862* (St. Paul, 1961); Robert H. Jones, *The Civil War in the Northwest: Nebraska, Wisconsin, Iowa, Minnesota, and the Dakotas* (Norman, Okla., 1960); C. M. Oehler, *The Great Sioux Uprising* (New York, 1959); and Louis Pfaller, "Sully's Expedition of 1864: Featuring the Killdeer Mountain and Badlands Battles," *North Dakota History*, XXXI (January 1964), pp. 25–77. On Navajo Warfare, see: Lynn R. Bailey, *The Long Walk: A History of the Navajo Wars, 1848–68* (Los Angeles, 1964); Lawrence C. Kelly, *Navajo Roundup: Selected Correspondence of Kit Carson's Expedition against the Navajo, 1863–1865* (Boulder, Colo., 1970); Frank McNitt, "The Long March: 1863–67," in Albert H. Schroeder, ed., *The Changing Ways of Southwestern Indians: A Historic Perspective* (Glorieta, N.M., 1973); Clifford E. Trafzer, *The Kit Carson Campaign: The Last Great Navajo War* (Norman, Okla., 1982). The Sand Creek Massacre is the subject of Raymond G. Carey, "The Puzzle of Sand Creek," *Colorado Magazine*, XLI (Fall 1964), pp. 279–98; Stan Hoig, *The Sand Creek Massacre* (Norman, Okla., 1961); Harry Kelsey, "Background to Sand Creek,"

Colorado Magazine, XLV (Fall 1968), pp. 279–300; Janet Lecompte, "Sand Creek," ibid., XLI (Fall 1964), pp. 315–35; Michael A. Sievers, "Sands of Sand Creek Historiography," ibid., XLIX (Spring 1972), pp. 116–42; and Lonnie J. White, "From Bloodless to Bloody: The Third Colorado Cavalry and the Sand Creek Massacre," *Journal of the West,* VI (October 1967), pp. 535–81. Hostilities on the Great Plains and in Texas are treated in the following: D. Alexander Brown, *The Galvanized Yankees* (Urbana, Ill., 1963); Marvin H. Garfield, "Defense of the Kansas Frontier, 1864–65," *Kansas Historical Quarterly,* I (February 1932), pp. 140–52; LeRoy R. and Ann W. Hafen, eds., *Powder River Campaigns and Sawyers' Expedition of 1865: A Documentary Account Comprising Official Reports, Diaries, Contemporary Newspaper Accounts, and Personal Narratives* (Glendale, Calif., 1961); W. C. Holden, "Frontier Defense in Texas during the Civil War," *West Texas Historical Association Year Book,* IV (June 1928), pp. 16–31; Robert M. Utley, "Kit Carson and the Adobe Walls Campaign," *American West,* II (Winter 1965), pp. 4–11, 73–75; and Eugene F. Ware, *The Indian War of 1864,* 2d ed. (New York, 1960).

The Modoc War is treated in the following: Richard H. Dillon, *Burnt-Out Fires: California's Modoc Indian War* (Englewood Cliffs, N.J., 1973); Keith A. Murray, *The Modocs and Their War* (Norman, Okla., 1959); and Erwin N. Thompson, *Modoc War: Its Military History and Topography* (Sacramento, Calif., 1971).

On the final Great Plains wars, see: Dee Brown, *Fort Phil Kearny: An American Saga* (New York, 1962); Marvin H. Garfield, "Defense of the Kansas Frontier, 1866–67," *Kansas Historical Quarterly,* I (August 1932), pp. 326–44; Marvin H. Garfield, "Defense of the Kansas Frontier, 1868–69," ibid., pp. 451–73; W. A. Graham, *The Story of the Little Big Horn* (New York, 1926); W. A. Graham, *The Custer Myth: A Source Book of Custeriana* (Harrisburg, Pa., 1953); John S. Gray, *Centennial Campaign: The Sioux War of 1876* (Fort Collins, Colo., 1976); Jerome A. Greene, *Slim Buttes, 1876: An Episode of the Great Sioux War* (Norman, Okla., 1982); James L. Haley, *The Buffalo War: The History of the Red River Indian Uprising of 1874* (New York, 1976); Grace Raymond Hebard and E. A. Brininstool, *The Bozeman Trail,* 2 vols. (Cleveland, 1922); Stan Hoig, *The Battle of the Washita: The Sheridan-Custer Indian Campaign of 1867–69* (Garden City, N.Y., 1976); Donald Jackson, *Custer's Gold: The United States Cavalry Expedition of 1874* (New Haven, Conn., 1966); De B. Randolph Keim, *Sheridan's Troopers on the Borders: A Winter Campaign on the Plains* (Philadelphia, 1885); Charles Kuhlman, *Legend into History: The Custer Mystery, an Analytical Study of the Battle of the Little Big Horn* (Harrisburg, Pa., 1951); William H. Leckie, *The Military Conquest of the Southern Plains* (Norman, Okla., 1963); Robert A. Murray, *Military Posts in the Powder River Country of Wyoming, 1865–1894* (Lincoln, Nebr., 1968); Wilbur S. Nye, *Carbine and Lance: The Story of Old Fort Sill* (Norman, Okla., 1937); Wilbur S. Nye, *Plains Indian Raiders: The Final Phases of Warfare from the Arkansas to the Red River* (Norman, Okla., 1968); J'Nell Pate, "The Battles of Adobe Walls," *Great Plains Journal,* XVI (Fall 1976), pp. 3–44; Rupert N. Richardson, *The Comanche Barrier to South Plains Settlement* (Glendale, Calif., 1933); C. C. Rister, "The Significance of the Jacksboro Indian Affair of 1871," *Southwestern Historical Quarterly,* XXIX (January 1926), pp. 181–200; Edgar I. Stewart, *Custer's Luck* (Norman, Okla., 1955); Robert M. Utley, *The Last Days of the Sioux Nation* (New Haven, Conn., 1963); Robert M. Utley, ed., *Life in Custer's Cavalry: Diaries and Letters of Albert and Jennie Barnitz, 1867–68* (New Haven,

Conn., 1977); J. W. Vaughn, *The Reynolds Campaign on Powder River* (Norman, Okla., 1961); J. W. Vaughn, *With Crook at the Rosebud* (Harrisburg, Pa., 1956); J. W. Vaughn, *Indian Fights: New Facts on Seven Encounters* (Norman, Okla., 1966); and Ernest Wallace, *Ranald S. Mackenzie on the Texas Frontier* (Lubbock, Tex., 1964).

On warfare in the Rocky Mountain and Great Basin region, see: R. Ross Arnold, *The Indian Wars of Idaho* (Caldwell, Ida., 1932); Merrill D. Beal, *"I Will Fight No More Forever": Chief Joseph and the Nez Perce War* (Seattle, 1963); George F. Brimlow, *The Bannock Indian War of 1876* (Caldwell, Ida., 1938); Mark H. Brown, *The Flight of the Nez Perce* (New York, 1967); W. C. Brown, *The Sheepeater Campaign* (Caldwell, Idaho, 1926); Robert Emmitt, *The Last War Trail: The Utes and the Settlement of Colorado* (Norman, Okla., 1954); and Marshall Sprague, *Massacre: The Tragedy of White River* (Boston, 1957).

For wars in the Southwest, consult: Eve Ball, *In the Days of Victorio: Recollections of a Warm Springs Apache* (Tucson, 1970); Eve Ball, *Indeh: An Apache Odyssey* (Provo, Utah, 1980); Keith H. Basso, ed., *Western Apache Raiding and Warfare: From the Notes of Grenville Goodwin* (Tucson, 1971); Jason Betzinez, *I Fought with Geronimo*, ed. Wilbur S. Nye (Harrisburg, Pa., 1959); John G. Bourke, *On the Border with Crook* (New York, 1891); John G. Bourke, *An Apache Campaign in the Sierra Madre: An Account of the Expedition in Pursuit of Hostile Chiricahua Apache in the Spring of 1883* (New York, 1891); Britton Davis, *The Truth about Geronimo* (New Haven, Conn., 1929); Dan L. Thrapp, *Al Sieber, Chief of Scouts* (Norman, Okla., 1964); Dan L. Thrapp, *The Conquest of Apacheria* (Norman, Okla., 1967); Dan L. Thrapp, *General Crook and the Sierra Madre Adventure* (Norman, Okla., 1972); and Dan L. Thrapp, *Victorio and the Mimbres Apaches* (Norman, Okla., 1974).

U.S. military figures are subjects of many volumes, but see: Don E. Alberts, *Brandy Station to Manila Bay: A Biography of General Wesley Merritt* (Austin, Tex., 1981); Robert G. Athearn, *William Tecumseh Sherman and the Settlement of the West* (Norman, Okla., 1956); John W. Bailey, *Pacifying the Plains: General Alfred Terry and the Decline of the Sioux, 1866–1890* (Westport, Conn., 1979); John A. Carpenter, *Sword and Olive Branch: Oliver Otis Howard* (Pittsburgh, 1964); George Crook, *General George Crook: His Autobiography*, ed. Martin F. Schmitt (Norman, Okla., 1946); Richard N. Ellis, *General Pope and U.S. Indian Policy* (Albuquerque, 1970); Richard N. Ellis, "The Humanitarian Generals," *Western Historical Quarterly*, III (April 1972), pp. 169–78; Richard N. Ellis, "The Humanitarian Soldiers," *Journal of Arizona History*, X (Summer 1969), pp. 53–66; Max L. Heyman, Jr., *Prudent Soldier: A Biography of Major General E. R. S. Canby, 1817–1873* (Glendale, Calif., 1959); Oliver O. Howard, *My Life and Experiences among Our Hostile Indians* (Hartford, Conn., 1907); Aurora Hunt, *Major General James Henry Carleton, 1814–1873: Western Frontier Dragoon* (Glendale, Calif., 1958); Virginia W. Johnson, *The Unregimented General: A Biography of Nelson A. Miles* (Boston, 1962); James T. King, *War Eagle: A Life of General Eugene A. Carr* (Lincoln, Nebr., 1963); James T. King, "George Crook: Indian Fighter and Humanitarian," *Arizona and the West*, IX (Winter 1967), pp. 333–48; James T. King, "Needed: A Reevaluation of General George Crook," *Nebraska History*, XLV (September 1964), pp. 223–36; Marvin E. Kroeker, *Great Plains Command: William B. Hazen in the Frontier West* (Norman, Okla., 1976); Jay Monaghan, *Custer: The Life of General George Armstrong Custer* (Boston, 1959); and Otis E. Young, *The West of Philip St. George Cooke, 1809–1895* (Glendale, Calif., 1955).

Index

Abbott, Lyman, 210, 219
Abert, J. J., 2, 3
acculturation, xx, 7, 11–30, 131, 218, 236 *passim*, 251, 267, 272
Ácoma Pueblo, N.M., 27, 56
Adams, John Quincy,
Adobe Walls, Tex., Battles of, 95, 175
agreements, with Indians, 154, 184, 232, 246. *See also* treaties
agriculture. *See* U.S. Indian policy
Alamosa River (N.M.), 136
Alaska, 261, 266–68
Alaska Native Claims Settlement Act of 1971, 268
Alaska Organic Act of 1884, 268
Aleut Indians, 266
Aleutian Islands, 266
Alexander Archipelago (Ak.), 266
American Fur Co., 18, 28–29
American Horse (Sioux), 234–36, 234, 249, 262
American River (Calif.), 3
Anadarko Indians, 56
annuity system, 45–46, 47, 76, 78
An-pay-kau-te (Kiowa), 164
Anthony, Scott J., 92
Apache Indians, xvi, 4, 8, 12, 20, 22, 31, 67, 95; and Peace Policy, 135–39; raids, 55, 56–58, 122, 134–35, 193 *passim*; reservations, 56–58, 139, 158, 193 *passim*; treaties, 56–58; wars, 65–67, 71, 134–35, 157–61,

186, 193–201. *See also* individual Apache tribes
Apache Pass, Ariz., 66
Apache Pass, Ariz., Battle of, 67, 71
Apache scouts, 157–58, 167, 197–201
Apache Springs, Ariz., 66, 67
Appomattox Court House, Va., 75, 95, 101, 130, 164
Arapaho Indians, 4, 90–92, 99–101, 125; reservations, 61, 86, 173–74, 178–81; treaties, 61, 86, 112, 114–16; wars, 87–95, 103–5, 109–12, 174–89
Aravaipa Apache Indians, 139. *See also* Apache Indians
Arctic Ocean, 266
Arikara Indians, 11, 61
Arikara River (Colo.-Kan.), 124
Arizona (territory, state), xvi, 20, 65, 72, 139; reservations, 140, 158, 193, 196; wars, 122, 134, 157–61, 193, 197–201
Arizona Rangers, 67
Arkansas (state), 59, 73
Arkansas River, 1, 19, 61, 62, 86 *passim*, 95, 97, 109, 110, 112 *passim*, 122
Armijo, Manuel, 31
Armstrong, Samuel C., 210
Army and Navy Journal, 101, 102
Army Medical Museum, 171
Army of the West, 1–3, 31–32, 37, 60
Arthur, Chester A., 217

307